CW01502160

Preface by Steve Newman   7

Introduction by Martin Val Baker   9

The Sea's In The Kitchen
    Chapter One - Art Colony by the Sea   15
    Chapter Two - A House Full of People   27
    Chapter Three - At the End of the Land   41
    Chapter Four - The Trees Came Tumbling Down   55
    Chapter Five - The Dear Golden Years   71
    Chapter Six - The Life and Death of the Cornish Review   87
    Chapter Seven - The Dream and the Reality   103
    Chapter Eight - A Potter and Her Helps   117
    Chapter Nine - Journey into the Interior   135
    Chapter Ten - The Sea's in the Kitchen   155

Bonus Material

    Steve Newman on Denys Val Baker   173

    Other Denys Val Baker Titles   181

THE SEA'S IN
THE KITCHEN

The Sea's In The Kitchen

Denys Val Baker

Preface by Steve Newman
Introduction by Martin Val Baker
Illustrations by Donald Swan

Humdrumming Ltd.
75 Withermoor Road
Bournemouth, Dorset
BH9 2QN

This Paperback Edition, Published by Humdrumming, 2006
ISBN 1-905532-18-0 - Classic Cover
ISBN 1-905532-24-5 - New Cover

First published by Pheonix House Ltd, 1962

Published 2006 by Humdrumming
www.humdrumming.co.uk
www.denysvalbaker.com

ISBN 1-905532-18-0 / ISBN 978-1-905532-18-6 - Classic Cover
ISBN 1-905532-24-5 / ISBN 978-1-905532-24-7 - New Cover

Printed and bound by CPI Antony Rowe, Eastbourne

Preface

I first came across Denys Val Baker's name in the 1970s when I heard one of his short stories read on my car radio. Although I can't remember the story, what I do remember is the effect it had on me, causing me to pull over, get out, and gulp in some deep breaths of fresh air. It felt as if I had come across one of those small secrets of our existence, of life itself. I quickly made a note of his name, a name that sounded slightly foreign and familiar. I wanted to read more by this writer.

Back home and looking through my bookshelves I realised I had read his work, and the work of others gathered together by Denys as an editor, whose introductions were scholarly gems that filled me with his own passion for writers and places.

By the late 1970s I was living in Plymouth and taking every opportunity to explore Cornwall, and it was in a second-hand bookshop in St Ives that I discovered a handful of Denys' autobiographies from the 1960s, the first of which, *The Sea's in the Kitchen*, you're holding in your hands now. Those books were a revelation to me, their simplicity of style (something very hard to achieve) speaks directly to the reader - as did that BBC short story - as if listening to Denys talking at the Val Baker kitchen table. They were a delight and heralded a new literary genre - they were also delightfully funny too. They are still delightfully funny, and forty plus years after they were first published they are now important social documents of the 1950s and 1960s.

Over the years I've collected many of Denys' titles in the second-hand market - they continue to fetch high prices - but became extremely frustrated that the titles, which were good earners for the publishers in their day (one of his early novels had initial hardback sales of 100,000 copies in the US) were not being re-published.

With the publication, in 1994, of Tim Scott's lovely biography of Denys, and the re-publication of Denys' 1959 title, *Britain's Art Colony By The Sea,* in 2000, I was delighted to see Denys Val Baker's name prominently displayed in book shops once more, which made me realise I had to try and do something (I didn't know what of course) to get Denys' work back in print.

But it was only with the creation of Humdrumming Ltd that I was able to get (with Martin Val Baker's and Jess Val Baker's own enthusiasm for the project) this important and long neglected (by the publishing industry) author re-published at last.

Consequently I hope you enjoy *The Sea's in the Kitchen*, which has been a labour of love to bring back to life.

Steve Newman
Senior Editor, Humdrumming

Introduction

Denys Val Baker was not a Cornishman, but he did live in the county for most of his life and could thus be reasonably considered an adopted son of Cornwall. In fact he came from a Welsh background, both his father and mother having been born at the North Welsh coastal town of Llanfairfechan where his grandfather had been headmaster at a local primary school. Denys was always very proud of his Celtic roots, the fact that his mother's family were Welsh speakers and that she herself had played harp in the Eisteddfod at the turn of the century.

Denys' father, Valentine Henry Baker, was working at a local bank in North Wales when the Great War broke out in 1914 and he immediately enlisted in the forces where he stayed for two years until being invalided out in 1915 after the battle of Gallipoli. After recovering from his wounds Valentine rejoined, this time becoming a pilot in the newly formed Royal Flying Corps - later to become the R.A.F. Flying a fighter at the front at that time was a very hazardous occupation and many of his fellow flyers were shot down. In late 1917 Valentine, as a relatively experienced surviving pilot, was withdrawn to teach new recruits at a base in Yorkshire.

A year earlier Valentine had married his childhood sweetheart Dilys Eames who was now able to join him in Yorkshire and it was here at Poppleton that Denys Val Baker was born on October 24th 1917. After the war, Valentine worked on as a flying instructor teaching people to fly at first in Chile and Java, eventually settling just outside London. So Denys grew up largely in the London suburbs though he did attend Grammar School in Sussex where he edited the school magazine - probably his first literary experience. However it seems that Denys was determined to be a writer from the off and he was soon busy writing short stories.

Throughout his childhood and adolescence Denys made regular trips to North Wales to stay with his Eames relations and many of his early stories and indeed his first novel were based on Welsh people and themes. Throughout his life Denys Val Baker, a keen observer of human nature and its foibles, would often use his friends and family as a basis for his fictional work. A very early story 'The Return of Uncle Walter', which tells the story of a ship's captain who returns to Wales to retire and finds that he cannot settle after so much time at sea, seems to be based on Denys' own great grandfather William. There is a also graphic description of the boating lake at Llanfairfechan in this story.

In the late 1930s, after a spell on the Derby Evening Telegraph, Denys started work as a journalist in London and, after registering as a Conscientious Objector, he was based there through most of the war. It was whilst staying at Youth House, a pacifist community in Camden Town, that Denys met his first wife Patricia Johnson a librarian from Leeds and they married in 1942. During this time Denys worked furiously as a writer and editor - many of his own short stories were published and he was running a literary quarterly Opus, (later to be renamed 'Voices') during the early forties.

It was through these experiences that Denys became an expert on the 'Little Review' genre as well as picking up a mass of contacts on the literary scene that were to last him a lifetime. As a result a series of annual collections of 'Little Review Anthologies' edited by Denys Val Baker began to appear. In 1945 his first novel 'The White Rock' was published to great acclaim and also his first proper collection of short stories, 'World's Without End' - it seemed that the literary career of Denys Val Baker was on the way to great things. He was still only in his twenties but in those pre-television days poets and writers were the equivalent of today's pop stars but he was never again to equal the earnings he made in the mid-forties.

In fact there were drastic changes ahead. By 1948 his marriage to Pat was collapsing and Denys moved on his own to Cornwall for some time to recuperate whilst working as a publicity officer for theatre companies in Camborne and Falmouth. In happier times Denys and Pat (with me) had rented Dora Russell's cottage in Porthcurno for six months so he did have some experience of the area.

In 1949 my father and I finally moved permanently to Cornwall, soon after finding happiness with his second wife Jess Bryan and her two daughters Gillian and Jane in a little cottage at the bottom of Trencrom Hill, and this is the story that his first autobiography 'The Sea's in The Kitchen' tells.

In the early sixties, encouraged by his friend Bill Picard, Denys began work on an autobiography and was delighted when it was accepted by Phoenix House for publication in 1962. From the start 'The Sea's in the Kitchen' went down very well with readers and attracted good reviews in the press. It was to be his best selling book since the forties, although Kenneth Allsop in the Daily Mail did suggest that 'Mr Baker's description of the life of a freelance writer seems to be of the freedom of a stoker in hell'. This book lead eventually to another twenty five volumes as the Val Baker life story became a sort of soap opera and we, his children, became characters in it. I think we all hoped secretly that we would be the victims of some dreadful libel and could sue for thousands of pounds - but we never were. It is wonderful to see some of his books being republished after so many years and congratulations to Humdrumming for having confidence in them.

Martin Val Baker, March 2006

To the Memory of
Len Missen

The Sea's In The Kitchen

AUTHOR'S NOTE

After working for many years in London as a professional author and editor I responded to a call which many writers and artists have felt and went to settle 'away from it all ' in Cornwall. As this autobiographical account of the ensuing ten years will show, life cannot be escaped from in Cornwall any more than anywhere else. But in fact Cornwall offers many precious things to the creative worker, quite apart from its inspiring natural background - not least a more sympathetic and tolerant attitude than is generally found in provincial England. For this reason I have tried in this book to capture a portrait of Cornwall in our life as much as of our life in Cornwall.

Chapter One

ART COLONY BY THE SEA

When Jess and I were married it seemed perfectly natural to me that we should settle down in Cornwall. But then perhaps I was a little prejudiced, for I had long ago deserted the literary world of London for the wilder and much more exciting world of Cornish cliffs and carns and moors, and everywhere the booming echoes of the restless sea. Like many other professional authors before me l had made the welcome discovery that one of the writer's most precious gifts is that of freedom of movement. I could, of course, have travelled farther a field, wandered the world, but the fact was I had for a long time been conscious of feeling drawn westwards to this strange and rather primitive and mysterious land of Celtic mythology. This may have been partly due to Celtic sympathy, as I am Welsh. Whatever the reasons I felt happy and satisfied in Cornwall, whether living in a tiny castle on the cliffs at Portquin or working with a repertory theatre at Camborne or writing novels in an attic bedroom looking over the serene beauty of the Carrack Broads at Falmouth. I could not, in fact, imagine living anywhere else, or how anyone could wish to live anywhere else.

It was true that Jess and I met far from this magic land. At the time I was spending Christmas up in London and one evening my friend Ross said: 'Do you remember I told you about a little Sagittarian with two small daughters who has a flat off the Fulham Road? Well, it's only round the corner - come on, I'll introduce you.'

As I followed Ross I could not help recalling that not only had he told me several times about this same little Sagittarian but that he had been to great pains to explain we would be ideally suited as companions, since we had both been through the emotional upheaval of broken marriages. Such precise forecasting on the part of Ross was something I had become accustomed to, and yet . . . nobody really likes to have his personal life quite so organized. I was prepared to be unforthcoming and antagonistic to this unknown female who, just because she was 'a little Sagittarian' was recommended as my lifelong partner.

The trouble with astrology is that its predictions are usually so right. Jess and I might have been made for each other: and so we felt almost from the moment we met. It was never a question of getting to know each other or making any decisions. We just were suddenly together, and we could not imagine life had ever been otherwise. Of course, we had many things in common. We were both Welsh, with all the inbred and intuitive ties of the Celtic race. We had much the same attitude to life, being what might be termed humanist socialists - that is we had a reverence for the dignity of the human being and a belief that the world should be organized by the people for the people, and not by a few monopolies and capitalists for their own gain. On the other hand in many ways we were apparently opposites (or perhaps, as experience was to suggest, complementary). Jess was an extrovert, I was an introvert. Jess assessed people as they seemed, my judgments were arrived at by a more tortuous caution, an intuitive feeling. Jess made friends very easily, I could only do so over a long period of time. Jess was a product of Cardiff University and a long history of activity in university debating societies had helped to make her an incisive and logical and forceful talker. Being a writer I was much more forceful and effective on paper than in conversation. Not that I lacked conversational fire with Jess. We often became involved in the most fantastic arguments and wrangles - part of a sparking off process which has continued to some degree through all the years. In one sense perhaps we were fighting to be free, in another we were weaving the bonds around us. That is all part of the wonder and fulfilment of being in love.

Six weeks after meeting, Jess and I were married at South Kensington Registrar's Office in a flurry of agitated relatives and friends. We enjoyed a hilarious wedding tea at the Blue Cockatoo on Chelsea Embankment and in the evening celebrated more merrily with a huge party attended by nearly a hundred friends and relations including writers, publishers, actors, musicians, and painters. It was a good party, I remember, the sort of sophisticated gathering that typifies the most pleasant side of London life. All the same I was already looking forward to our coming journey westwards, to our new life in Cornwall.

It was going to be a little different from my previous life, of course, for ultimately there would not only be Jess and her two small daughters, Gill and Jane, but also my own 3-year old son, Martin, of whom I now had custody. We would be starting off life much more soberly and realistically than many much younger married couples: for one thing, with a ready made family to support from the beginning we should need to find a home and plant some roots. But then Cornwall was just the sort of place where this could be done in a positive, even romantic way. For children it would seem to offer everything one could wish for in the way of sunshine, clean air, lovely country, and other pre-requisites of a healthy life. While Jess had never been to Cornwall before, surely a Celt would respond to a Celtic country?

Poor Jess was hardly given a chance at first. From the moment of our arrival, over-anxious to make her like Cornwall, I brazenly over-sold my commodity. Day after day - especially as they were lovely sunny days when Cornwall flowers into full beauty - I organized her life.

'Today I thought we might drive along the coast road to Land's End.

I want to show you Zennor on the way, and the climber's hut by Morvah - maybe Cape Cornwall, too. .

Or again:

'I don't think you've seen Newlyn and Mousehole yet. There is a lovely harbour at Newlyn - second biggest fishing fleet in the West Country, they say.' And again:

'How would you like to see Chysauster? That's a Roman village settlement up near New Mill - not far from that there's the Lanyon Quoit.'

No wonder that on one occasion when I grimly drove her over to see the famous Minack Theatre the dutiful honeymoon worm turned, resolutely sitting in the car reading the daily paper and refusing to budge!

Naturally I meant well but my unsubtle propaganda probably delayed Jess's reactions by a year or two. I think it was only when we finally settled in a permanent home at the Old Vicarage, St Hilary, that she felt able to relax and put down her roots, and began to appreciate Cornwall.

Our first, if rather temporary home together was an old Cornish cottage on the side of Trencrom Hill, in the heart of what might be called Penwith country. What had originally been a cowshed was now converted into two long low rooms, one above the other, with a steep stairway connecting. I was used to living in such places, but Jess was not. I was able to feel romantic about a home tucked away down a lane and one and a half miles from the nearest main road, where the only water was obtained in buckets from a stream a hundred yards away, where cooking was done on a Primus or on a ferocious old paraffin stove, and lighting was equally dependent on the same fuel, plus the temperament of two Aladdin lamps. For Jess it was a form of purgatory, and she reacted accordingly. We had many momentous rows glaring at each other across the inefficient smoking futility of a stove whose wick was burned out, or after I had tired of carrying innumerable buckets of water which, it appeared to me, Jess wantonly wasted.

But then things often seemed different at night. Outside all was dark and mysterious - inside the long low room was lit by a cosy stove at one end, and the friendly light of the Aladdin on the centre of the long scrubbed oak table. It was somehow rather a romantic room at night, even the whitewashed walls took on a soft glow. At that time Jess's younger daughter Jane was still being looked after in London, so we had one child each, but enough to remind us of the extra need for stability in this, our second marriage. Martin and Gill slept in the upstairs room, and sometimes we would climb up and peep at them. They were both then about 4 years old; lying there they would look infinitely tender and appealing tucked deep into the bedclothes. We used to creep away down the stairs back to the warm room below and forget all our petty quarrels thankful for the wonder of being alive and in love, and embarking on such an adventure of life.

And of course we were living in a truly beautiful position. It only required a few minutes clambering up the gorse strewn and boulder-studded hill to reach the rocky pinnacle of Trencrom and enjoy that superb view stretching from Godrevy Lighthouse on the north coast to Mount's Bay and the glittering spectacle of St Michael's Mount on the south coast. Often when we felt tired or depressed we had only to make the short climb to enter a different atmosphere, in more senses than one. On top of Trencrom, several hundred feet above sea level, the air was crystal clear and even the light seemed brighter. Walking on the soft grass plateau that wound among the huge mounds of rocks it was impossible to remain low in spirits - especially if it was a sunny day and not only the sea coast but the inland areas could be followed clearly to the horizon. I can remember many times lying on the grass and watching the first puff of smoke as a train from 'up country' snaked across the landscape, over the viaduct at Hayle and then through the junction of St Erth and on past Marazion to the end of the line, those final buffers at Penzance. Was it possible that train came from some other reality? Here, now, the only reality seemed these hills and slopes of West Cornwall, these familiar wandering outlines of cliff and coast and white-capped seas. In Cornwall, of all places, it is not difficult to forget the less attractive harsh realities of the outside world. For there is so much all around one, whether it be the restless ever-changing sea with its eternal mysteries, or the wandering ageless landscape, with all its own strange and brooding reminders of the past. Everything seems so peculiarly charged with a vibrant and often secret life that it is hardly surprising if Cornwall makes a violent impact on people. As John Heath-Stubbs wrote:

This is a hideous and wicked country
Sloping to hateful sunsets and the end of time,
Hollow with mine-shafts, naked with granite, fanatic
With sorrow. Abortions of the past
Hop through these bogs; black-faced, the villagers
Remember burning by the hewn stones.

At Barn Cottage our full postal address was Trencrom Hill, Lelant Downs, Hayle, Cornwall: in fact this represented three very different areas. Trencrom was the inland area of stark hills and hidden lanes, of tiny half-hidden valleys and lonely moors. Lelant Downs led to Lelant and the sea - we often took the sandy path leading under Lelant railway bridge down to the sands. I found the area around Lelant church and the ferry crossing immensely interesting. There were a few indeterminate chalets, one or two boats pulled up out of the water, across the way the extraordinary hotch-potch of Hayle Towans - and in between the ever-changing Hayle estuary, which was a mere trickle when the tide was out, yet rose to a tremendous swirling torrent with the incoming tide. After school we often took the children there and wandered out to the mouth of the estuary, a part which holiday-makers usually miss. Sometimes it is possible to obtain the most extraordinary effect; standing on the white sands and looking up to see the enormous hull of an oil tanker apparently gliding along beside as the ship comes steaming in on the evening tide. The experience can be even more striking on the Hayle side of the estuary where from certain positions it is possible to look across the sands and see the clustering houses of St Ives rising up out of the water, like some medieval city of old.

Hayle itself, too, laid its almost perverse charm upon us: a most misleading town, outwardly rather drab and ugly and symbolized by its ghastly yellow street lighting - yet in fact full of relics of gracious living, lovely old Georgian manor houses now turned into fiats or scrap yards, quiet and rather beautiful backwaters, and not forgetting the bird watcher's paradise, the inland lake of the estuary, bordering the A30 road from Hayle towards St Erth. Sometimes I used to stand where the Hayle docks merged into the sands of the Towans, or over by the Lelant ferry boat, and it would seem as if I was enclosed in a curious forlorn world all of its own. More than once I have tried to use this setting in a story, but I always feel that perhaps it was captured best of all in some rather vivid and startling paintings done by Tom Early, who has long since, unfortunately, left Cornwall.

It must have been about this time that I wrote a story called *Death at the Carn* in which I used as a setting the carn cottage of a painter, Bryan Wynter, up above Zennor. In my story, which was published in the *London Mystery Magazine,* I tried to capture something of the elemental side of life in Cornwall, as suggested by the ancient hills and moorland - and I coupled it with the bohemian life of the artists, culminating in a mock observation of the old druidic sacrifices. In my story there is a death - I was a little shaken to find out later that in fact there was a not dissimilar case of someone going to spend a night at the carn and being found dead the next day. This, I suppose, might be called a sort of pre-vision on my part. Certainly I have on several occasions written a story or a novel, and later found events following a similar pattern. For instance, I set a satire on cummunity living, *The More We are Together,* in Cornwall - but I wrote it before coming to live in Cornwall. *The Awakening,* a short story of mine that has been extremely popular, having been published several times, and broadcast on the radio, was written around my conception of a woodchopper at work being watched by a rather nervous and subdued woman, whose spirit is somehow lifted up by the man's gaiety and the beauty of his movements. Some years after writing it Arthur Slater, one of our woodchopper friends from Lamorna, told me of an incident almost precisely the same which actually happened. But I must not push the analogy too far. At the time my first marriage was in distress l wrote a novel, *The Widening Mirror,* about a marriage which is threatened but finally works out to a happy ending. The real life ending was sadly different.

For a while our life at Barn Cottage fell into a sort of routine. Each day Martin and Gill attended the nearest local primary school, one of the smallest and prettiest I have ever known -Trevarrack. This was situated on the other side of Trencrom Hill, and though in the mornings I usually took the children the long way round by car, most afternoons Jess and I would stroll across the hills to meet them out of school. When the sun shone and the sea stretched blue and untroubled to Godrevy Lighthouse it was impossible to wish we were anywhere else. The difference between the high clear air, ranged with a scent of the sea, and the diesel-laden fumes of London, must have an enormous effect on a child's health. At a later date our children attended an L.C.C. school in the heart of London, and indeed they have been to several other schools, but I have yet to feel that any suited them better, at least at an early age, than this tiny school of Trevarrack, with about twenty pupils from scattered country homes, looked after lovingly by an enlightened headmistress. When nature study period came, then it was simply a question of taking the children wandering down the lanes strewn with hawthorn and blackberry bushes, or among the near-by woods of Lelant Downs.

While the children were at school Jess and I were free if we wished to visit Penzance or St Ives. The latter was not only much the nearest, but our more natural port of call. This was a time when I was planning the *Cornish Review*, the literary magazine whose history is described in detail in a later chapter. This involved quite a few discussions with authorities on Cornish affairs, like the late R. Morton Nance, then Grand Bard of Cornwall, with craftsmen such as Bernard Leach, the master potter who was always very keen to encourage any cultural movement in Cornwall, with modernist artists like Sven Berlin and Bryan Wynter or John Park and David Cox of the more traditional school - and of course with fellow writers.

Like any concentrated centre of artists St Ives suffers from over-population - every year a kind of flotsam of art students and worse, pseudo art students, descends on the existing art colony, so that life becomes very difficult for genuine workers.

There is a tremendous world of gossip and chatter, everyone's movements seem to be watched with a telescope and reported upon. It was rather amusing to notice this kind of thing in action now that I produced Jess. Hitherto, as an unattached male, I had found myself excessively popular, especially among that strange community, the ex-wives of St Ives (there are a surprisingly large number of wives separated from their husbands, who seem to retire to St Ives as a kind of resting centre). Now that I was safely tied up, I was no longer of such interest; but of course Jess was. I shall always remember the first time we walked along the front at St Ives towards the sloop Inn, on a sunny day. There they were all lined up outside, those ex-wives, like an inspection squad.

On the other hand the social life of St Ives could be very lively and amusing. These were the days when Sven Berlin, a huge, handsome sculptor, lived and worked at The Tower, a small studio on the side of the island, and this was a favourite centre for parties. St Ives is one of those queer hangovers from the days of Primitive Methodism, and though it has been pretty thoroughly infiltrated by artists, retired people, and others there is still a strong underground activity against sinful enjoyment, as any noise after ten o'clock at night is termed. As a result places like Sven's Tower, which had no neighbours, were very popular. Every now and then, if he sold a sculpture or if there was a crowd of convivial visitors, Sven would invite everyone back. As the Tower consisted of two small rooms about twelve by fifteen at the most, and these half occupied by pieces of alabaster and rubble, it now seems incredible to recall that as many as seventy people would attend one of these parties. Of course, if it was a warm summer evening, then it was always possible to relieve the congestion by a quick dip in the sea off neighbouring Porthgwidden Beach. In those days Porthgwidden was a quite delightful unspoiled little Atlantic cove; now in the cause of commercial enterprise the St Ives Council have reduced it to a yellowbrick eyesore.

We now became great friends with Sven who, as his name suggests, is half Swedish by birth. Sven was a romantic not only in his work but in his life and appearance. He was a big powerful man, as befitting a sculptor, and he usually went about dressed rather like a swash-buckling pirate of old. He had a luxuriant black beard, and with his open shirt revealing a bushily hairy chest he made a striking and handsome figure. He looked quite a fiery and formidable man, but in fact was one of the kindest and gentlest of creatures, with great sensitivity to other people's problems, though inclined perhaps to over-dramatize his own. Not that they didn't lend themselves to melodrama! During the whole of his twenty years at St Ives Sven was constantly involved in situations of one sort or another, culminating in a comic opera tussle with the St Ives Council over the tenancy of the Tower. Despite letters not only to the local papers but to *The Times* and other national newspapers, as well as protests by local groups of artists, Sven was finally forced to leave the studio where he had worked for so long (and proved incidentally quite an attraction to the visitors)-and the St Ives Council, in their wisdom, incorporated it into the building of some new ladies' and gentlemen's toilets! Somehow to me that has always symbolized the local council's true attitude to the artists from whom they have derived such benefit.

Like most of the genuine artists of St Ives, Sven worked hard and painstakingly, and personally I admired his sculpture very much, far more than his paintings. I liked, too, the way he wrote about his work, and in particular the effect that Cornwall had upon it. He was one of the first people I asked to contribute to the *Cornish Review,* and I always like to quote a paragraph from his article 'My World as a Sculptor':

My taste was always for the primitive and early creations of any civilisation. It led to Cornwall, the most primitive of all places, where one can recapture the delight of playing with a crystal as a child and watching the arms of the lighthouses divide out the night when the sea is oily with moonlight and the angels and dragons are slumbering on the cliffs. This is truly a sculptor's country, itself made of granite, but few have realised it. The terraced landscape of the little fishing towns and the geological nature of the rock at once become operative, along with the submarine cargo of shells, skulls, fish and plants, in orientating one's vision back to the fundamental shapes of nature as was the case with the sculptors of earlier civilisations. This added to the peculiar influence Cornwall has upon the unconscious mind of man brings into line once more the ancient forces of creation which, it may be surmised, have a close affinity with the spirit of life. In such an environment it becomes possible for modern man to make a statement

about humanity penetrating its mechanical armour and seeing it once again as a
dynamic part of the universal order governed by the mystery of God.

Some readers objected to the supercharged style of Sven Berlin's writings, but these same people would no doubt have complained of the way people like Sven walked or dressed or talked. To me Sven's writing is in its own way as vivid and striking as his sculpture. Even if his flamboyancy and perhaps, conceit, rubbed some people up the wrong way, one has to recognize a sensitivity and a tenderness for the good things of life in such a man. He was very much a character, the sort of creative eccentric which I have said Cornwall attracts. I think in fact most of St Ives were sorry at heart when finally he and his wife Juanita left the district to settle in the New Forest.

What was so fascinating about these periodical forays into St Ives-apart from the striking contrast between the vast silence of Trencrom and the loud arguments in artists' studios -was the way in which life became a series of encounters. It was only necessary to stroll down St Ives' tiny Fore Street to meet not one but perhaps half a dozen friends, a painter, a potter, a writer, a critic, a printer. Where else in the British Isles, I used to wonder, was this possible, out of London. Perhaps I would come across a little group in earnest conversation: Canadians Norman Levine and Christopher Wanidyn discussing with Guido Morris the setting of a book of Norman's poems, to be printed by Guido on his printing press set up in a cottage on the island looking right out over St Ives Bay. Next, there might be another little group, several bearded young men in blue jeans and coloured shirts, members of the New Crypt group, arguing about policy. In a near-by bookshop a couple of young writers would be drinking cups of tea with the proprietor, Bill Barnes, whose second-hand books always drew us like a magnet. A little farther on in the Gay Viking cafe, which Elsa and the Saint ran, a group of gay young art students might be laughing over coffee in Norwegian mugs. That tall rather distinguished looking man walking along might well be Bernard Leach, the world-famous potter. Around a corner came a small dapper bald-headed man - Ben Nicholson, winner of many international awards for abstract painting. Up at Carbis Bay his wife Barbara Hepworth the sculptor might be working on some of those strange shapes, impregnated with a feeling of Cornwall, which have won her great acclaim. Out at the Carn Bryan Wynter would be working on his new picture, 'Seagull Over Water', while David Haughton may have travelled out to his favourite setting, St Just-in-Penwith. Somewhere along the Wicca coastline local-born Peter Lanyon might be found studying the rock formations which were such a feature of his work.

And then there were the pubs. At that time Endell Mitchell, brother of the sculptor, Denis Mitchell, was landlord of the 'Castle Inn', and this was for many artists their 'local'. It was a small and rather uncomfortable pub, but its walls were lined with exciting new paintings and the talk was good. For a change we would sometimes go to the 'Queen's', in the days before it was modernized, when there was a back room which the painters had to themselves, squatting round upturned beer barrels. And on a fine sunny day there was, of course, nowhere like the 'Sloop', whose windows look out on the waters of St Ives harbour. Here, fifty years ago, Sir Alfred Munnings, Louis Grier, Julius Olsson, Alfred East, and others held regular sessions in the Round Room: and something of that atmosphere has been carried on ever since, despite the summer swamping by holiday-makers. Once a haunt of smugglers the 'Sloop', being the only pub in the centre of the 'Downalong' part of St Ives, has remained a favourite with the local fishermen - many of whom, like 'Jimmy' and 'Matt' are commemorated in a series of famous portraits by the late Harry Rowntree.

It was very much a time of the painters. We writers were very much in the minority; though scattered about Cornwall as a whole, there was quite a large number of well-known authors, Winston Graham at Perranporth, Walter Greenwood at Polperro, Howard Spring at Falmouth, Daphne and Angela du Maurier at Par and Fowey, A. L. Rowse spending his holidays in his old home at St Austell. But few lived around St Ives, though many came to visit - for instance at various times the poets George Barker and John Heath-Stubbs and David Wright had cottages out at Zennor. Like D. H. Lawrence before them they were all quite profoundly affected and influenced by the Cornish landscape. So, too, was one writer who came to stay, W. S. Graham, the Scottish poet, who over perhaps fifteen years has soaked himself in the world of the sea and the cliffs, of Cornish landscapes and Cornish fishermen. It was he who wrote the very beautiful memorial poem to Alfred Wallis, an old St Ives fisherman who took up painting at the age of 70, and whose cantankerous, slightly crazy personality, fiercely daubing away with boat oils on old pieces of cardboard, reflects something of the unique childlike quality of the Cornish people:

> World hauled, he's grounded on God's great bank,
> Keelheaved to Heaven, saved into boatfilled arms,
> Falls his homecoming leaving that old sea testament,
> Watching the restless land sail rigged alongside
> Townful of shallows, gulls on the sailing roofs.

Another local writer whom we became friendly with - and about whom I have written in more detail in the chapter on the Cornish Review - was Arthur Caddick. Sometimes that booming voice could be heard coming half a mile away and the man fulfilled the expectations it aroused. With his expressive eyes, his high forehead, his wild greying locks, his manner of striding along and brandishing a walking stick as he spouted satirical lines from his own head, he seldom failed to dominate the company. An erudite and learned man, with an ironic wit, Caddick had a sharp gift for rattling off amusing verses about the artists, but more especially about the philistines of West Cornwall. He wrote a very funny and possibly libellous novel about life in the art colony, Two Can Sleep Cheaper, which I think has never been published. But his real gift is for poetry. We once used a long poem of his in the Cornish Review, 'Ode on Becoming Respectable', in which he looked back with tender but ironic regret to past days - to Amanda whom he loved one spring, but who 'lives no more in sin but Putney now - Her husband has a convex sort of waist'. Later in the poem Caddick bemoans how Bacchus sets the heart of man on fire and then robs the lover of his finest powers, yet he ends, weakening, with a cry that perhaps he'll pop into town for just one more drink...

For some fifteen years Caddick, with his wife and five children, has survived a life of constant worry and distress, up at a small cottage above Nancledra. Originally the cottage was associated with a part-time job in charge of a small electricity power station, the sort of bizarre side-line which poets are often forced into taking. At various times Caddick has undertaken other subsidiary occupations - writing commercial limericks, correcting correspondence-school papers, teaching, lecturing, selling advertisement space, making wooden models, acting as curator to an art gallery - through it all, including illnesses and the inevitable troubles of bringing up a large family, he has continued to write. Locally he has inspired many famous legends, for he is one of the best-known characters in West Penwith. Children who hear him declaiming Shakespearean sonnets (or more likely his own) on the bus from Penzance are sometimes a little shy of him - yet in them, as in others who have similar encounters, there exists an instinctive respect. For people like Caddick, with all their personal failings and difficulties, represent what I suggest are an important minority in this standardized world of ours - the individual, eccentric artist at work. Cornwall is the richer and wiser for being the chosen home of so many such people.

Like Sydney Graham, like Norman Levine, like myself - like painters such as Bryan Wynter, John Wells, W. Barns Graham - Caddick became involved in Cornwall in some curious, almost subterranean way - and here we all are. Something in this land must give the artist a kind of sustenance, I think: and if I wonder about this, I find my mind always goes back to the time when we lived high up on Trencrom Hill, in a world lingering with memories most ancient and powerful. It was then I became seeped more than ever in the strange lore of the land. In particular I came to feel very conscious that *West* Cornwall, that tip of the county which is almost cut off by a narrow line from Marazion over to Hayle, is the hub of all that is most ancient and mysterious about Cornwall. Although I had already lived in several other parts of the county I knew now that I wanted to settle at the western end. This was where I felt spiritually at home. This has frequently put me into some difficulties. For instance, about this time I received a commission to write a book on Cornwall - *The Cornish Scene* it was to be called. Acutely aware of my prejudice towards the West I resolved at all costs to write about Cornwall as a whole. Instead of writing the vivid and imaginative kind of book which at that time and in that mood I think I could have done, I produced a weighty, factual plodding tome which, though it contained all kinds of facts and figures about fishing and mining and so forth, completely failed to grasp the more striking images of Cornwall. I could hardly complain when the publisher came to the same conclusion and turned the book down.

Soon after this disappointment I found a much more suitable subject, namely the revival all over Britain of regional activities, and I wrote a book about this. My own title, *The Regional Renaissance,* was I think the best one, but in the end the publishers brought it out under the slightly pompous title of *Britain Discovers Herself.* I enjoyed writing this book very much, for my mind was greatly on this subject at the time. I surveyed the theatre, literature, art, music, broadcasting, crafts, education, and industry, and showed the very encouraging developments that were being made in various regions. I concluded that:

The Briton of old was the regional man. He knew no grey and smoky cities, paved with mythical gold. He did know his own home, his own village, his own locality; where to find food, how to build a home, how to create the necessary conditions of existence. Above all, he knew personally the people of his locality, with whom he lived, worked and played. He was not, as so often his successor has become today, an anonymous flat-dweller among a colony of anonymous flat-dwellers living in secretive worlds, seldom knowing one another's names. He did not, as today most of us do, depend on some remote monopoly for the provision of a synthetic form of heating-he went out and chopped wood and made his own fire. In the earliest days, instead of eating his frozen Argentine beef and opening his can of carrots he went hunting for his food. And if he wanted to entertain himself or his friends, he did not switch on a button or put on a record-he stood up and sang, or joined with others in dancing around a fire, or maybe to a pagan god.

And at the end of the book, claiming that the regional renaissance was now in full swing, I pointed out that its strength lay in the fact that it sprang from the earth, a familiar geographical background, and is fashioned and expressed by craftsmanship and other creative faculties. Naturally I cited Cornwall as an example of a strong regional entity, and I have no doubt that my experiences of living there helped to add colour to my writing. But I wasn't only thinking of Cornwall, but of Wales, of Scotland, of Ireland, of East Anglia, of the West Riding, and so on. Altogether I felt strongly, and still do, that regional independence is an excellent and positive thing.

Now I felt even more encouraged to go on with my projects for a Cornish magazine. I had often contributed stories to *Welsh Review* and *Wales,* and through my work as editor of the *Little Reviews Anthologies* I was familiar with many other such regional magazines, and I knew how important a part they had to play in keeping regional life aglow. So now, in our tiny Trencrom cottage, I often worked late into the night drawing up plans and circulars for the *Cornish Review.* At the same time, however, our family life in such a remote spot was becoming increasingly strained. We were now expecting the first baby of our own, and as Jess grew heavier and heavier, the pleasures of country life were los, and only the difficulties left. Everything became more and more of an effort, and our daily lives were frequently dependent too much on one rather dilapidated old Austin Seven. With the prospect of the children home for the seven week summer holidays we suddenly longed for space and comfort, for a more civilized life. We would have liked to move into St Ives, but not only were houses there hard to find but their prices reached to the sky. As time ran short, regretfully we turned our search elsewhere. At last, about three months before the baby was due, we moved into 16, Morrab Place, Penzance.

Chapter Two

A HOUSE FULL OF PEOPLE

Although it can fairly claim to be 'the last town in England' Penzance almost ties with Falmouth for the largest population of a Cornish town. It has a harbour and docks, is a centre for several light industries, and also the market town for a very wide agricultural area. With the fishing port of Newlyn to its south-west, and the famous towering peak of St Michael's Mount reaching up to the sky on the east, Penzance holds a glorious situation on the sheltered inside of beautiful Mount's Bay. Standing at the top of Paul Hill, Newlyn, and looking down, one might be surveying some jewel city of the Mediterranean. It is only later, on ground level and closer acquaintance, that one discovers that Penzance has the inevitable limitations of so many provincial small towns. Nevertheless, with all these, it is a very pleasant and climatically attractive place, notable for its famous tropical Morrab Gardens, its unique Morrab Library (which houses the country's finest collection of sixteenth-century books), its many surrounding beauty spots -and of course the Penzance-Newlyn Pirate Rugby team.

At our new home, a Georgian terraced house, we were fortunate in being in the centre of things and yet partially sheltered down a quiet cul-de-sac. Only a few yards away the buses ran up and down Morrab Road, with its long line of doctors and dentists and guest-houses, and, at the top, the Penzance Art School; behind us were the offices of the *Cornishman;* sloping away, easy of access, were the Morrab Gardens themselves, a wondrous place of camellias, magnolias, and sub-tropical plants of all kinds - while in the distance, visible from the top floor, stretched the vast waters of Mount's Bay, with the Lizard Lighthouse winking in the distance at night time.

At first we had the house to ourselves. It had been bought pretty cheaply at an auction by a local speculator who had done it up a little and then put it on the market at a much higher price. We haggled about this, but being by this time desperate we had to clinch the deal, so we approached a building society and arranged a mortgage of 80 percent (later to be our downfall). Finally in the middle of a hot August we moved in, householders at last. The house was certainly big enough to hold us all comfortably, for altogether there were eleven rooms occupying five floors - basement, ground, first, second and third. For a time we wallowed in the luxury of sheer space, plus the conveniences of constant hot water, electric light, and gas cooking. Jess and I lay around in lazy comfort in a lovely big Georgian bed-sitting-room on the first floor, while we put in fitted carpets in the sitting-room below, which had an old-fashioned coal fire. I made an office for myself in one of the rear rooms with a somewhat unedifying view of a white-washed backyard (we had no garden, alas). Here I was able to work in peace, and to go on with the work of the *Cornish* Review, which had just been launched. Through all the upheaval of the past few months I had managed to carry on writing - not such a praiseworthy achievement as it sounds, perhaps, since it is almost a pathological necessity for me to be writing: after two weeks holiday I become restless and fidgety until I can get back to work. Unfortunately, since my new married life began with all its increased responsibilities, my earnings, always variable, had to stretch to keep a family of five, soon to be increased to six. As far as possible I attempted to write stories or articles that would bring in a quick return, but it so happened that I had had to spend many months writing books, and these seldom earn a great deal of money. The trouble is that, for me, writing a book has to be a full-time occupation while it lasts. Many's the time Jess has practically stood over me begging me to write a story and earn some money, while doggedly I have hammered on with the next chapter of the book under way (this one, needless to say, being no exception!). The only time I felt I found a satisfactory solution was when a London publisher agreed to pay me L10 a month for a year on condition I delivered a novel at the end of that time. This system seems sensible - though I must confess that when I finally delivered my novel it was turned down, and shortly after the firm ceased publishing fiction!

It wasn't long therefore, before our family life at 16 Morrab Place began to run into the type of financial 'problem' which has dogged us relentlessly for the past ten years namely too little earned money chasing too much owed money. The position of the writer is the position of most self-employed men, but whereas the cobbler or the blacksmith, and various other kinds of self-employed businessmen are usually in daily contact with their customers and able to collect payments within a reasonable time, the author is entirely dependent on the whims of people who may be hundreds of miles away. While things have improved and many publishing concerns now pay on acceptance of an article or story, there are still some who cling to the inconsiderate practice of paying only when a manuscript is actually published. Thus a story which I write today, and which the editor of a magazine accepts, may not actually bring me its cash return for a year or more. In the same trend, publishers only pay royalties due to authors twice a year, although at least these payments are regular. Lack of *regular* payments is, I am sure, the free-lance author's greatest bugbear. He never knows from one week to another where his next penny is coming from.

If I dwell here for a while on this problem it is because in my experience it is one whose implications are not fairly considered by other people. Bank managers, for instance, who cheerfully grant over-drafts of £2,000 to farmers or owners of factories, begrudge a mere £5 over the limit to authors whose 'potential', did they but know it, probably rates far and away above farmer or factory. Many other business men who are as impressed as bank managers by any show of visible wealth and property are equally unsympathetic to any member of what is generally termed the artistic community. Yet these same business people are often high on the list of what I term 'culture snobs', and would if they could afford it pay £20,000 or more for a tiny painting by poor dead (and in his time scorned) Van Gogh: it would, of course, be a good 'investment'. Such anomalies are part of the sickening hypocrisy of our modern society which reaches its high peak - I nearly wrote high priest-hood-in political leaders proclaiming their desire for peace while authorizing the spending of another billion on rocket missiles.

So, although pleased with a wide-spread friendly reception to my regional book, I had reason to be alarmed at the general financial position, and Jess and I were forced to sit down and consider our assets, such as they were. They boiled down in fact to one very old and rather tired Austin Seven, now gaily decorated with a map of Cornwall and the emblem, *Cornish Review,* and the house we lived in. Desperate situations demanded desperate remedies. The house was obviously too large for our requirements. Why not then augment our very shaky income by letting out a room? Or, upon reflection, even perhaps two rooms.

Once born the idea germinated quickly. For one thing it would bring us nearer to the dream of a regular weekly income. Another aspect that appealed to us at that early stage of our residence in Penzance was that it would bring us some company: most of our friends seemed to live over at St Ives, and as yet we had not seemed to find a niche in Penzance life. So Jess, who is extremely practical in such matters, began to plan a general re-arranging of the house. We went along to one or two furniture sales and bought a few extra items, a couple of beds and a couch and so on. After a lot of consideration we decided the simplest arrangement would be to keep the top three floors of the house to ourselves, and let off the two ground-floor rooms and the basement, which made a self-contained flat. We had just finished redecorating the rooms and putting in the furniture, and I was vaguely wondering about forming an advertisement for the local paper, when there was a knock at the front door and a friend of ours produced a rather shy young couple with two small children.

'This is Anthony and Dorothy Richards. They're badly needing somewhere in Penzance to live, and I wondered if maybe you could help them?'

Anthony Richards was a neat, almost dapper figure of a man, dark haired and with a carefully trimmed dark beard that made him look rather older than his twenty-eight years. His wife Dorothy, by contrast, was a lush Rubensesque type, half Greek by birth and reflecting this Eastern influence in her dark skin and almost jet black hair. Anthony was a potter who like many other craftsmen before him had been attracted down to Cornwall, and was now working at the Lamorna Pottery about five miles from Penzance. We were only too pleased to offer them the flat, and they moved in almost immediately.

For a while that was the extent of our adventure into landlordship. We didn't see a great deal of Anthony then, as every morning he departed at the fantastically early hour of 7 a.m. to catch the early bus out to Lamorna, where he worked terribly hard and very long hours for a somewhat meagre wage of £7 a week. But Dorothy and the two children were now very much present all day, the latter contributing about another 10 per cent to the noises of the day. What with them and our children, life at Morrab Place was never exactly quiet. Sometimes in the evenings we would share a cup of tea together with our new lodgers, whom we liked as simple and unspoiled people, vaguely groping towards some sort of satisfying life, like ourselves.

Unfortunately Anthony's monetary problems became ours. Gradually we became accustomed to the sheepish manner in which he would shuffle into our room every Saturday morning bearing his rent book and mumbling apologetically, 'Er, I'm afraid it's a little bit short this week.' With a total wage of around and a family of four to support, it was not surprising that Anthony had difficulty in finding even a comparatively low rent of 3os. This we quite understood, but as things hadn't improved for me, we felt the only thing to do was to rent off another room at Morrab Place. We decided, rather regretfully, to move ourselves out of that lovely first-floor front room, and let that-the best in the house. Only this time, we decided firmly, we would advertise the room and let it not to someone happy-go-lucky like ourselves, but to some normal everyday respectable type, the sort who would pay the rent like clockwork.

In this way we welcomed into our midst Miss Frost, a short stocky lady who seemed eminently respectable, indeed who was eminently respectable, one might almost say painfully so. With Miss Frost we learned, if we had needed to, that no one is really normal, and even the most prim and proper have curious neuroses of their own. Miss Frost was one of those women who spend half their lives polishing brass and cleaning furniture and brushing away imaginary specks of dust, while yet somewhere in their inner life there are inexplicable shadows. Miss Frost, we discovered, had her skeleton in the cupboard, a middle-aged gentleman who called regularly every Tuesday and Friday and whom quite primly she explained as her fiancé It was only accidentally that we learned that the gentleman fiancé was in fact a married man. During the whole tenure of her stay she maintained the illusion of herself and her fiancé, and would discuss, but with guarded vagueness, plans for their marriage. Unfortunately, Miss Frost carried her primness as a weapon of war aimed very positively at Dorothy, the two being complete opposites. Almost every day there were complaints from our first-floor lodger about the behaviour of our ground floor lodger, and sometimes, in exasperation, vice versa. By an unhappy circumstance both shared the same bath-room for their washing. Frequently I would be sitting working in an upstairs room and I would hear the angry voices rising from the yard below. Sometimes when the Greek side of Dorothy's blood was up the pace would hot up, and Jess or I would have to rush downstairs to prevent actual physical violence.

All in all we were not sorry when finally Miss Frost departed. We decided we would celebrate our freedom from respectability by letting the room to someone with more open and bohemian tastes. There was no need to advertise, for as soon as the word got round we were presented with Anna, one of the innumerable wives separated from husbands who seem to gravitate to Cornwall. In no time Aima transformed Miss Frost's room from a sterile sort of show place into a more living thing - still more so when she acquired a sympathetic boy friend with whom she would listen to symphony concerts and read her books and generally pursue a worthy intellectual life. As we had gathered that Anna's separation from her husband was because he insisted that in order to write a great novel they must have no sexual intercourse for six months we certainly felt no great sympathy towards this unknown and somewhat obsessed being. All the same we felt rather alarmed one night, very late, when there was a thunderous knocking on the front door and the said husband made a dramatic arrival after catching the last train from London. In the best style of old-fashioned melodrama he entered Anna's room to find her and her friend cosily together, whereupon he immediately produced a knife and threatened to use it. Things were eventually smoothed out a little and the final result of it all was that Anna returned to her husband, possibly a little flattered by his positive action.

As time went on the list of Morrab Place lodgers got longer and longer, and even more varied. What with losses on the *Cornish Review,* and a steady downward trend in my own earnings, we were coming to depend more and more desperately on our rents, even if some of them were often rather delayed ones. Soon we executed some further shifting around to enable us to let off yet another room-this time the small rear one on the first floor. This certainly seemed to attract an odd series of characters, mostly for some reason male. One that always sticks in my mind was a strange little man whom I never saw except wearing a trilby hat and usually a flapping raincoat, and who persisted in keeping in his room a bicycle permanently undergoing repair.

Then there was Carl, a blond and beautiful young man with a cult of the healthy physique, who would spend hours doing complicated athletic feats in front of a full length mirror; Rodney, owner of a huge ostentatious American car which he left outside the house for weeks on end, a sort of big business type of man who was perpetually on the point of negotiating sole contracts with the local council for the beach rights or something of that nature; and later a friend of his who actually did take up the photographic rights of Penzance promenade, a somewhat doubtful money spinner which he wisely gave up for a more lucrative beat at Land's End.

And then, of course, P. Words almost fail me in my efforts to describe P., a responsibility we were somewhat tricked into. Around that time we had met a bearded psychologist-philosopher called Alf Knowles who had under his wing this mixed-up young man, son of a General, who had revolted against home discipline and became very confused in the process. Somehow Alf had come into the picture and was being paid by the family to look after P., and keep him out of harm's way. Upon closer acquaintance with P. we had every sympathy with Alf quickly tiring of this somewhat onerous duty; but we subsequently took a rather dim view of the arrangement not only suggested but positively begged of us by Alf that we should let our little rear room to P. Not to worry, Alf assured us, he would look in regularly to see P. was all right. Somehow once P. was installed Alf's appearances became few and far between. Meanwhile we and the other lodgers were left to cope with the eccentricities of an over-grown schoolboy with a mother complex who preferred to mumble incoherently rather than speak clearly (as he could perfectly well if he wished), whose favourite occupation was to wander the streets at early hours of the morning until picked up by the police and politely delivered to our front door, and whose main delight, otherwise, was in the malicious misuse of any articles he could get hold of. We were heartily glad when finally P. ran away altogether and was last heard of at Newton Abbot, hotly pursued by a worried Alf.

Most of our lodgers seemed to come and go at intervals of a few months, but one other long-term lodger of whom we grew very fond was Amy. She was one of those delightful, slightly eccentric English ladies who tend to do good works, take up crafts, try to help their neighbours and often, as in her case develop a very real devotion to some form of religion or philosophy. For a long time, after we had done some more shifting around and decided to let out the top part of the house, Amy rented a four-roomed flat at Morrab Place. There she often entertained some of the young students from the near-by art school. Indeed, after this, what with another student on the floor below, our house became quite a centre for the art students of Penzance, many of whom used to combine resources to cook a quick cheap lunch, either upstairs or downstairs. Amy quite rekindled my interest in psychic affairs, in which she was very interested. I always remember an occasion some years later when she had decided to rent a flat in the old vicarage at St Hilary; but on spending a night out there she mysteriously, yet meaningly, announced that she wouldn't be able after all to take the room. Later I discovered a man had jumped to his death out of the window of that room, and this sent up my opinion of Amy's psychic powers enormously.

But at Morrab Place there were no psychic problems, only purely physical ones. The time came when Dorothy ran off with a young painter called David who had rented the big room on the first floor, and we thus lost not only her but another lodger, too, while Anthony was left very unhappily on his own. Fortunately at about this time Anthony was very fully occupied with giving up his underpaid job at Lamorna, and starting a pottery of his own with another of the Lamorna potters, Len Missen, who had also taken a room at Morrab Place - so although Anthony was naturally upset emotionally, he was forced to occupy himself with more material things. The Penzance Pottery, as it became known, had many teething troubles. It first saw light in the upstairs loft of an old warehouse down by the harbour which could often only be reached when the tide was out! The kiln and wheel were both home-made, built with enthusiasm and hope, but they worked - and soon a more central workroom at the Greenmarket enabled the P.Z.P., as it became known, to get really established. We often remember that familiar corner cottage, the two tiny rooms like a furnace, Anthony practically chained to the wheel turning out orders, Len busying himself with the decorations - work, work, work, often late into the night, but readily undertaken because the boys felt they were building up something of their own.

Where Anthony was essentially a primitive and simple person, instinctive and fairly uncalculating in his approach, Len was quite the opposite - very much a thinking man. Fair haired, almost baby-faced but with an old mouth and sharp eyes that belied any innocence. Len had a most attractive personality, to men as well as women. There was somewhere about him a natural charm, and ageless grace, as well as a warmth and vitality that made him an irresistible companion. He was extraordinarily mature for his tender age of 27, perhaps because all his life had been a relentless struggle to raise himself from a comparatively working class background. During the war his school was evacuated to Bedfordshire, and there he was billeted with a cultured family from whom he developed a taste for reading and similar pursuits. He had a year as a Bevin Boy, which helped to clarify his left-wing political feelings, and after that he took up painting, and became a member of what was loosely known as the Euston Road school under David Bomberg. During this period Len married and lived with his wife's parents off Fulham Road, but spent most of his time, when not doing odd jobs like making lamp brackets or masks, in the company of painters. Finally, after his marriage had broken up, he decided to come and live down in Cornwall, and went to work at the Lamorna Pottery. He was never a craftsman-potter in the sense that Anthony was, the latter having served seven long years apprenticeship and having an automatic feeling for throwing. Len had learned to throw, and understood the various processes of pottery making, but his main interest was in design. He also had a good head for business, which was just as well since Anthony had no head for it at all. It was Len who did the planning for the Penzance Pottery-Len who worked out the types of pots they would make, and the designs to be made on them - Len who grappled with all the economics. Yet it was Anthony who did the basic function of throwing the pots, with almost effortless ease. They made, indeed, an excellent partnership.

Does the list of our lodgers at Morrab Place sound too much of a catalogue? The fact is it was that sort of house, a place where a bizarre collection of people came and went, each leaving something of his personality behind-so that the house itself became a little the total of all its denizens. By Penzance standards it was quite a bohemian household and I have often wondered how it was looked on in official quarters, especially by the police who had the job of bringing back such characters as P. What mattered, however, was not whether it was a bohemian sort of place, but that during our ownership it became a house that was alive and living-and, I like to think, a happy house. To this day I often bump into someone who lived there for a time, and their eyes brighten as they remember and say: 'Ah, yes, I miss the good old days at Morrab Place.'

From our own point of view it was a period notable for laying the foundations of a tenuous link between a group of people who subsequently captured that secret of true friendship that eludes many people throughout their lives. It was also, more practically, a time of great activity and even greater worry over the *Cornish Review.* And it was, finally, the time when jess and I experienced the very great joy of having the first child that we could truly call our very own - Stephen Ross Val Baker, born during a wild night in early November. He weighed over lb., had a tuft of blond hair and a pair of bright brown eyes, and in no time at all was yelling his little head off - possibly to demonstrate his apprehension of the somewhat impoverished family life he had joined.

I found Stephen's arrival unsettling rather than the reverse -knowing that it was really time we dug in our roots, I became all the more conscious that! didn't want to plant them in this particular spot. Though, as I have explained, it became a very happy house, I couldn't suppress a feeling of being stifled by living in the heart of a town, or at least that town. Instinctively I longed to get back to the romantic Cornwall that I had known at Portquin and Trencrom. At least I suppose so. Not long ago I came across an essay by my son Martin about different homes he had lived in: it began quite baldly, and perhaps a little sourly, 'For some reason my father was obsessed with a wanderlust'. Perhaps that is true, also; though I am not the normal sort of wanderer, I like comfort and routine and am most chary of hazardous expeditions. Still, now I come to think about it, I have spent most of the past ten years either moving house or planning to move house or even, for one exultant period of six months, contemplating settling the whole family on a large Thames barge. So perhaps Martin has something.

Whatever the reason or motive, the fact was, shall I say, that I was keeping my eyes open. In these matters I am a great believer in things happening because they are meant to happen; or as one might put it, apparently aimless incidents that really have a purpose. The advent to stay with us for a few days of one Norman Potter was an example of this. I had known Norman in London many years ago, though not very well, but now that he too, had been bitten by the Cornwall bug and had come down to look for a home, he remembered my name and called on us. Norman was a little like myself in that his enthusiasms seemed to take possession of him quite violently. Since I had first known him he had developed a talent for producing hand-made furniture, very contemporary in style, and his idea now was to set up in business in Cornwall, where rents might be cheaper than in London. While his main purpose in coming down was to find living accommodation for himself and family, he was also already thinking in terms of obtaining wood suitable for hand-made furniture. He noticed one day that there was a big sale of household goods and furniture at a local auction rooms and suggested we went along. Norman's idea was that there might be a few pieces which would be worth buying for the quantity of good wood contained: he could then strip them down and reuse the wood.

My presence, of course, was purely fortuitous. But once there my eye roamed round curiously and came to rest on a grand piano. For most years of my life, I have had access to a piano of one sort or another, though I do little more than strum out tunes. Since coming to Cornwall I had been rather cut off from this amusement. Suddenly I became fascinated by the idea of owning a grand piano of my own. It certainly was an impressive one, a huge positively grand-grand piano made of rather unusual light coloured wood. I moved over to the piano and tried the keys, and realized it would need tuning. However, a grand piano . . . . Ah, but of course it would no doubt fetch some stupendous price. All the same I would have a go, just out of curiosity.

When the number of the piano was finally called I nearly missed it through just waiting to see how the bidding went. In fact, there was no bidding at all. The auctioneer was about to pass on to the next item when I collected my wits, and rather foolishly stammered out a bid of five pounds (I have learned wisdom since then: recently I paid 5s. for an upright piano). In no time the bid had been accepted and the piano knocked down to me.

'Mmmmmmmm!' said Norman, examining the piano thoughtfully. 'That's a nice piece of wood you've got there, you know.'

At the time the significance of his remark was lost on me. I was caught up with the exhilaration of my dramatic purchase, and sent Norman hastening off to fetch some help from among our friends at Morrab Place. Half an hour later four of us wheeled a grand piano across Greenmarket, Penzance, and down side roads towards Morrab Place.

I had imagined the journey would be the worst part, but when we reached the steps of the house we discovered the piano was too large for the hallway. Then Norman came to our rescue.

'Wait a minute. We'll unscrew the legs, and then take away the lid, and I think if you take out those two window frames we might just about manage. . .

In the end we got the piano into the house but found it quite impossible to take it upstairs as I had vaguely intended, and we were compelled to put it in the rear end room, which was now once again my office. This was a pleasant enough room, about 13 feet by 12, into which quite

comfortably fitted myself and a desk, some files and an easy chair. But it was hardly designed for a grand piano as well. However, by a process of manoeuvring we managed to angle the piano so that the door could just be opened about eighteen inches, while space was left in one corner for a huddled cramped gathering of desk, files, and me. When the piano tuner arrived - visible evidence of my dogged determination not to be defeated! - he had to perform acrobatics to get at the piano. Still, after that we aere able to have some fine impromptu concerts, especially when the children came home from school. This halcyon state lasted, or perhaps I should say was persevered with, for a couple of weeks, during which time life in the office became more and more difficult. Then one day the piano got out of position and I found it impossible to get into the office at all and had to get a ladder and climb up and force the window to make an entry.

'Mmmmmmm', repeated Norman later that day, rather cunningly. 'You know there's a lot of very good wood in that piano. I was wondering...'

'Five pounds and it's yours,' I said abruptly.

And the deal was done, thank goodness.

That was a minor example of how Norman's arrival affected our life. The other example, however, was to have a major influence on our life. At this time Norman's main preoccupation was finding a home, preferably out in the country, and one day he wished to visit two prospective houses, one at Sancreed, about five miles out, and the other much farther, at Sennen Cove, near Land's End. It was a fine sunny day, and I said I would drive him out. Norman had already seen the Sancreed house once and it was very much what he wanted. This time the owner was going to be there to discuss things more fully. The upshot of this was that by the time Norman came back to the car he had more or less settled on renting the house.

'We can go back to Penzance if you like.'

'No, come on, we've come this far, let's look at the other,' I replied. I had been browsing through the sheaf; of details from the auctioneers, and something had clicked in my mind as I read: '. . . set on cliffs over-looking Whitesand Bay glorious Atlantic views . . . one mile from Land's End...Yes, there could be no harm in looking'.

The road to Sennen, which is that same one that so many thousands of holiday-makers follow every summer on their way to Land's End, is normally a lonely one, contributing to the sense of penetrating to a very isolated part of the world. When finally one comes in sight of the sea there is a panoramic view of craggy cliffs and white-crested waves, and in the distance the promontory Cape Cornwall. Then the road winds away from this to turn through the tiny village of Sennen itself; with its 'First and Last' church, its 'First and Last' pub, and so on. Sennen Cove, however, lies down a turning reached before Sennen, with a finger pointing to the 'Old Success Inn'. By the time Norman and I took this turning we were very hazy about how to find our objective and went all the way down the steep hill into the Cove itself before finding a kind soul who told us that we must go back up the hill and then turn right and follow the lane to the end.

When we had literally followed this advice we found the lane petering out into the soft mossy turf. There was nothing for it but to park the car there and get out and forage on foot. As far as we could see we were standing on Cornish cliffs with a magnificent view over Whitesand Bay, but little evidence of the house we were looking for.

'Just a minute,' said Norman, pointing. 'Do you see down there! Isn't that a roof?'

I have never known whether to be glad or sorry that my first approach to Peter's Cottage was the essentially romantic one, coming over the top slope of the cliffs, along a winding tortuous cliff-path, to find the grey-slated cottage almost beneath our feet. For a while both Norman and I could only stand and stare, lost in admiration of one of the most beautifully situated houses we had ever seen. Other parts of Sennen Cove have arisen haphazardly, often consisting of badly built bungalows and shacks, but Peter's Cottage was all on its own, the very last cottage along the cliff top before the mile walk to Land's End itself; and it was, outwardly at least, one of the old style Cornish granite cottages that seem to blend naturally into the Cornish landscape. Directly below the cottage, several hundred feet below, reached by twisting stone steps, was the village of Sennen Cove itself, mostly built around a tiny harbour and the Sennen Cove lifeboat station, which served the Land's End area.

It was a majestic, panoramic view, and as I say I have never known whether it was a good or bad thing that I came upon the cottage in such circumstances - for the fact is I knew at once in my heart that I wanted to live there. Going on down the path and knocking at the door and introducing myself to the owners and being shown all over the cottage - that was all merely a perfunctory going-through-the-motions.

'And what's the lowest you would consider taking?' I heard myself saying suddenly.

It wasn't as simple as all that, of course: by no means. First, there was the problem of Jess, who was rather enjoying the convenience of civilized things like constant hot water and electricity and so on. Peter's Cottage was quite well equipped in the practical matters, being all-electric, but I knew that Jess might not fancy going to a comparatively isolated spot. I could only go back and enthuse as effectively as I could, and pray that it would be a lovely sunny day when I took Jess out to see her prospective new domain. Fortunately it was; the air was full of the scent of honeysuckle and seapinks, and everything looked rather like a cliffland paradise. There was even a lovely sunlit patch of lawn built into the cliffside where baby Stephen could sleep all day in his pram - yes, even Jess's romantic soul, more cautious than mine, was suitably stirred. I was in any case assaulting her at an unfair time, when she was still all soft and tender and motherly after the birth of Stephen. All the same there was a certain hesitation, I fancied.

'But what about Morrab Place?'

'Ah!' I produced my master-stroke. 'That's just it - we'll be able to let out all the rooms. We'll have a *regular* income!'

Those were magic words in Jess's ears, as in mine, and I saw the last of her real objections vanishing. I can't say she was ever a hundred per cent sold on the move to Sennen Cove but at least she bore yet another upheaval womanly, if a little resignedly.

We had now dealt with the first and second problems, but our third one seemed more difficult altogether. It was brief and to the point. How on earth were we going to raise the money to buy Peter's Cottage? The most obvious method, selling the Morrab Place, was one I had quickly explored, only to find that the market had slumped and that in the agent's opinion it might take a year before we found a buyer, and then at a low price. As this was precisely the same gentleman who had persuaded me into buying the house in the first place I was not amused, but there was little I could do about it. However, he did redeem himself somewhat by managing to obtain for us a mortgage of 80 per cent of the purchase price of £2,000.

We were still left with the problem of finding a remaining balance of about £500, with the legal charges. It was a problem that worried the owners as much as us, for they were very anxious to leave the district to settle in Devon, where they were starting a new business. At last after we had made several wistful visits to Peter's Cottage and stood around looking sadly at our home that might be, Mr and Mrs White took pity on us and said they would be willing to regard the balance as a loan.

In the end we improved on that by making the £500 a second mortgage on the Morrab Place house, which gave more security to the mortgagees. The fact remained, and often it dazed us slightly, that we were able in the end to buy Peter's Cottage without any cash being paid out at all, apart from the usual lawyer's fees.

It all took time, of course, and meantime there were complicated arrangements to be made for letting out the rest of Morrab Place, but finally everything was settled. Early one morning a huge furniture van arrived to collect our worldly possessions, and later that day we drove out in its wake - in brilliant sunshine again, I was relieved to note - to supervise the somehow unusual removal operation down the side of a Cornish cliff. By night-fall we were living, as near as needs be, at Land's End.

Chapter Three

AT THE END OF THE LAND

Living at Land's End has its drawbacks, to be sure. It is a long way from anywhere: Penzance, the nearest large town, is almost ten miles distant and bus services, though reasonable in summertime, in winter end at the absurd hour of 6.30 p.m. Then there are the holiday-makers, teeming crowds of them arriving in long queues of garish coloured motor coaches every hour of every day from May to September - so that Land's End itself is engulfed in a nightmare world of car parks, gifte shoppes, wayside stalls, ice cream vans, placards, posters, and other unwelcome symbols of commercialism which seems especially revolting in such a beautiful setting. Yet worse than any of these things, I think, is one of Nature's own hazards, and a peculiarly torturous one. I refer, of course, to the wind. Not an extraordinary wind, by any means, though sometimes, on exceptional occasions, it can rise to truly homeric proportions; but in general just a wind, a mild, pernickety, poky, querulous, irritating and constant factor in daily life.

At Land's End one has to learn to live with the wind, with the profusion of damp mists that settle like a plague. But there are compensations, as we began to find out during the next two years. Once we had settled in at Peter's Cottage and the three older children were attending the village school, there was only baby Stephen for us to worry about. Every morning, after a good feed, he would go off into a deep sleep tucked into his pram parked in the middle of our tiny lawn. Often, about mid-day, Jess and I would seize the opportunity to slip out along the cliff path, leaving Stephen peacefully dreaming while we strolled along the short cliff walk to the Land's End point. These walks are something we shall never forget, for during them we became conscious of a tremendous solitude, of our being literally alone with the mysterious universe. Everywhere the cliffs ended abruptly in steep precipices, granite slabbed slopes down to jagged rocks and swirling waters. Rounding the curve towards Land's End we could see the huddle of odd shaped rocks leading out to the famous Longship Lighthouse, and beyond that the Armed Knight, Doctor Syntax, and several other rock formations which the guide books have given popular names. Invariably we would throw ourselves down on a grassy slope and stare up into the azure sky, while the music of the sea and the seagulls'

cries blended harmoniously in our ears and the scent of seaweed and wild thyme tickled our nostrils. Then the gentle walk back, this time with quite a different panorama; the huge sweep of Whitesand Bay, with the sea travelling across in steady long lines of swell, to pour itself upon the wide golden sands of Sennen, while on the horizon Cape Cornwall, the only Cape in England, poked outwards like a humped fist. After a stroll such as this one felt invigorated not merely by the fresh Atlantic breeze, but by an awareness of the joy of living itself. Sometimes, of course, on a blustery day when the wind whipped at your feet and cut into your cheeks and the sea roared and raged, one's awareness was tinged with fear. How often have I watched several small tankers and cargo vessels fighting their way around Land's End and marvelled that their frailty could withstand the elemental forces unleashed by rough weather. Yet even on wild days the district reflects a kind of terrible beauty which is paralleled probably only by such places as the Welsh mountains or the Western islands. The whole of the peninsula is pervaded with this quality, so that as far as outings were concerned we were confronted with endless delights. In one direction we could drive out to St Just, that rather lonely town on the north extremity of the peninsula, notable for its large square, the meeting point of five roads, with four pubs, perhaps taking the turning that led out along the hump to Cape Cornwall with its picturesque cliff setting. Or if we liked to follow the coast road farther there was the valley at Kenidjack or, past Pendeen with its tiny mining houses and tiny people, the lovely moors around Morva and Gurnard's Head. Taking the south and west direction even livelier experiences awaited - for instance the cliff walk past Nanjizel Bay and round past the coast-guards to Porthgwarra, a tiny cove and beach tucked between the cliffs. A little farther on lay the cliff top church of St Levan and beyond that two beautiful sights, Porthcurno Bay, with its translucent white sands (out of which pass the cables on the first stage of their tremendous journey across the Atlantic to America) and the famous

Minack Theatre, set on the cliffs.

Porthcurno Beach - and when the tide allowed the two smaller beaches leading eastwards to the Logan Rock became a favourite haunt of our family. Nowhere else in Cornwall is the water quite so clear, a ravishing greeny-blue of Mediterranean intensity. Sometimes we would spend stolen days of bliss there, sunbathing and swimming, and eating our sandwiches, and then the more energetic ones climbing the stone steps winding up to that strange phenomenon, a theatre on the cliffs. I feel sorry for anyone who has never paid a summer visit to the Minack to watch the work of Shakespeare or Euripides, or perhaps Fry or Ibsen or Shaw, played in that romantic setting. They have missed a unique occasion. There cannot anywhere in the world be quite such an experience as to sit in the amphitheatre with the play outlined on the spot lit greensward below, while a vast backcloth of moonlit scenery stretches to the horizon, broken perhaps here and there by the flickering lights of the Newlyn fishing fleet steaming out to sea. It is magic, pure magic!

Nanjizel, Porthgwarra, Porthcurno, Logan Rock, Penberth, Lamorna . . . truly the Land's End dweller is surrounded by beautiful things. Of course we were lucky in being able to take the romantic view. Down in Sennen Cove many of the old cottages were inhabited by families of fishing folk whose weather-beaten faces and guarded expressions bore eloquent testimony to the hard lives they led. In-shore fishing is a hazardous occupation at any time, and especially so around the Longships and Sennen. The Cove, of course, is the place famous for the annual casting of the seine net, a local custom that has been carried on for generations by the combined efforts of local fishermen. When shoals of mullet are due in the vicinity a watch is kept night after night from high on the cliff top (the phosphorescent glow of the mullet can be seen in the dark). Finally a great shout of 'Hulla! Hulla!' is heard, whereupon every available man leaves whatever he may be doing and runs down to the boats. An enormous and very expensive seine net is thrown across the bay and, when the mullet are safely enclosed, the haul is steadily pulled up on the shore, where fishermen's wives and children are helping to gut and pack the fish for dispatch to Newlyn market. As can be imagined the whole operation is very tricky. Sometimes luck is in, and a catch may net some unusually high figure, but in general the result is perhaps to £400, and by the time the takings have been equally divided each family may only pocket about £25.

Even that has been in jeopardy lately for, as has been made pretty generally known in the national newspapers, fishermen from another Cornish fishing port, Par, have developed a habit of turning up with boats of their own, claiming that the mullets were fair catch for anyone. The last visit of this kind needed the combined efforts of forty policemen to keep the peace!

Living at Semien I soon learned to appreciate how centuries of hard living made the local families - the Georges, the Nicholases, the Laitys and so on - a trifle insular. Folk who have had to fight literally for their very existence find it hard to get out of a suspicious attitude, even if times - as represented by the influx of holiday-makers staying at fishermen's cottages - seem a little easier. This of course is a wide-spread problem in Cornwall, but one that was especially emphasized at Sennen. It often seemed to me an impossible task to make contact across such deep-rooted barriers as existed between locals and aliens like myself. Perhaps one came nearest to achieving it during some of those convivial evenings at the 'First and Last Inn' just past Sennen parish church. At that time the pub was run by three brothers from the north country, and what with their natural cheeriness and hailfellow-well-met attitude, plus the infectious high spirits of holiday-makers, even some of the local fishermen and farmers who used the pub seemed to thaw out. In the summer the pub would fill with a most varied collection - fishermen, farmers, painters, commandos, R.A.F. men, commercial travellers, coach parties, and visitors of all kinds including Americans and other overseas parties. There was always singing, ending with 'Abide with Me' or 'Auld Lang Sync'. And then one came out to a view across slopes to the winking red light of the Longships Lighthouse - and perhaps a glimpse of the more distant lights of the Scilly Isles.

The 'First and Last' was one of three hotels at Sennen Cove: the others were the 'Old Success' down in the Cove itself, which catered then mostly for visitors, and the 'Sennen Cove Hotel', a very modern looking black and white super luxury hotel, built into the cliff-side not far from our cottage. This latter building appeared to be empty most of the year, but for a period often weeks or so suddenly sprang to life, filling up with staffs of foreign embassies and other parties down from London. I was assured by the proprietor that it did quite well but I sometimes wondered. Somehow it never seemed quite to belong to the Cove-but then, I realized on reflection, neither did we, or several other non-Cornish families I knew. Even Ruth and George Manning-Sanders, the writers, had to live many years at the Cove before they were really accepted. By the time we lived there they had achieved this unusual distinction, I think, although Ruth, a very fine writer whose best-known books have been about circus life, always seemed to keep rather to herself. Sometimes I would see her taking long lonely walks out along the cliffs and it was interesting to come upon the sensitive result in this description of such a walk in her book *The West of England*:

It is then that the drowned sailors of the past can be heard hailing their names above the moaning of the waters. It is then that the sense of the primordial, the strange and the savage, the unknown, the very long ago, fills the dusk with something that is akin to dread. It is then that the place becomes haunted; a giant heaves grey limbs from his granite bed; a witch sits in that stone chair on the cliff.

By contrast George Manning-Sanders was a gregarious soul and though for many years a cripple, sustained a very lively interest in life. It was a familiar sight around Sennen to come upon George in his motorized wheel-chair taking an outing - though usually more than an outing, for he had taken up painting as a hobby and loved to paint the local Cornish views. At home, along the same Maria's Lane which led eventually to our cottage, George had a workroom at the bottom of the garden, and sometimes we would visit him there in the evenings for a chat. He had a sharp eye for character, which revealed itself in many short stories, but in fact, as he often said, fiction was hardly to be compared to the bizarre reality of life in an isolated fishing community. The Manning-Sanderses were one of a number of non-Cornish families settling in the Cove who might be taken to represent the other side of Land's End population. There are the locals - and there are the solitaries and escapists of one sort and another, who are impelled to choose this outlandish haven from the world. It is an area, for instance, that has always drawn its quota of writers, many of them very eccentric creatures. I think what attracts so many people is this very sense of being at the end of it all, of being face to face with the huge, ponderable infinite ocean, so that at any moment one only has to walk along the cliffs or across the wide sands of Sennen to get the world into perspective and see ourselves as the minute pitiful species we are.

We, too, were very much influenced by this atmosphere. I can remember sitting in my small box of an office, looking out on the great waves roiling over Sennen Sands, and being inspired to write a talk 'At the End of the Land', which later I gave on the B.B.C. West Region. In this talk I tried to suggest that even though we seek to escape to our own solitary beauty spots, we cannot forget that in truth we are all of the same world: as John Donne says, there is no need to wonder for whom the bell tolls - to some degree, it tolls for each one of us. At the same time, though I expressed and indeed felt such sentiments, I have always derived some of my greatest moments of happiness from being alone with Nature, especially by the sea. I seem to share those almost incommunicable feelings of which Richard Jefferies wrote so marvellously in *The Story of My Heart*, the one book above all others which, at the time I read it, had the most profound effect on me as a writer.

My writing career was following its usual undulating course. For some time past I had been concentrating on short stories and articles, partly to earn more money. Every now and then I would manage to get a story taken by a magazine which had not previously used my work, and I would feel pleased at this achievement - unfortunately only too often I would find that some other paper, on which I had come to rely, had closed down, or had a change of policy. Time and again I have had this experience, and that is what I mean by undulating course! At this time I had contributed a large number of stories to the B.B.C. Mid-Morning Series - to date I suppose I must have had about sixty stories broadcast in this series. I do not read them myself, as I think actors make a far better job of putting across a spoken story. Many of my stories, I am sure, have been twice as effective thanks to the creative interpretation by actors such as Hedley Goodall, Valentine Dyall, Paul Rogers, Frank Duncan, David Enders. Writing for the wireless is, of course, a specialized art and one which even after all this time I am not too sure I can command. But I do know that among the stories I have done for wireless have been some of my best.

Writing for the B.B.C. was interesting, but not especially rewarding, I found. It took me about ten years to be raised in price from £15 15s to £21. Sometimes I would get better prices from magazines such as *Argosy*, or *Home* or *Good Housekeeping*. The highest price I ever had for a short story, I think, was about £50 from the American magazine *Esquire* (today of course their prices are far higher than that.) Recently I went through a record of my stories and earnings, and it was significant that at least a dozen have individually earned maore than several of my books. Nine stories have earned more than £100 over the years (one has earned £150) and there is always the prospect of further sales. In writing, the subject which interests me more than any other is that of the relationship between human beings, often between man and woman, and some of my best stories have been around such themes. But they have not often earned much money. The stories which have earned money, in general, have been studies of childhood or of old age, sometimes written perhaps with rather too much sentiment. When they come off-as for instance in two popular ones, *The Big Wheel*, a study of a young girl at a fair, and *The Clay Pool*, a portrait of the flowering of a friendship between a boy and a girl - they are what I would most like to represent my qualifications as a writer.

During a short visit to London we had at last given up our ancient Austin Seven and obtained in its place an even older car, a 1929 Rover coupe. For two very good reasons I have always preferred old cars to new ones. First, because we have never been able to afford anything else, and second because they seem to me to have far more character and even road worthiness. At the time of writing I have owned eleven cars, and all but one has been a real veteran, full of extraordinary idiosyncrasies and wayward ways, yet, once known and understood, a friend for life. The Rover was such a car, and now that once again we lived in an isolated place we came to depend on it very much. I don't remember it ever letting us down at Land's End, though for nearly two years it was left parked on top of the cliffs facing the wild Atlantic.

One of the reasons we badly needed the car was to be able to keep in touch with Penzance, not only for business and pleasure reasons, but also in our new roles of absentee landlords. Some time later I once read in one of the children's schoolbooks an essay on 'How I spend my Saturdays', which began something like this: 'Every Saturday morning we all get in our car and Daddy drives us to Penzance and we collect our rents.' This was a state of affairs of which, morally, I do not really approve, anyway, but I have to admit that for the short period it endured, we were often desperately dependent on these Saturday morning visits. In fact my writing was going through a very sticky patch financially, with cheques few and far between, and often our weekend food depended on safe collection of our rents. In the long run we were to pay dearly for this little extravaganza of owning two houses at once, but as yet we did not visualize the end to the story of 16 Morrab Place and meanwhile were grateful for small mercies every Saturday morning five separate ones in fact, as of course by now we had let out the whole house. With the sort of tenants we had, a rather happygolucky lot like ourselves, this meant that we could never be quite sure that we were going to get our rents exactly when due. I well remember how nervously each Saturday I would begin my 'round', secretly keeping my fingers crossed, not only about the rents, but lest some unforeseen disaster had befallen, such as a ceiling collapsed, a washbasin cracked, lights fused, furniture burned, gas cookers broken and so forth (all of which happened at one time or another). In general our tenants were pretty good: no doubt all kinds of odd happenings took place there at one time and another, which fortunately I never knew about, but at least to the end the house remained standing in one piece. Sometimes, I must admit, I was surprised.

Now that we lived some way out it was difficult for us to get out in the evenings except by making special arrangements for a baby sitter. If they wanted to see us people began to get the habit of coming out to Sennen. It could anyway, in the right weather, be an exhilarating trip, and it was always cosy in Peter's cottage - once you got there. Remembering some of the ferocious gales that blew up I am relieved to think that none of our friends actually got blown away. In fact there was a later occasion, while we were away, when a friend of ours who was in charge of the house unwisely opened the front door at a time when the back door was also open. She swore ever after that the ensuing gust of wind lifted the roof up several inches! Peter's Cottage certainly had quite an atmosphere, though it looked much more romantic outside than it was inside. We discovered that it had really been built by a Peter, an old fisherman, and from that I developed an idea for a play which I wrote about a family coming to live in a cottage impregnated with the spirit of its past owner. It is one of a number of manuscripts I have by me - every writer has his little collection! - which I feel will eventually see the light of day if not in one form then in another.

This was a period when we became friendly with the woodchoppers of Lamorna, or the Ancient Orders of Britons as I think a local wag termed them. They were a group of young men, some of them with girl friends, who originated mostly from the midlands and the north. They really were professional woodchoppers and had come together during the war when they were all working in forestry in North Wales. But they were also philosophers of a sort; one or two of them had been to university, others had read voraciously, and they had arrived at a very positive outlook on life. They wanted to opt out of the rat race, to live naturally, to work with their hands, to enjoy sunshine and laughter of life, and not grovel in the cesspools of modern civilization. In a way they were an earlier version of today's rebels, the bohemians and the beatniks and the angry young men, only perhaps they were a little more happy-go-lucky, a little more tolerant in their attitudes. But then they were in a better position to be tolerant: today's rebels , who are even more numerous, have little time to be tolerant in the face of such an incredible race of mankind towards self-destruction. Whenever I look around at the immoral mess which 'statesmen' have made of the world and the inconceivable sangfroid with which they gaily await the inevitable atomic warfare, I do not join those who, peeping desperately in dark corners for something nasty in the woodshed, bemoan the fallen bad behaviour of our teenagers or the wicked ways of the young. My sympathies are all with the innocent young to whom we dare bequeath such legacies.

Cornwall had attracted the woodchoppers not so much because it is a particularly good place for forestry (it isn't) but for the same reason that it attracts so many others who rebel against standardization - because it offers a free and easy atmosphere, spaciousness, a slower and more tolerant tempo of life. For some years now they had centred themselves around the beauty spots of Lamorna Cove, made famous by the paintings of Lamorna Birch, and before him Laura Knight, Harold Harvey, Alfred Munnings, the Procters, and others. Their great aim was to live a natural life, as much as possible in the open air. During the summer they slept out on the cliff tops in sleeping bags and tents, and they spent a great deal of their spare time either sunbathing or bathing off the rocks - preferably in the nude. Although most of the men were fine looking physical specimens, bodies tanned a golden brown and trim and taut from their work, their inevitable beards enhancing a certain aesthetic look, they nearly all responded to curiously humdrum names - Syd, Reg, Alf, Ray, Harry, and so forth. Personally I found this endearing: there seemed an extra warmth about discussing Jung and Freud, liberty and freedom, Communism and Fascism, God and Mammom, with a bearded philosopher who still responded to such a stark prefix as Reg or Syd.

Our particular friend among the woodchoppers at that time was Ray, a tall, lean, blond exBirmingham University student who had, I think, the most dedicated attitude of them all to the forester's life. Subsequently he went with Richard St Barbe Baker on the latter's famous expedition to plant trees along the edge of the Sahara Desert. At the time when we knew him Ray was very much immersed in literally planting his roots in Cornwall. He had acquired a plot of land at Lamorna, some way back from the sea, leading off the valley and alongside one of the main streams. Ever since he came to Cornwall, Ray had dreamed of owning such a plot, and of building there a red home for himself and his wife and children. Although a dreamer, Ray was also quite practical, and gradually he had accumulated wood and other materials to build his dream home. The first time we visited him and Biddy, picking our way along a muddy footpath across the wooden bridge over the stream, it was the huge piles of planks that at once caught my eye. It was summer time then, and very pleasant to sit around sunbathing, listening to the music of the dancing stream: but Jess and I both noted, with some sympathy for Biddy, that the kitchen consisted of a ramshackle halfcompleted hut with the awning flapping in the wind. Several other woodchoppers lived there, sharing a converted bus as sleeping quarters, and altogether, with several small children around, it seemed to us that life must often be difficult, especially when it rained. If we raised such practical points we were scoffed at, however, and we assumed that everyone liked it like that and we felt rather ashamed of our more conventional liking for conveniences. We had to admit that the suntanned kids running about barefoot and often naked looked the picture of health. Ray himself, tall and blond and sunburned like a Viking of old, and Biddy, his wife, lovely to look at, with long flowing hair befitting a mermaid, fitted ideally into the idyllic picture.

And of course it was delightful to be there, especially in the evenings when the woodchoppers would light a bonfire there was never any shortage of wood - and we all sat around talking and drinking beer or some of Biddy's hot soup. I remember in particular a birthday party when there was a bigger gathering than usual, with Ray and Biddy, Arthur and Elizabeth Slater, Syd and Jean, Connie, Martin, Keith Gardiner, Sven Berlin and Juanita from St Ives - in the firelight the bearded figures of the men and their women, wearing colourful gypsy costumes, made a striking picture. Perhaps some of it was a little self-conscious, but in this world of miserable conformity let us welcome all who strike a different path. The woodchoppers, with their muddled groping for a more natural way of life, were at least being courageous compared to most citizens of our land. The odd thing was that having made such a gigantic effort to break away they often became immersed in squabbles as petty as any indulged in by lesser mortals. There is nothing so comic, and yet so tragic, as the story of how one of them laboured for years to provide a modern house with all conveniences for his wife - and when finally it was achieved, his wife refused to inhabit it, and went on living in a tent on the land outside.

At this time a newcomer attached himself to the woodchoppers in the form of Alf Knowles, the psychologist I mentioned earlier, who had brought with him his charge, P., one time tenant of ours at Morrab Place. Alf had some idea that it might do P. good to rough it on the land with the woodchoppers, and they certainly toughened him up. Air himself, though he looked like a woodchopper with his tweed sweater and corduroys and almost biblical beard, was not really so. He was a man almost totally immersed in philosophical abstraction, talking largely in psychological slang, and far from leading the tough life, one of his favourite weekly experiences was Saturday morning coffee at Chirgwins in Penzance, when he was quite likely to wolf down half a dozen cream buns. Like myself, Alf was a vegetarian (though I hasten to add that cream buns are not a normal part of vegetarian diet!) and this gave us something in common. He was also, perhaps inevitably, interested in Theosophy and Buddhism, and that much neglected prophet, Krishnamurti. At times when I feel really despondent in life I renew my spirits by re-reading some of those slim volumes of Krishnamurti's works. Not that he has any easy advice to give or free cures to offer; it is merely that he repeats, so relentlessly and so wisely, the simple truth - be responsible for your own actions; or, to put it the popular way, to thine own self be true. I have a nasty feeling that the sort of people who are drawn to Krishnamurti's teaching, of whom Alf and I are probably typical examples, make very half-hearted practitioners. But then perhaps even that is better than to be whole hearted devotees of capitalism, militarism, sadism, capital punishment, and all the other isms which seem to govern our world still.

At that time Alf and Ray would often walk over from Lamorna, via St Buryan, to visit us at Peter's Cottage. We grew to look forward to these visits. Perhaps the wind howled outside and the sea could be heard breaking below, but inside all was snug and warm while the four of us argued and talked into the early hours of the morning. I used to wonder a little about this rather new companionship of Alf and Ray, especially as we would find ourselves involved in what often seemed discussions within a discussion - in short, while arguing about some general subject, such as the meaning of love, or the validity of marriage, Alf and Ray would talk in such terms that they almost seemed to be having some private argument at the same time. As I remember, Ray was in a state of turmoil about his personal life, and Alf was constantly urging Ray to stop doing what he thought he ought to do, to make a break, to follow out his individual destiny, and so on.

This was all discussed in such abstract and philosophic terms that it is difficult even now to realize that we were in fact witnessing the disintegration of a whole pattern of life. Not long afterwards Ray went off to North Wales with a beautiful South African girl from St Ives - while Alf neatly stepped into Ray's place with Biddy, continuing to dispense philosophy and psychology to all and sundry, until finally he, too, disappeared into the mists of Wales. As a final irony Ray sold his Lamorna plot and the new owner, Janet Gibbs, went ahead with the building of Ray's dream house - and ever since has lived there and run the market garden that somehow Ray never brought to fruition. Whenever I enter the lovely long wooden bungalow and sit before the roaring fire with its surround faced with granite lumps specially picked out by Ray, I am always reminded of this ghostly past, always impelled to ask myself - were things *meant* to work out in this pattern anyway, or did individual actions *cause* them to do so? A question I often ask, about many events in life, without ever knowing the answer. My friend Ross would say confidently that it was all foretold in the stars: but I fancy Krishnamurti would say it was all reflected in our souls.

We missed the woodchoppers very much, though fortunately from time to time we were able to entice other friends out for a night. None of them, however, chose such a delightfully flamboyant method of travel as Sven Berlin and Juanita, who came over from St Ives on horseback. Juanita, who believes herself to be descended from an old Romany family, certainly looks the part of a gypsy, with her jet-black hair and dark skin and dangling ear-rings, usually wearing a bright blouse and dirndl skirt with riding boots. She has had a lifelong passion for and affinity with horses, and has held several exhibitions of drawing and paintings, as well as writing a beautiful radio programme, with music by Vaughan Williams, *Stallion Eternal.* The sight of Juanita on one horse, followed a little gingerly by Sven on another, looking like a cross between a pirate and a country squire, must have caused quite a lot of comment on the twenty-mile route. They certainly caused commotion enough at Peter's Cottage when they arrived, for horses cannot just be parked like cars, they have to be put out in a field, and I feared that not every farmer in Sennen would welcome such a responsibility. However in the end we always managed to tether them somewhere, and then the four of us settled down for a stimulating evening's talk.

Jess was now expecting another baby, but hadn't been feeling very well for some time. One afternoon she had gone into Penzance shopping, and decided she would spend the night with her mother, who had recently moved to Penzance. At eight o'clock the next morning she had a severe haemorrhage and was rushed into Penzance hospital for immediate blood transfusions. I knew nothing about this until about eleven when her sister rang me up, and I dashed into Penzance by car. When I got to the hospital, Jess was very ill with blood transfusions still going on - she had at one stage been so bad that a priest had (without being invited!) said the last rites over her. If she had had a miscarriage out at Sennen Cove she would undoubtedly have lost her life - only the fact that, for no particular reason she chose to spend the night in Penzance, and was close to the hospital there, saved her life. This sort of thing makes one wonder. Once again, was it pure chance that prompted Jess to choose to spend the night in Penzance! I cannot be sure, but I do know that incidents of that sort, where life and death are acutely counter-played, make one see things in their proper perspective. I felt utterly lost and bereft, as did the children, and once we were all together again Jess and I felt for a long time a new undercurrent of closeness.

Soon after this we began to have frequent visits from an old friend of ours, Lisa of Lelant, who had for some years been a favourite model of many of the St Ives artists, but now spent most of her time looking after a 3-year-old girl, Pandora, relic of a broken marriage. Lisa had long dark hair that made her look wildly romantic, and so in many ways she was, but she also possessed a vivid sense of humour and something of a grasshopper mind. One way and another she was delightful company, and we always welcomed the sight of her bravely climbing the stone steps from the bus stop, carrying Pandora in her arms. Indeed, after a while it began to seem to us all that this tiring journey could easily be avoided.

'Why don't you come and live with us!' said Jess, ever the practical one. 'I mean on a business-like basis - you can help look after the children, and in return well pay you and give you board and lodging, that sort of thing.'

'Yes,' I said, getting interested as ever at any new venture. 'There's that tiny house outside, it'll just be right with a few improvements.'

Lisa was only too pleased to agree, and meanwhile we got a local builder in to work on what we had vaguely called the outhouse. This consisted of one downstairs room, and two inmate bedrooms. The main drawback was that the rear of the place was built against the steep walls of granite, and consequently there was a general atmosphere of damp-and across the centre of the bottom room a decided trickle of water pursued its course along a worn groove in the cement. We had always assumed that when we came to do the place up it would be easy to get rid of this, but now in practice this proved quite impossible. During the whole of Lisa's tenancy, though she was quite happy in her tiny cottage, she had to live with a perpetual stream running across her living-room floor, though mostly covered up by straw mats.

It was one of the delightful things about Lisa that she always took such things in her stride. She always saw the funny side of an incident, however upsetting at the time. Both Jess and I swarmed to her presence in the house, and the three of us got on very well indeed, while the children and Pandora also seemed to take to one another.

It was, of course, probably because of the children that we had been encouraged to suggest Lisa's joining us. The idea was that she should help Jess about the house, and do some baby sitting at night. Lisa more than did her share of helping about the house: what we had not quite allowed for was the precipitate development of her own separate life in the locality. Perhaps we made our first cardinal mistake, one evening when another friend was available to baby-sit, when we invited Lisa to come with us for a drink at the 'First and Last'. The result was a very gay evening, during which Lisa became quite the belle of the pub, an evening that ended with Jess and I returning, a little uneasily, on our own, while Lisa was wafted off for a joy ride on a local boy's motor bike.

After that, somehow, we began to see less of Lisa in the evenings. It began innocently enough with her poking her head round the kitchen door one evening and calling out cheerfully; 'Just going for a stroll to the "First and Last" perhaps you'd keep an ear open for Pandy! I left her fast asleep.' This was reasonable enough one or two evenings of the week. We did not even complain of the fact that, no matter how asleep Lisa thought her child was, invariably about half an hour after her departure Pandora would wander into our kitchen in her dressing gown saying she wanted a drink, or couldn't go to sleep. But gradually the whole process became speeded up, and one day we suddenly woke up to the fact that Lisa had been out ten nights in a row, while we ourselves had stayed in, baby-sitting for her for ten nights. At this we felt bound to stand up for our rights to get out just a little. Lisa was perfectly apologetic and a new approach to the problem was essayed by Lisa having her boy friend come back to visit her several evenings, so that once again we were free to go out. As frequently we didn't particularly *want* to go out on specified evenings, the net result generally was that the four of us would join forces in a scrap meal and a talk around the fire. So I suppose the problem was never really solved, for not long after Lisa's mother died and she had to go away from us.

Before that happened, however, there occurred the famous instance of our £80 August, or the Val Baker trip to Paris, call it what you will. Up till then we were comparatively innocent of what goes on in the Cornish holiday world, of how tiny little cottages, no matter how isolated, are let for enormous sums of money during the holiday seasons. The idea that anyone would be interested in renting our place just hadn't occurred to us. And then one day we happened to see an advertisement in the *Cornishman:*

'£80 offered for Cottage by the Sea, August, Cornwall. Send details.'

'Eighty pounds,' exclaimed Jess excitedly. 'Why for that amount we could have a wonderful holiday somewhere. Why don't we write?'

So we wrote. A few days later we received a wire saying that the advertisers' wives were *flying* down from the north, where they lived, to inspect Peter's Cottage. We rushed round and tidied away as many signs as humanly possible of children's inhabitation, washed all the bedcovers and generally gave Peter's Cottage a sprucing up it had never known. On the day of arrival Jess and Lisa busied themselves in preparing a sumptuous lunch, and I drove to the railway station to meet these affluent wives.

Fortunately it was one of those perfect Cornish spring days, sunshine bathing the lanes and bringing out the fresh green. I took care to drive the Newlyn-Lamorna-Porthcurno route, thus exhibiting, as if it was my own private property, some of Cornwall's most lovely countryside. Finally I drove to Peter's Cottage by the top road, so that the visitors arrived, as I had first done, to find this lovely cottage set in majestic beauty.

The ladies were, of course, quite overwhelmed. We made them comfortable in our romantic sitting-room, where they could hardly stop staring in wonderment out upon the panorama of sea and cliffs. We plied them with wine and roast chicken and then, after allowing them a very cursory turn round the house we settled them down again by the fire, and tried to look blasé as one of the ladies pulled out a cheque book and inquired sweetly: 'I expect you'd like a deposit, wouldn't you!' In the end it was agreed that they should pay £40 in advance now and the balance of £40 the week before they arrived. In our elation at bringing off this coup we threw in all kinds of extras, constant hot water, telephone, electricity - even casually, the services of our 'house-keeper', Lisa.

In the meantime, confronted with £80 which somehow began to dribble away alarmingly, we kept revising our ideas about holidays. As Jess was rather run down at the time anyway, we decided it might be a good idea for the children to spend three weeks or so at a children's holiday home, while Jess and I had our first proper holiday alone for five years, and paid a visit to Paris. We took farewell of the children in Devon and drove off to Southampton to catch the night boat to Le Havre and on to Paris.

Just about the time we reached Paris it began to dawn on us that what with the school fees and the travelling and so forth, that famous £80 had dwindled alarmingly - so alarmingly, indeed, that we could hardly afford to come to Paris, let alone stay there a month. While this was a depressing factor, it also had its stimulating side. Somehow we felt rather young and naive and enjoyed our time in Paris almost without relation to where we were. Simply to be on our own again was wonderful and we used to walk about hand in hand as if we had just met. We rented a room in an apartment house whose windows opened out on two or three cafes and bistros from which excitable French voices and the inevitable music seemed to rise up at all hours of the day and night. In that room we spent much of our Paris holiday, eating wonderful cheese and swiss rolls and fresh fruit, and drinking cheap but delicious wine, talking and reading and making love indeed the sort of second honeymoon which every married couple needs every year.

Needless to say, it couldn't last. In fact events had taken place some hundred of miles north-west which, if we had known then, would have had us rushing home: but fortunately owing to the vagaries of the French postal system, we did not know. What happened to us was that one day we woke up and found we only had about 500 francs left between us and starvation, and there was nothing for it but to catch the next boat train. When we reached Southampton we had about 2s. 6d. and the old Rover, fortunately with enough petrol in it to drive us up to my mother's home at Surbiton. And there, living on borrowed money, we had to spend the remaining two weeks of our famous holiday.

By then, the wandering letter which Lisa had written us, having followed us to Devon and over the sea to France, finally caught up with us. We learned the sad story of how on arrival the holidaymakers had turned out to consist of nine people and not as we had assumed four - how they had come earlier than they stated anyway, to find Lisa in her bath and a boy friend playing games with Pandora in the sitting-room (not J suppose a good reception in an £80-a month-holiday home) and how the water supply had sunk very low and was a bare trickle - and how, in short, after various recriminations and threats of legal action, the whole crew had departed to find hotel accommodation. No doubt we should have felt more guilty, but by now we were so exhausted by the whole project that we could not really care. All we wanted to do was to collect our children, if still alive, and creep home. And this we did, thank goodness.

It was good to be back, to sniff the wonderful sea again, to see the children running down again to play around the little harbour, to feel autumn in the air and order logs from our woodchopper friends to build up great fires in the evenings. We both felt so much better for the break, despite all the worries involved, and I celebrated my new found good spirits by doing something I had never done before. This was to sit down after supper, and each evening write a chapter of a new book in an ordinary exercise book. As a working professional author I keep fairly regular hours, and do the bulk of my writing in the mornings, revision and correspondence in the afternoon. As a very young man I used to like starting to write very late at night and working on in the early hours of the morning, but now I much prefer more orthodox hours. However, this was to be the exception to prove the rule. The fact was I had been thinking and talking quite a bit about the comic hazards of an author's life with all its curious problems. Suddenly one day Jess said: 'Why don't you write a book about it'

And so I did. It was called *How To Be An Author,* and consisted of about twelve chapters, all fairly short, and the whole book. was written in a fortnight - what's more, only in the evenings, as an addition to my ordinary day's work. It was one of the most enjoyable experiences I have known. From the moment I penned the first sardonic words, 'It is a well known fact that all great writers had unhappy childhoods. ..' I felt I had struck just the right note, and I think I managed to keep this up right to the last chapter sections 'Games with Rejection Slips', 'Relations with Publishers', and 'Behaving at Literary Parties'. As the titles suggest it was a funny, indeed a comic book, but I think it gained from being written from experience. Some of the chapters, such as 'How to be a Bestseller' and 'Life and Death as an Author' were very bitter indeed, under their humour: and I was always amazed that one of the book-trade magazines reprinted the chapter on 'Capitalizing Your Local Fame', for it had a go at booksellers on behalf of all authors who have suffered by being completely ignored by local booksellers on their own doorsteps.

I wrote the book with such a rush of enthusiasm that I felt this must communicate itself, but I was pleasantly taken aback by the way it found a publisher. I had to pay a visit to London, so took the manuscript up with me. I had been studying the lists of publishers who specialized in funny books, and after choosing one I made an appointment and took the book in at 11 a.m. At lunchtime I received a telephone message to call round that afternoon: when I did I was greeted enthusiastically and received an immediate offer.

'We think it's marvellous, very funny indeed. We'd be *delighted* to publish it.'

My friend Val Biro, a very gifted Hungarian artist who is well known for book jackets and illustrations, supplied some excellent humorous drawings, and when *How To Be An Author* was finally published it had many long reviews in various national papers. Most authors seemed to appreciate its humour, and I was especially pleased to hear Charles Causley, in a review on the B.B.C. West Region, draw attention to the fact that the book's comic quality was enhanced because it was so obviously based on bitter experience. The book had a good deal of publicity and many reviews, though its sale was fairly modest. Possibly this was in part the fault of booksellers. It seemed to me ironically in keeping with the theme of my chapter criticizing their attitude to authors that, apparently, many booksellers were found to have tucked the book away on educational shelves as an instructional manual!

Not long after the appearance of this book we began house hunting again. This time, if anything Jess was the instigator, though I was quite in sympathy for I realized that she found Sennen altogether too bleak and lonely as a home. So far the children remained young enough for us to be able to move around without much damage to their own lives, but we realized that our next move would need to be a more permanent one. By a stroke of luck, through hearing a chance remark from Martin Lambourne, one of the woodchoppers, who had decided against it as a 'white elephant', we heard that the Old Vicarage at St Hilary was coming on the market. I shall describe our campaign to buy this property in the next chapter, but the fact that the Vicarage was to be auctioned meant it was imperative that we should obtain a quick sale for Peter's Cottage. The sale of outlandish houses, even at Land's End, is a task that often takes a year or two, and ours was so isolated from a convenience point of view, that we knew our only hope was to find someone rather like ourselves, romantics and rather optimistic, to whom normal considerations mattered very little. As in the best adventure stories, we did make contact with such a purchaser precisely six weeks before the auction of the Old Vicarage was to take place. Like myself, Donald Cresswell was a writer, and his wife an actress, and just as I had done, they obviously fell hook line and sinker for the position of Peter's Cottage. But alas they were like us in other ways; their only hope was to raise a large mortgage, and so the drawn-out process began of getting a surveyor's report and applying to a building society. Gradually the date of the auction drew nearer and nearer: finally the building society O.K. that enabled the Cresswells to buy our house came through a mere day before the auction. One of the almost unbelievable results of this process was that for a period of two weeks we found ourselves temporarily owning three houses at the same time!

But in the end things worked out to a more bearable result.

Chapter Four

THE TREES CAME TUMBLING DOWN

'Mother' I said, 'It's a wonderful place. Seventeen rooms. Some of them are enormous. Why, the kitchen's twenty feet long. There's a beautiful lounge with an open fire place. And a study for me to work in.'

Jess took the phone from me.

'And lots and lots of bedrooms - the children can have one each.'

'And a tower.' I grabbed the phone again. 'Right at the top of the house there's a real tower. They say it's haunted just a little. And then just outside the back door there's an old magnolia tree growing out of a wall. Isn't that extraordinary?

'Grounds,' whispered Jess. 'Tell her about the jungle.'

'Oh, and yes, mother,' I went on, 'there are lots of grounds -three acres the agent says. Outhouses, henhouses, stables the whole shoot.' I cleared my throat-avoided Jess's eye. 'Er, it's a little wild now, of course. But it must have been beautiful once. All terraces and lawns . .

'What about the dried-up well?' hissed Jess.

I shook my head.

'And the cesspool that doesn't work?'

I shook my head again.

'And those lavatories!' Jess managed to impart the full implication of horror to her voice.

But I merely shook my head again, and answered my mother's anxious query.

'Oh, yes, mother. All modern conveniences and so on, of course.'

There was a pause. Jess and I looked at one another in an agony of uncertainty as we waited for what is now known as the 64-dollar question. When it came at last my mother's voice sounded curiously sad and resigned, and somehow that seemed to give me new strength.

'Well, the agent thinks about two thousand, mother, but perhaps less. Now this is the point . . . . We've discovered we can raise a mortgage of 80 per cent, and we've got three hundred pounds. But we still need a bit more. Do you think perhaps . . . ?'

My mother, sounding even more resigned, acquiesced to a loan of two hundred and fifty pounds; and over the tenuous phone wire from Penzance I poured a stream of thanks.

'I'll let you know how it goes,' I promised, just before ringing off, ' the auction's on Thursday.'

The auction was held in a big hall in the centre of Penzance. It wasn't by any means the first auction we had attended since settling in Cornwall. On and off during the past three or four years we must have attended a dozen or more - invariably as mere spectators, knowing our inability to make an effective bid, yet drawn like moths to the flame by the tantalizing temptations.

But now, at last, we were active participants. The Cresswells' confirmation had solved the problem of Peter's Cottage and we should have a few hundred pounds from that. We had managed to get a building society figure of £1,600 towards the Old Vicarage, and my mother's loan, we hoped, would enable us to seal the deal. And so here we were to fight all kinds of unknown forces in a bid to purchase our most ambitious home, the former vicarage of the parish of St Hilary, some two miles beyond Marazion - a large rambling old house of seventeen rooms standing in three acres of pretty overgrown land.

It all, now, depended on the auction. As we approached the hall, on the fatal morning, we felt like nervous wrecks. Our spirits weren't raised by seeing an enormous crowd of people gathered in the hall, even though we should have known from previous experience that in Cornwall attending auctions is for many people a form of light amusement, like going to the cinema, only cheaper. Supposing they had all come prepared to bid for the Old Vicarage? How could we compete, when we knew that on no account could we bid more than £2,000. Our hearts sank as we looked round these potential competitors. With something like hatred we contemplated possible buyers who, without a qualm, would rob us of our heart's desire.

Our hearts sank a little further as we became aware that a number

of good friends had come along, presumably to give us moral support. During our years in Cornwall we had naturally gravitated to the bohemian world of painters and writers, potters and poets, and woodchoppers. This was our world, indeed, and grateful we had been for their friendship. But just today, just this one occasion when bank balances, sober appearance, civic responsibilities and all other attributes of the more conventional world were things that were bound to count...

There they sat, almost like a row of soldiers: four beards, one eccentric poet, a bald literary critic, and two brazen hussies in tight-fitting jeans. We could not avoid them, we could not refuse their kindly, well-meant greeting. They had saved two seats of honour among them, in the very front row. Furtively we slunk down the corridor and into our places, conscious of the curious eyes of the auctioneer and several solicitors watching us.

But, as the proceedings began and it became apparent there were several other houses to be disposed of first, and the tension relaxed, we too recovered our sense of proportion, and began to be glad our friends had rallied round. For Jess, who gets wound up with inner tensions on such occasions, it was difficult to relax; but I began to warm to my temporary spotlight.

And then suddenly with a suspicious glance at our group, the auctioneer, Thurstan Lane, cleared his throat and announced that he would now put up for sale the Old Vicarage, St Hilary. He then proceeded to give a brief history of the place, explaining that for six years during the war it had been used as a hostel for Land Army girls and that since then it had been empty. A condition of sale was that it should not be used as a hotel or public house.

'And now gentlemen, what am I offered? Come on now, it's on the market.'

I waited, nervously, for someone to start the bidding. After a while, finding the silence more terrifying than a bid, I found myself stuttering:

'A thousand pounds.'

At this a pained smile passed over Thurstan Lane's face, as if to say, the gentleman will have his little joke. However, to my astonishment, he accepted the bid, and asked for any advance.

Now our hearts, which had begun to lighten, felt weighed down with despair, for from another part of the hail a strong Cornish accent said:

'One thousand and two hundred and fifty pounds.'

I looked at Jess. This was it. The battle was on. Around me I felt the beards wagging and my friends egging me on with their kindly thoughts. 'One thousand five hundred pounds,' I said, marvelling at the steady note of my voice.

'One thousand six hundred pounds,' returned the Cornish voice, rather defiantly.

'One thousand seven hundred pounds,' I said firmly.

'One thousand seven hundred and fifty,' spoke up the, now more cautious, rival bidder.

We began to creep along in fifties and then twenty-fives. Now and then the bidding hung fire altogether, and Thurstan Lane, in his jovial manner, tried to liven things up.

It was at one of these stages that Arthur Caddick, stirring from his reveries, stood up, his gaunt shape swaying slightly, and asked in his booming voice:

'Sir, is it true that there are two curates locked in a cupboard, and if so do they go with the Vicarage!'

There was a stir and a ripple of laughter, but, I fancied, a slightly uneasy ripple, as if most of the people could not allow their ingrown suspicions of the bohemian world to be overridden by the sheer humour of the remark. It was then, I think, that I suddenly began to feel that we could get the old Vicarage. It was such a white elephant, such an extraordinary hotch-potch both to look at and in its history. It was a place already famous for having been a home of a succession of rather eccentric priests, including Bernard Walke, famous for his Nativity Plays broadcast by the B.B.C., and Sandys Wason, turned out of the neighbouring parish of Cury-by-Gunwalloe and arriving at St Hilary with all his belongings piled in a furniture van. During Walke's incumbency many famous artists and writers had dined with him at the Vicarage - among them Compton Mackenzie, Bernard Shaw, and Alfred Munnings. Now that the Vicarage was to become worldly, signified (by legal agreement) by the prefix 'old', it seemed only right that it should be inhabited and visited by writers and artists and other rebels against the orderly, imprisoning routines of life.

'One thousand nine hundred and fifty pounds,' I said firmly.

There was a pause. A very significant pause.

I felt strangely like some boxer in the ring who knows instinctively he has got his opponent groggy. Perhaps one more rally and then

'One thousand nine hundred and seventy-five pounds.'

There - that was it- the last despairing punch. I knew it, somehow I sensed it in the tone of his voice, in the slightly wild way of utterance.

I waited, purposefully, to make my kill. Then:

'Two thousand pounds,' I exclaimed, trying to pack into my voice all the confidence of a man prepared to bid for thousands of pounds more.

And then, of course, my balloon collapsed, and I positively wilted under the terrifying tensions. Supposing the bidding went higher after all, Supposing, supposing…?

It seemed to me a most awesome few moments of silence. Jess and I both went hot and cold all over, we dared not look at one another. Beside us we felt the tension spread right along our row of friends: even the beards quivered with fearful anticipation.

Then somehow the atmosphere changed. Almost imperceptibly, there was a slackening of tension. Suddenly I became aware that the silence was continuing, that there had been no answering bid; that there was not going to be an answering bid

'Come now,' said Thurstan Lane with a last attempt at persuasiveness. 'Two thousand pounds I am bid, by the gentleman on my left. Any advance on two thousand pounds?'

With an air of impending finality, he picked up his little mallet and brandished it in the air. I watched its flickering movements with absolute fascination.

'For the last time gentlemen. Two thousand pounds is the bid. Going at two thousand pounds - once.' Crash went the mallet. 'Twice.' Another crash. 'Going for the third and last time -'

The mallet fell decisively on the table, and almost in the same gesture Thurstan Lane waved in my direction.

Sold to the gentleman over there for two thousand pounds.' He put down the hammer, and nodded; and then, so I am reliably informed, muttered discreetly: 'And God help the Old Vicarage!'

Buying an old vicarage at an auction is one thing: getting into the place quite another. It was to be nearly two months before the lawyers had finished their leisurely corresponding over the deeds and articles of our new home. In the meantime, twiddling our thumbs at Peter's Cottage to the accompaniment of gale winds and white-crested Atlantic rollers, Jess and I thought we should go quite crazy with impatience.

I expect we should, too, if we had not one morning, somewhat guiltily, remembered the kitchen window with the broken catch. When we had originally viewed the Old Vicarage, complete with agent's permission and key, I had happened to notice that one of the kitchen windows did not quite shut, because the catch had cracked. Presumably it was still in the same condition? In which case -?

Two minds with a single thought, Jess and I drove over to St Hilary. In the strict legal sense, although we had purchased the Old Vicarage we were not supposed to enter the premises until the various documents had been signed and exchanged, and we felt that in their hidebound way lawyers would adhere to the letter rather than the spirit of the law, in this matter as in others. However it seemed a very academic point and I cannot pretend that it was with any great sense of guilt that, leaving our car in the lane, we slipped into the wild grounds and made our way over to the kitchen window.

It opened at the first effort! Of course the wood was stiff and jerky, but I was able to lift the window half way up and in a matter of moments Jess and I found ourselves standing inside the big, bleak, bare room looking round wonderingly at our biggest-ever kitchen.

We had of course been thoroughly round the house before, but not since the auction. This was our first visit as owners. Somehow that knowledge seemed to make everything quite different. No longer was it some strange, rambling, unfamiliar building that seemed not quite of our world. It was ours, our home to be.

And what a home it was to be, too. Not only was the vicarage old, it was definitely odd. It rambled all over the place with rooms jutting out here there and everywhere, and little flights of steps darting up unexpectedly, so that almost every room seemed to be on a different level. The kitchen was

in quite a different part of the house from the sitting room. The bathroom was over the coal cellar - and, of course, miles from any of the bedrooms. Although nearly all the rooms were roughly on two floors, there were still two higher floors to the house, the top one devoted entirely to one long room with a high ceiling, and above that yet another loft. These latter floors, it appeared, had been added on as a Victorian afterthought to a Georgian type of building - the result being most offensive, aesthetically. Viewed from the lane, the vicarage looked rather like a huge aircraft carrier whose superstructure rears up out of all proportion to the rest.

There were many other oddities which we were to discover; but naturally, on this morning, we were not in a critical frame of mind. We wandered about from one empty room to another, marvelling - after our cramped cottage at the spaciousness. Mentally we were allocating rooms. The bedroom facing south with three windows and a glorious view over sloping fields to St Michael's Mount in the distance - that would be ours. The children were scattered about, each would have a room of his or her own. Of the three ground floor rooms, apart from the kitchen, one would be a playroom (as a consequence it was never used at all), one would be my study, and the really big room, of course, would be the lounge.

It was standing in the middle of this enormous long room, with its ceiling-to-floor high windows looking out on a stately vista of circular drive and, beyond, the steeple of St Hilary Church, that Jess and I began to get down to realities. The whole house would have to be redecorated. At the moment everywhere was a faded, peeling cream and chocolate brown, legacy of the Land Army days and the Ministry of Works style of decoration. Some of the work was going to be most intricate, especially the main hall with its winding stairs and its great glass window overlooking the top landing. Some of the work we could do ourselves, but we decided it would be wise to employ someone else as well.

At once we thought of K. We knew he was out of work, we had heard he was something of a handyman, and it seemed an excellent arrangement that we should buy the materials and that for two or three weeks he should come every day and decorate the rooms. One day we ran over to fetch K. and installed him in the great lounge with pots of paint, new brushes, a ladder, and various other instruments, then off we went cheerfully to get on with our own business elsewhere.

We realized that painting the sitting-room was quite a large task, and so left K. on his own for a couple of days. When we came back on the third day, full of excitement, we saw absolutely no change in the room.

'But K.- the painting'?

'It's all in hand,' said K. calmly. 'I've been estimating and measuring.'

Estimating and measuring . . . we reckoned that at three shillings an hour, this was going to be rather more expensive than we thought. Still we bottled our disappointment, and went off to do some decorating of our own in other rooms.

So it went on for two or three weeks. Jess and I splashed away merrily, painting room after room. And painstakingly K., the perfectionist, painted the sitting-room. After five days he had completed one wall. During the second week he completed another, then began the third. After that he looked rather exhausted and was missing for several days. However, manfully, he returned, and finally three and a half weeks after we had first engaged him, K. finished the sitting-room. It looked, we thought, much the same as if we had done the job. But K. apparently felt pleased with his progress.

'Now,' he said cheerfully, 'which room shall I do next?

Somehow we managed to extricate ourselves from our formidable new financial burden. K. was a little hurt, but no doubt not half as hurt as he would have been if he had stayed a moment longer and Jess's long pent-up exasperation had overflowed.

Meantime, our own work had progressed, and before the month was up we had decorated all the rooms that we were going to need for immediate use. During this time, too, there had been a steady coming and going of plumbers and builders and electricians. One of the exasperating but typical last actions of the Ministry of Works had been to remove all the plumbing which they had originally installed for the benefit of the Land Army. As the plumbing had been practically nonexistent before, that was once again the general state. Water could only be got up by bucket from a well 100 feet deep; around the top remained the scaffolding and structure of what had once been a highly efficient electric water pump.

There was nothing for it but to order a new one. That, we found, owing to the depth of the well, would cost us something like £150. Having no alternative, we went ahead. At first there was delay, delay - but after we had begged and implored, and emphasized the largeness of our family, so dependent on water, things were speeded up, and our water pump was finally installed. It was indeed a most impressive affair which automatically started working once the water in the tanks fell below a certain level. All through our years at the Old Vicarage, that noise was one of the most familiar. Sometimes it would startle us in the middle of the night if someone unwisely pulled a lavatory chain - Boompety, Boomp, Boompety Boomp - once it started it went on for at least fifteen minutes.

All this time, the lawyers were still gravely meditating and corresponding, arguing and agreeing. Every now and then a document would arrive to be signed, or I would be called in for a consultation. Officially we were still waiting to get into the Old Vicarage, unofficially the only thing we weren't doing was actually sleeping there.

At last came the great day for moving in. At our lonely cottage on the cliff; we waited in great excitement for the furniture van. It loomed up against the skyline, parking as near the edge as was safe, and the men began carrying our stuff up and down the steep cliff path.

When everything was loaded, the van set off, and we assembled for our own journey. At last we were ready, and set off along the bumpy private road. We reached the main road and chugged up hill and down dale to Penzance, and then along the coast road to Marazion, past the wide sweep of the bay and the steep sloping island of St Michael's Mount, and on to the pasture land of Goldsithney and St Hilary.

At last we turned down the pot-holed lane leading to the Old Vicarage. It was a brilliant spring day, and all along the lane were primroses and daffodils. Sunshine poured down, the sky was blue, everywhere there was an air of peace and contentment. I swung the car into the drive, and round the sloping bend to the front of the house - the imposing, Georgian front to be seen from the church, a view which relieved the ungainly shape of the house at the rear. I jammed on the brake and gave a flamboyant toot on the horn.

'Well - here we are!'

But the words were hardly out of my mouth before the children were out, racing across the drive and banging on the great blue door.

'Let us in! Let us in! We want to see our new home!'

Smiling, I admit rather sentimentally, Jess and I went across and let them in.

Almost the first thing we did after moving into the Old Vicarage was to increase its population. Although she had helped so manfully in the work of getting the Vicarage ready, and then packing up for the great move, Jess was in fact within a month or so of having our second baby. Somewhere around this time I had come across the books of Winston Graham, a popular author well known for his thrillers, many of which have been filmed, but less generally known perhaps for a series of novels of family life in Cornwall during the eighteenth century - the Poldark novels as they are known. Later on we had the pleasure of meeting Winston Graham, who lives at Perranporth on the north coast of Cornwall, but at this time I had no reason for reading the Poldark books other than their sheer fascination. Winston Graham gave flesh and blood to some very real characters. Particularly Demelza, the warm-hearted, impulsive, mischievous, wayward, and wholly delightful heroine . . . . She seemed to me every man's ideal.

'If it's a girl, let's call her Demelza.'

'What a beautiful name,' said Jess. 'What does it mean?'

'It's a Cornish word. It means, "Thy Sweetness".'

So Demelza she was called, when she first opened her eyes to the world in that gracious bedroom with the magnolia tree writhing its way up the side and filling one of the windows with its soft blossom. Demelza Ann Val Baker, neat and plump and as dark as her brother Stephen, now romping around with a 3-year-old's curiosity, was fair.

From the beginning, then, the Old Vicarage was very much a children's house, and this was as it should be. For too long the house had stood empty, although in years gone by, we gathered, the Vicarage had reverberated to the sound of childish laughter from a succession of large families. Indeed one of the previous vicars had been responsible for the addition of the curious square tower that had been erected on top of the Vicarage - an escape room to which he could flee from the ravaging of his brood. Sometimes I, too, cast an envious eye on that room, but I was for ever put off attempting to settle in it by the revelation, which I mentioned in an earlier chapter, that it was possibly haunted by the spirit of some unfortunate person who had jumped to death out of the big bay window. In fact this window - which looked out over fields and down to St Michael's Mount rising out of the sea in the distance - was the only window that really had an impressive distant view. For the rest the windows of the Old Vicarage tended to look more inwards, to the more immediate reality of our life there and in its three acres, enclosed either by moss-covered walls or rows of old trees.

A large family, above all, needs large space to move around in, and at last we were lucky enough to have that. For the children the Old Vicarage was something of a paradise. They could disappear for hours down among the undergrowth, following in single file between the trees, playing cowboys and Indians. There were out-houses abounding, some of them full of old bedsteads and lumps of coal. There was a derelict walled orchard next door which offered tremendous temptations to adventures (seldom resisted, I regret to report). And, in the house itself there were seemingly endless corridors leading to room after room. No wonder the children, under such circumstances, seemed to blossom out and assert themselves more as individual units of the family.

So far I have managed to keep our children out of this book, though goodness knows it is difficult enough to keep them out of anything. But I think with the coming of Demelza and the settling into our first real family house we became much more aware of ourselves as a family. And indeed, quite a family. The oldest child, my son Martin, was already developing the tendencies which have since reached maturity - that is, he showed every sign of being an ingrained tactician, a superb practitioner of evasive action. If we decided to ask Martin to do something arduous or unpleasant he would never refuse, he would just take care not to be there to be asked. For one of those exquisitely torturous 'family outings' which we occasionally, rather foolishly in my opinion, embarked on, there was never any need to press Martin to come along: he had long since wisely departed on some more interesting project. Where some aim of his own was involved, such as going fishing or watching his favourite football team, Martin's energy was prodigious. In later years he cycled forty miles to Mevagissey and forty miles back in one day and lived to tell the tale. But if we were to ask him to fetch some butter from the grocer's around the corner, a glazed look of utter exhaustion transfigured his 10-year-old face with such suffering that, abjectly, we felt we had to apologize for insulting a sick man, and turn to some other less delicate plant. On the other hand, being a boy with a mind of his own, he was already beginning to develop qualities of intelligence about world affairs, as well as an ironic sense of humour, which have strengthened his character subsequently.

Gill and Jane, Jess's two daughters, were a complete contrast. From the age of one day onwards Gill had been a frilly, pretty little thing, with blonde curly hair and blue eyes, a somewhat limited intelligence but absolutely sharp as-a-needle intuitive reactions, so that she could get her own way about almost anything, be at home in any situation - for her we foretold a life of titillation and flirtatiousness, and felt rather sorry for whatever young man she eventually acquired as a husband. By contrast Jane, eclipsed in the sunshine of Gill's good looks, took to competing by dressing herself in tattered clothes and misshapen shoes, anything, in the true psychological pattern, to attract attention. She also developed a habit of conducting her life on a histrionic level - for instance, when the postman called Jane would rush through the house screaming 'The Post, The Post!' just as a distraught person might scream, 'Fire! Fire!' (This talent, not surprisingly, fulfilled itself in later years in amateur dramatics.)

Next in the age group came Stephen, as yet a mere infant about to join his elders in the morning walk along past St Hilary Church to the rather delightful village school which looked out across flat fields to the Penwith hills. In later years Stephen was to attain renown, not only in family circles, alas, as the boy who broke seventy-two windows', and as somehow this incident sums up his character perhaps I can recount it out of context. At the time of the occurrence Stephen's participation seemed laughable. When a police officer called inquiring about the breakage of seventy-two windows at a nearby warehouse we were somewhat offended that he should suspect any of our children. However, we promised to ask them, and received indignant denials from the others. From Stephen however - and our hearts sank - we received no denial, merely a curious, slow, rather wicked smile. *'Seventy-two, was it? Fancy, seventy-two windows! I must tell Michael.'* But why? - how? - what? It turned out that Stephen and his friends were playing a game called 'Smash and Grab . . . .' Luckily Stephen was let off this somewhat untypical extravaganza (he is fond of practical jokes, but not generally of wholesale damage). From this story you may gather that Stephen is a typical, mischievous, naughty, reckless, and rather attractive boy - and you would be right.

And now there was Demelza, as yet no more than a gurgling blob lying in her pram in the Cornish sunshine. Naturally we could not as yet read into her future, see her dark and elfin-like, a sensitive and rather nervous child with a vivid imagination, showing, along with an elemental and romantic nature, a shy gentleness, also a surprising tomboy attraction, symbolized by her wearing a Red Indian hat and brandishing a tomahawk and yelling out bloodthirsty threats. We did not yet know of the surprising religious streak in her nature which, coupled with great excitability, could lead her to come running into a room, eyes shining brightly, crying out: 'I've just been to Holy COMMOTION!' These Characteristics were to appear some years later - as was, did we but know it, the sixth and last member of the Val Baker family, Genevieve.

Perhaps I have said sufficient for the moment to indicate why life at the Old Vicarage was unlikely ever to be on the dull side - or, alas, at all inexpensive. Six months after we had moved in Jess and I held a little round-table conference with ourselves, and were somewhat alarmed at the general position. My own career was progressing satisfactorily, and indeed there had been one or two encouraging developments. For many ears I had written short stories about the often mysterious relationship between men and women. Because I believe sex is very often the key to such relationships I have felt it impossible, in a serious story, not to touch on this subject. If we are to understand ourselves then we must surely be honest about these things. I can conceive that a marriage may go wrong between two people, who are ideally suited sexually, for some other reason: but equally I would find it very hard to believe that a marriage could normally prove satisfactory where the sexual relationship was a bad one. Writing stories about such matters I had naturally found it very hard to get them published in the rather prudish British magazines. However, through a chance suggestion from a friend of mine in America, I had been put in touch with Samuel Roth, an American publisher who held similar ideas to mine. What was more he was prepared to publish my stories, in a quarterly magazine he ran, called *American Aphrodite*. This was beautifully produced and I was delighted to find my work alongside stories by Rhys Davies, Henry Miller, Frank O'Connor, James Hanley, William Sansom, Gwyn Jones, and many other excellent writers. Possibly the knowledge that at long last I had a definite market for this kind of story stimulated my creative ego, for during the next year I supplied Samuel Roth with about fifteen. On one occasion an entire issue of *American Aphrodite* was devoted to my work. I couldn't help feeling exasperated that British magazines should turn down some of my best stories, but at least they *were* being published, and indeed to a far wider audience. I was grateful for this, although unfortunately Sam Roth's rate of payment, about ten pounds a story, was no great help to our economic situation. This was now rather desperate, for the expenses involved in installing the water pump, decorations, and so forth, had eaten up our capital - while I was continually losing money on my own 'baby', the *Cornish Review*. For some time past now we had often kept going only thanks to the weekly rents from 16, Morrab Place, although uneasily aware that by spending these each week-end we were letting the Building Society repayments mount up alarmingly. When finally one or two long-standing creditors became belligerent in their demands we knew we had reached the stage where desperate ills demand desperate remedies.

That evening Jess and I took our usual stroll in the grounds of our new domain. There was a wide sweeping drive round to the front of the house, bordered by shrubs and trees, and this front part of the house seemed to grow out of the land as if it had always been there. But at the rear, parallel to the vegetable garden, the path ran under a long avenue of tall beech trees which seemed curiously artificial - though of course they must have been planted at least fifty years previously.

I had already noticed that these trees, standing so close to the house, kept out a lot of light.

'What are you looking so thoughtful about?'

'I was just thinking. These trees.'

I took Jess by the arm and led her close to one of them.

'See if you can get your arms round that? You can't, can you? It must be nearly ten feet in circumference. I wonder how tall they are?'

'Tall enough,' said Jess. 'But what -?'

'I was just thinking - supposing we sold these trees? It would be a way of raising money quickly. It would get us out of the mess we're in.'

Of course it never did, quite, because a self-employed writer and his family are bound to exist in a financial mess from beginning to end, one way and another. But it certainly helped. The next morning I rang up the manager of a local timber yard who came out and inspected the trees and quoted us a price, if I remember rightly, of about ten pounds a tree. We decided to sell twelve trees and gave him the order to go ahead with the timber felling.

The next day the men came out. Timber-felling is one of those professions that still carries a romantic aura about it, woodchoppers always seem rather wild and gypsy in appearance. Our own friends were unfortunately not available at this time, but the group of three who turned up in an enormous old lorry, itself containing two or three smaller mechanical instruments, were true to tradition. They managed to invest what might well be a perfectly simple and humdrum operation (to those who know) with an air of mystery. For hours after they first arrived they seemed to do nothing but pace out measurements, take angled alignments, and tie ropes out in all directions.

At lunch-time I became a little impatient and asked when the trees would be coming down.

'All in good time, mate, all in good time.'

Mid-way through the afternoon we were startled to hear the crackle of a combustion engine spattering across the still air. 'Brrhmm-brrhmmmmmm-brrmmhh - ' Ah, we thought, circular saw at work. Now something will happen.

Alas, after a few hours' 'brrmmhs' there was silence for quite a while. Then a few more 'brrmhs'. Then silence.

In the end, unable to concentrate on anything else, we went out to investigate. It turned out there was mechanical trouble. Meantime the circular saw was embedded about six inches into a very formidable tree trunk.

Later on there was a further hold up. We kept hearing furious cries.

'Wedges ! -Wedges!'

Rushing out, we found quite an amicable discussion going on about what apparently was one of numerous terms peculiar to woodchoppers.

In the end, by a complicated combination of ropes, pulleys, wedges, occasional jabs with a circular saw and sheer man power, the woodchoppers brought down the first of our doomed trees. I shall never forget that first experience of the death of a tree. I had never expected to be so poignantly aware of it. What I think enhanced the sensation was the awful, seemingly infinite gap in time between the moment when the woodchopper's saw suddenly stopped crackling and when the tree hit the ground. That silence was uncanny and sinister: one knew that something was happening, something rather awful - and then came that frightening rush of air and that terribly final, irrevocable thump. It was certainly much more like an execution than I had imagined. Although, later, we were told by the woodchoppers that the trees were in fact on the point of decay and were over-ripe for cutting, this never quite allayed our feeling of remorse.

In the end the cutting down of the trees not only brought us in about £120 to help clear off our immediate creditors and had the expected result of flooding the house with new light - it also, after all the manoeuvring of the men and their machines, resulted in a clearing away of most of the mysterious jungle that had covered our land. Suddenly we realized that at the rear we had about two acres of potential market garden.

'Of course!' declared Jess, who once worked in the Land Army and has a more practical attitude to the land than myself. 'We'll make our land pay its way. Just think of the possibilities!'

What a lot of harmless fun we had sitting round the big log fires in that long sitting-room at the old Vicarage! Vegetables, chickens, potatoes, early lettuce, fruit, anemones, violets, corn on the cob, even tobacco - we toyed with all kinds of ideas. But of course we had no capital, and so Jess's vague dream of hundreds of poultry living in little wooden huts boiled down (not literally!) to a handful of about five or six sad looking hens who used to peck their way around the estate morosely, occasionally chased by quite the most vicious cockerel I have ever seen. We did get a few eggs, but one by one the hens died off or were eaten by marauding dogs, and the end to that story was a Christmas execution of the cockerel by a friend of ours - after which no one could face the result, and I was able to smile the smug smile of the superior vegetarian.

Vegetables petered along in the same desultory way. We did manage to keep a small patch going for our own use, but weeds defeated any larger efforts. With violets, however, we made a really determined effort, after discovering, somewhat to our mortification, that almost every Cornish back garden supported a family's winter in violet sales.

'We must think big - plant them on a big scale. We'll make a fortune.' This I hasten to explain was Jess speaking, not me. She brimmed over with confidence and vitality about the prospects . . . who was I to voice a vague half intuitive idea that no good would come of it all

In Cornwall violets are planted in the early summer with a view to flowering in the late autumn or winter, to catch the great Christmas market. So early in July we spent afternoons and evenings hard at work digging up the land and at last planting in neat rows the two thousand violet plants which we had bought. It was indeed a laborious task, and by the time it was finished we ached in every limb. But we thought avariciously of the delightful sums of money that would be due just before Christmas.

'Mind you,' said Jess warningly, 'it's essential to keep the ground hoed. Violets must have plenty of air and space.'

But of course, yes, we agreed. We would hoe them most diligently. And so we would have done . . . if it had not been for the bees. They were not our bees, dear me, no. If they had been we might have been able to do something about them. They were the bees belonging to the gentleman who had rented the next door walled fruit garden. Day after day great swarms of bees abruptly deserted the humdrum existence of their fruit garden to explore the more interesting world of our garden. Later we were told that the real cause of the trouble may have been the introduction of the wrong strain of Italian Queens into the hives, thoroughly upsetting the entire family.

Anyway, the cause didn't matter, what was so disastrous was the result. This was, quite simply, that every time Jess or I, or any other grown up, appeared in the back garden, he or she was immediately attacked by a vicious swarm, or at least a posse, of angry bees. It became quite commonplace for me to hear a bloodcurdling scream and look up to see an agitated screaming human figure wildly dancing a jig in the garden. The bees were quite relentless: it was impossible even to venture twenty feet into the garden without their zooming up from nowhere and launching their attack. No adult was sacred. My mother, down for a summer holiday, tried in vain to take a deck chair in the garden. For some reason the bees were particularly incensed by the colour blue, which was hard lines on our friend Donald, who ventured into the garden in blue shirt and jeans. Only the children escaped - a mystery for a long time, until Jess worked out that the line of the bees' flight was about four feet from ground level, so they passed over the children's heads.

The strange finale to all this was that the bees discovered we had a small cement bathing pool in the garden, measuring about four feet square and filled with about two feet of water. Every day they made straight for this plot and hovered over the surface of the water. In their excitement dozens were drowned, others helped on their way by sadistic children or infuriated, recently stung adults. At the very end a Ministry of Agriculture Adviser arrived at our summons, and finally had the hives removed, and we were at last able to venture into our garden in peace. But as for the violets...alas, they had vanished forever into a jungle of weeds, all two thousand of them.

Chapter Five

THE DEAR GOLDEN YEARS

After the violets we gave up trying to explore the agricultural potential of the Old Vicarage. We realized sadly that we were just not cut out for this sort of thing. We were very worried about money matters, particularly the problems of day to day living. No matter what else, five small children have to be fed and clothed, and it is not always easy, more especially without any regular income. Once again we fell back on the temporary expedient of letting out a part of our home. Even though we now all had a room each, and there was a playroom as well for the children, and an office for me, there still remained the top floors, and also a large outbuilding with possibilities. Soon we let the top flat of the Old Vicarage (conveniently from the point of view of a large family!) to Nurse Ford, the local mid-wife. Like all members of her profession that I have met Nurse Ford was most expert and conscientious, and often out all hours of the night on her cases. She was a little elderly to be involved in the helter-skelter life of a family of small children, and had too long and disillusioning an experience of children and their little ways to be unduly sentimental about ours! But she delivered our two daughters, Demelza and, later, Genevieve, possibly the first births at the Old Vicarage for quite a few decades.

Our most vivid memory of the nurse is inevitably associated with the birth of Genevieve, by which time the nurse had just moved into a new house she had bought up the road from the Old Vicarage. Genevieve, who was to be our last, and certainly our most placid and equable child, true to her character arrived quickly and neatly and with the minimum of fuss. After hearing that inevitable strange cry which signified one more V.B. loose in the world I hurriedly made a pot of tea and arrived back in the bedroom bearing this welcome refreshment - almost at the very moment when the nurse, probably tired after her night's work, slipped over and fell with a resounding thud full length on the floor. What's more, she found herself quite unable to get up again, as she had obviously sprained her leg quite severely. Very thankful that it hadn't happened ten minutes earlier, when I should have had to deliver Genevieve myself, I had first to complete the general tidying up processes under the nurse's directions, then carry her to her car and drive her home, where she had to stay in bed for several weeks.

After Nurse Ford found a house of her own we let the top floors to a dog lover and breeder, Miss Grover, whose advent the children welcomed with some glee, for it meant there were always three or four huge boxer dogs bounding about the grounds. They were however inclined to express their feelings at all hours. Frequently I would wake up in the middle of the night in great alarm, wondering whether the strange disturbing noise that cut across my sweet dreams was (a) one of the children having a nightmare, (b) the electric water pump screeching into action, or (c) Miss Grover's dogs yowling to their absent lady loves. Usually, it was (c) I fancy: but in all fairness I must confess that we ourselves had by then acquired one of the most extraordinary canine animals in West Cornwall. This was Dina, a huge, fat, lazy, friendly Labrador whom the local vet described as a nymphomaniac. Dina quite overwhelmed us with her progeny - it seemed that she delivered a litter of about nine puppies every six months or so. Whenever her time arrived she would disappear and we would know where to look for her - deep in the hollow inside of an old oak tree in the garden. There she would be, curled up with her little new arrivals sucking away contentedly. They were always delightful puppies, usually being cross of Labrador and greyhound, what are called lurchers. We made desperate efforts to find homes for them, and for quite a while we succeeded. But gradually, inexorably, Dina's very prolificacy began to overwhelm, as well as exhaust us. Finally the R.S.P.C.A. ordered that she must be destroyed. I shall never forget the macabre morning that followed. I had been directed to dig a large grave deep in the garden. When the R.S.C.P.A. man arrived there was a thick mist and drizzle. Through this, he and I set out on Dins last walk. It was a humane and painless execution, I know, but a sad end to such a voracious life. For months, indeed years afterwards, whenever I walked about the district I kept corning across descendants of Dina's. Somehow their liquid brown eyes seemed to look at me with eternal reproach.

Finally, in our apportioning out of the spare rooms of the Old Vicarage, we decided to convert a large separate building standing beside the main one - I don't know quite what it had been, but it made a very good residential studio home, and we let it permanently to our old friend Donald Swan, a portrait painter. Donald was one of those warm-hearted, very sympathetic Scottish souls who take to family life like a duck to the water, and in no time he became an integral part of our life at St Hilary. Now and then he would join us in a meal or if there was any sort of gathering or party, but at the same time he was very proud of having his own little home in the studio. This was so big as to be almost like a miniature hall. This meant it could be cold in the winter, but Donald fixed that by installing a rather fearful and antiquated Belgian stove, which cost about £3, and had the most ferocious wind draught I have ever seen. Fortunately wood was endlessly available, especially after the advent of the woodchoppers, so Donald was always able to keep warm, though the rate of consumption of logs was formidable. At one end of the studio were some wooden steps leading to a loft room over the garage where we kept our car, and up here

Donald had his bed. The rest of the studio was for working in, and here he did many paintings, mostly portraits.

As a painter Donald belonged firmly to what is called the academic school: that is, he painted in the tradition of Rembrandt and Titian. When his portraits came off they were very good - I well remember his presentation portrait of the late judge Scobell Armstrong, and, more personally, a delightful oil painting of Jess, which he executed in an hour or so, and which has hung in my room ever since. But though academic in style (and what a good teacher he would have made, I always thought) Donald fully appreciated what modernists were trying to do. He jolly well had to - for periodically his girl friend Ann Holden would descend on him from London, where she studied at the Royal College of Art. And Ann was a modernist in the best and most vital sense of the word. Her paintings, even if sometimes obscure, always conveyed a vitality, a sense of force that would not be denied. Donald and Ann would spend hours animatedly arguing about painting and its ethics, but always with an inherent respect for each other's viewpoints. We always felt we understood just why Felix Topolski picked out Ann Holden as the most promising young painter of her year - and were as sad as Donald when she took herself and her unfulfilled talent, of all places, into the backwoods of British Columbia.

We liked very much having Donald around. We were of the same generation and, so far as the position of the artist in society was concerned, of the same general viewpoint. Donald had passed through lean times during the years he struggled to make a living as a painter, he understood the hardships and poverty that confront artists of all kinds. We knew what it was to borrow each other's last shilling indeed, on occasions when the car had broken down, we more than once would have been unable to get into Penzance to collect our desperately needed rents, had it not been for Donald searching through the pockets of his clothes and unearthing an odd coin or two. We learned to love even Donald's idiosyncrasies, such as his habit of glancing casually at a newspaper as he passed through a room and starting to read it and staying there for the next hour: or his incredible absent-mindedness. And he for his part *had* to learn to love our children's idiosyncrasies, for they were in and out of his studio like so many burrowing rabbits - the result being sketches and portraits of little Val Bakers all over the place.

Jess and I, Donald and Ann, we were all part of a group of friends, all of whom had come to settle in Cornwall because it was a place that drew them, because they appreciated its unique qualities, and because they found that here they could work best. Len Missen and Anthony Richards, the two potters at Penzance, were two others: another was Dennis Pattison, of Porthleven, a dreamer who on one level worked on the telephone exchange while on another was immersed in the world of films, planning all kinds of wonderful scenarios which alas would never be filmed. Later there were some of the woodchoppers, Ray Perry and Arthur Slater, and then Ray's former wife Biddy and Bill Pickard, with whom she eventually opened a pottery shop at Mousehole; and also Jack and Joan Richards, who made wrought iron down by the Quay at Penzance. The feeling of instinctive comradeship that developed was something quite intangible that could hardly be grasped at - if you did it might slip away. But it was there, somehow. We used to be especially conscious of it on Saturday mornings, when many of us would meet for a midday drink in Penzance, at the St John's House', or later the 'Star': and on Saturday evenings when it became a custom to link up with one another on a drive via the Tolcarne pub at Newlyn, to the 'Ship', Mousehole. It wasn't that any of us were heavy drinkers; quite the reverse - in our own case we could not have afforded to be, and usually only went out for a drink on these Saturdays. But in Cornwall pubs are very much a social centre and, among the artists, particular pubs come to be recognized meeting places.

Against this wider background we remained very much a group within a group, perhaps a dozen in all, several owning old cars of one kind and another, so that sometimes, indeed, we formed quite a crazy cavalcade. Once we dispensed with the cars in favour of hiring a motor coach for one new year's eve - it cost, believe it or not, only £3 for a coach that carried I think eighteen people. It is the only time I have taken part in such a communal trip and I must say it was quite an experience. We called in at the 'Wink' at Lamorna and picked up some of our woodchopper friends, then went on to the 'First and Last' pub at Sennen - where more appropriate to say goodbye to a dying year ! - ending up, of all places, at a night club at Cape Cornwall. That is typical of Cornwall, in the most outlandish spot you will often find some quite bizarre place or activity.

Another very entertaining experience was when we entered for the annual Newlyn carnival. In Cornwall, carnivals are still taken very seriously and entries are often intricate and impressive. At this time the Kon-Tiki raft adventure was very much in the public eye, so we decided to take that as a theme. We hired a lorry and Len, Anthony, Dennis Pattison, Bill Pickard, and a local basket worker, Ron Lander, dressed up in rags and coloured charcoal to look a real wild party of raft-ites. There was suitable decor, too, including a huge 'mast' which caused quite a sensation by getting entangled in the telephone wires going through Newlyn Narrows. As an extra twist to the presentation we had decorated my old Rover car as a second raft, and on that, bearing the banner: 'The Girls They Left Behind Them', reclined Jess, Dorothy Richards, Dorothy Missen, Joan Pattison and Anna - each one a delectable representative of a different nationality, French, Japanese, Russian, and so on. Our efforts were suitably rewarded for we won the first prize in our class, £3. Late that evening the annual dance took place at Newlyn Fish Market. The long hall had been washed down and cleaned and decorated, a local jazz band installed, sawdust thrown down, and everyone from miles around seemed to be dancing there, beside the rippling water of Newlyn Harbour. It was a gay unexpected evening that I always remember, especially turning for a moment from the whirling dancers to lean over the railings and stare across the harbour to the forest of masts of the fishing fleet, their moving lights reflected like stars in the still waters.

This spirit of companionship which I am trying to capture was reflected in innumerable ways - often over such a small matter as cars. Somehow one by one we had all acquired not just cars but very eccentric *old* cars that were always breaking down or nearly breaking down. I think it was J. B. Priestley who once wrote an interesting article suggesting that the cult of old cars was part of a protest against the terrible standardizing effect of our modern civilization. Whether rightly or not we seemed to find much more character and warmth in old cars with hoods frayed and washed-out colours, whose mudguards were rather bent, but whose hearts were indubitably in the right place. We were all proud of our cars, most of which were bought for sums of £10 to £30. But perhaps none of them provided such a vivid story - and, alas, such a short-lived one - as Jezebel, Jess's first and last car of her own.

We found Jezebel under some furniture in a second-hand shop! I was in there one day asking the owner, Mr Scrase, about a repair job when suddenly my eye was caught by a strange apparition peeping out from under an old bedstead. It looked like, well, undoubtedly it *looked* like the mudguard of a car. But of course it couldn't be Yet it was: there, hidden away, fading away one might say, was one of the famous Austin Seven 'Chummys', vintage 1928.

As soon as he observed our interest Mr Scrase let loose all his own former pride. My word, she was a wonderful little bus, he had driven her every day for thirty years, used to have her when he was fireman - then he had to pack up driving, and he had left her in the back of the shop ever since.

I didn't need to look at Jess, I could imagine the gleam in her eyes.

'Do you think she would go again?'

Mr Scrase looked at me in amazement.

'Why not? She'll go on for ever if you want. Austins always have done, haven't they?'

We arranged that Mr Scrase should unravel the car from the conglomeration of furniture, get the battery charged, and then we would return the same time tomorrow. When we did so and she started quite sweetly at a touch of the starter, we could resist her no longer. A brief but dignified haggle with Mr Scrase, and she was ours for £12.10s.

'A present for you, darling', I said, secretly rather envious.

Immediately of course, Jess looked quite scared. She has confessed that often in our life together she has dreamed vaguely of doing something: and then when I have somewhat impetuously brought the event about, she is never ready for the reality.

Now she protested weakly that she couldn't drive.

'Don't you worry about that,' I said airily, 'I'll teach you.'

In point of fact, I myself found it difficult enough to get the hang of Jezebel, as we renamed old Mr Scrase's car. Various parts worked by lengths of wire and string, and black smoke frequently belched out. But after we had taken her home and painted her a bright yellow she looked much more a lady of the road. I felt it was time to take Jess out on her first lesson. I was not happy about the prospect, I must confess. At the loneliest spot I could find, out on a wide, fairly quiet road, I stopped the car and said, like a man announcing the outbreak of war or a coming execution:

'Let's change seats, shall we?'

'Well, now - ' I began and then stopped; aware most uneasily, of Jess now in the driving seat. She was sitting forward, both hands gripping the wheel feverishly, one foot tapping the floor impatiently - in her eyes a strange, unhealthy, wild gleam.

'Come on,' said Jess briskly. 'Let's start.'

I embarked on a careful explanation of the basic principles of motoring, elaborating upon the complex techniques of changing gear, operating the clutch, accelerating, braking (especially the braking) painstakingly explaining what all the switches were for, and was leading up to the grave matter of the engine, when -

'Yes, yes, all right. *Do* let's get going. I know all that stuff.'

'But dearest, you can't possibly "know all that stuff" as you put it. Why, I've been driving for nearly twenty years, and *I* don't know it all myself.'

'Don't be silly. I've watched you dozens of times. You just press something and move this black knob and make a horrible noise, and do something else I've forgotten, and then the car moves. It's quite simple, I know. Do let's *start*.'

As time passed, and at the expense of much energy and patience, it seemed, rather to my surprise, that Jess was actually beginning to grasp the principles of gear-changing. Indeed, she mildly surprised me by driving several times up and down the road, and even round a bend or two. At last I decided the time had come to let her drive in traffic.

What followed was like a nightmare. First, Jess shot the car out of a side street into the centre of a busy main road. Breaking violently to avoid ramming a milk cart she swerved into the path of a huge diesel lorry. As the lorry pulled up with a screech of brakes Jess took fright and swerved into the opposite direction, on to the wrong side of the road.

What can be said of the next few minutes? As Jess aimed for a space between a bus and a taxi which I, the trolly-bus driver, and the taxi man all knew to be too narrow - as she swept across a pedestrian crossing filled with stout ladies wheeling prams full of innocent children far too young to die yet - as, finally, she glided regally past a red traffic light, smiling graciously at a policeman standing aghast at the side of the road - what words can possibly describe these peculiarly husbandly experiences? They must be lived through to be believed.

At last, with a sort of perverse expertness, Jess stalled the car exactly in the centre of a busy cross-roads. She did this, in the main, because she found an enormous double-decker bus within three feet of her bonnet on one side and a lumbering petrol tanker about to crash into her on the other side - while a second loomed up behind. For a few pregnant moments the scene remained static, like this.

All around fascinated pedestrians gathered.

I awoke as if from some dream.

'Into gear!'

'It's no good, I can't.'

'Of course you can't until you start the engine, idiot!'

'It won't start.'

'For heaven's sake - *start it up*!'

'I can't.'

'Into gear - into gear - into gear!'

'I can't!' Jess let out an agonized wail, the prerogative of all badly-done-by wives. 'Oh, you're beastly, absolutely beastly! You just don't want me to learn to drive, do you?'

In the end, indeed, Jess had to turn elsewhere for her lessons, and it was really after Len's tuition that she finally took the test. Unfortunately she had to take it in an unfamiliar car and was failed, so whenever she went out, though by now she was quite a competent driver, I usually had to accompany her. Since this was not really not the idea at all, as Jezebel was supposed to be Jess's symbol of freedom, she began to get a little disheartened.

There was, I must confess, another reason for this. His name was Ginger. This was a friend of ours who seemed to live and breathe cars, a mechanic of some genius who drifted on to the outskirts of our circle through beginning to do some repairs to one of our friends' cars. After that the word was suddenly passed round.

'Here, why don't you go along to Ginger? *He'll* put things right. And he doesn't charge much either.'

This was all true. Ginger had an old shed down a back street, and at all hours of the day and night he was to be found lying on the ground inspecting the bowels of some unfortunate car. When I first met him it was someone else's car: but almost ever after it seemed to be Jezebel.

I have often wondered if Ginger developed some kind of unhealthy passion for Jezebel. From the moment, quite unaware of what indignities we were condemning her to, we left Jezebel in his hands, she never quite seemed ours any more. At first Ginger was just going 'to look her over' and we hoped to pick her up a couple of days later. Alas, when we arrived, there was Ginger hard at work, his hands (which often looked like spanners) delicately manoeuvring among the intestines of Jezebel's engine.

'Afraid there's a spot of trouble here.' Then quite a reassuring nod of the head. 'Never mind - we'll soon have her right.'

First, I think it was little-end trouble. Then pistons. Then valves. Then something else. I am quite sure all these were needing attention, and I know from my own experience that Ginger devoted not merely hours, but days and even weeks solely rejuvenating Jezebel in readiness for the road. Indeed, he was himself so enthusiastic about her that, despite all the ominous warnings of the continual delays, we were provoked into announcing flamboyantly that we would drive to London in Jezebel.

As the great day drew nearer we got more and more anxious, as still the car was in pieces. The night before we were due to leave we called in at Ginger's garage at 11pm, and could only see his feet sticking out. He was too busy to appear, but a little muffled voice assured us that he would drive the car out to us first thing in the morning.

So he did. True, it was about 10 o'clock and we had hoped to start at eight. But there she was, dear little Jezebel. Our Jezebel...or was she? I stared at her unhappily. Somehow I could not feel I knew her any longer.

Still, Jess and I got in and gave our heartfelt thanks to Ginger. Then with a hearty wave we zoomed off...say about a hundred yards. There was a sort of whooof! a hiss, a cloud of steam - and Jess said plaintively:

'She's stopped.'

I looked around. There was that old trusty figure lumbering up, his tired greasy face full of concern. I shared that concern, as we opened the bonnet and found oil streaming everywhere. Something, I knew, was definitely wrong.

Two hours later, leaving Ginger plunged once more into the innards, we set off for London in my old car. Nothing was said openly, but in our heart of hearts we knew that the story of Jezebel was over. When we came back we towed her to the Old Vicarage, and parked her in the garden. Soon weeds grew higher and higher, winding themselves around the wheels. just when we thought she would disappear altogether, a friend called and said he would buy her. We handed over the log book, and said collect her any time . . . The odd thing is, he went away, and never came back. And there Jezebel stayed to rust and rot away.

Another sad car story was concerned with our friend Dennis Pattison, over at Porthleven. Dennis is one of those light-hearted optimists who is always thinking up wonderful schemes and urging people to embark on crazy ventures. At the same time, though he always talks about plans of his own - for making a film of Cornwall, for buying a house and turning it into a club, for starting a pottery shop, and so on - nothing ever materializes. So when after a lot of talk we found that in some way he had actually accumulated the responsibility of an old tourer we decided to try to make at least one myth turn into active reality.

'Yes, you see, I've got some spare parts and I'll put these in and then I'll have a car better than an original. Fellow I know makes a fortune doing that. All I need are the right tools. . .'

Dennis burbled on and we suspected nothing would happen, as usual.

'Where is your car?'

'Oh, it's in an old quarry at Porthleven. Pity, it's too wet to work on it there.'

'All right', said Len decisively. 'What say we drive over and tow your car to the Old Vicarage. You could work on it there.'

We could see that Dennis was a little taken aback, but he couldn't think immediately of an a answer. And so one fine Sunday afternoon we drove over, equipped with plenty of rope.

Of course, only Dennis could have conceived of putting a car down such a fantastic place. It was the inside shell of an old quarry, and the gravel and slush and grass leading down to it covered a surface like ice. First we tied the rope and tried pulling them. Then Len backed his little van down and tried pulling from there. The only result was that his wheels went round and round - and he too was stuck in the quarry.

Next it was Anthony's turn, in his Ford saloon. He revved and revved and slowly, instead of him pulling the car up, he too was pulled down into the quarry.

We now had three cars in a quarry, and I was the last hope. At all costs I was determined not to leave the road at the top. So we borrowed more rope, collected every available spectator to form a human tug-of-war team - and at last, as I pulled from the top, we managed to get Dennis's car up (afterwards Len's and Anthony's).

After that we all retired to Dennis's cliff-side cottage to recover our breath. At once our host was off on another tangent. 'How about a swim? It's only 60 degrees. We like swimming in the winter. How about -'

'No,' I said, 'we're going to get your car to St Hilary.'

Somehow, we did. There was a puncture on the way. and one or two snappings of the rope. But at last, triumphantly we drove up the drive of the Old Vicarage. Len and Anthony went off home and we all congratulated ourselves and looked forward to Dennis working on his conversion.

We had mis-read his character completely. The next day he got a friend of his with a lorry to come over and load up the car. That night it was back in the quarry.

'Er, you fellows rushed me too much. You see, it's no good unless I get the right equipment. It will all take time.' And then, his eyes gleaming, Dennis rushed on. 'Fact is, I hear there's a bloke up country who's

practically giving away crown wheels and pinions for old post office vans. Got so many he doesn't know what to do with them. I'm going to wait until one of the fruit lorries are going up to London and then I'll get a lift up...'

Needless to say the car remained in the quarry, where gradually it was stripped to pieces by local boys. Dennis was most indignant. He had, he said, all sorts of plans for that car.

Each of us could produce our favourite version of Dennis Pattison and his cars. I think I like best the story told by Donald Swan, of how one lovely sunny day he was driving back from Bodmin and gave a lift to a young New Zealand doctor and his wife. Wishing to impress them with the delights of Cornwall, as it was such a lovely day, Donald said: 'Look, I'll tell you what, I'll drive over to Porthleven. A friend of mine has a bungalow on the cliffs there. We'll have a nice lazy time...'

However, when Donald drove up the narrow lane leading to Dennis Pattison's house he found the way blocked by an old ex-Post Office van, and Dennis Pattison hovering nervously around. Apparently the car had been there for days blocking the way and now there was unrest among the neighbours. How fortunate that Donald should arrive - as it happened Dennis knew of a shed at the end of a field, a woman had told him it would be all right to put his van there. Could Donald possibly . .

Aided by the New Zealand doctor, Donald turned his car around and hitched up the van and proceeded to tow it by a difficult route up a narrow winding hill and out of Porthleven until they reached a large white gate opening on to a field, with a shed nearby. After much complicated manoeuvring they got the old van close to the shed and then went and opened the doors. Somewhat to their consternation the shed was full of a conglomeration of old motor cycles, garden machinery, wooden crates, and so forth. However, Dennis was adamant that it was quite all right to use the shed, so laboriously Donald and the New Zealander emptied the shed of its contents, piling them up on the grass outside.

Donald got back in his car and to the accompaniment of various shouted instructions was just manoeuvring the van into the shed when he became aware of a man's figure on the horizon, rapidly rushing across the field. He appeared to be waving agitatedly. Indeed, he was waving agitatedly.

'Stop! Stop! What on earth are you doing? How dare you!'

This, it transpired, was the owner of the property. He knew nothing about storing Mr Pattison's van, and he was not interested in such a crazy idea. What's more, he wanted his equipment put back into the shed at once.

There was nothing for it. Wearily Donald and the New Zealander loaded the motor bikes and the gardening equipment back into the shed. At last the task was completed, they re-hitched the rope and towed the van back to Dennis Pattison's cottage. There, waiting darkly in the background, were unseen but complaining neighbours. There was, as Donald wearily recalled, nothing for it but to tow the van down into that familiar repository, the old quarry. As for the New Zealanders, they decided they would be on their way.

Cars were by no means the only extent of Dennis Pattison's ventures into fantasy. For many years he talked volubly and persuasively about plans for developing Porthbeeny, his somewhat unsafe-looking bungalow posed over Porthieven Beach. It was going to be converted into a luxury chalet, into a holiday home, into a craft shop, into a tea shop, a night club . . . . When after some particularly violent storms, Dennis's wife put her foot down and insisted that they moved up the hill to a more permanent home, we thought that perhaps now the dreams would become reality. But the bungalow still stands in forlorn solitude.

Yet I do not want to belittle fantasy thinking (I do it myself a lot) for in two directions Dennis helped very considerably to further the golden days of which I write. First, there was Porthbeeny itself, where so often we would all drive out for a Sunday, to spend the afternoon sitting down on the sands, or walking along to Looe Bar, that strange beauty spot where the sea is divided from an interior lake simply by a bar of shingle (and beyond that Gunwalloe, with its lovely church half buried in sand). The outstanding annual gathering at Porthbeeny would always be on May 8th, that is Helston Flora Day. This ancient custom, now ballooned into a national institution and on the regular list of American tourists no doubt, can be a very exhausting experience, since the first dancers are out on the streets at 6 a.m., and very pretty, too, the children all in their white dresses with garlands of flowers in their hair. At intervals during the day there are a series of dances, in which columns of couples wind their way up and down the streets, and in and out of houses. The most popular one is the midday one, the Ladies' and Gentlemen's Dance. We used to arrive in time to see this and then gather in the 'Angel Inn', before returning to Porthbeeny for a spread lasting perhaps till four. This was usually a family occasion, and sometimes as many as twenty or more gathered in those tiny rooms. At night we would all descend on Helston again, ending up in the huge fair that is an essential part of the day, whizzing around on dodgems and whips and octopuses and other horrid machines for upsetting the digestion.

Dennis Pattison's other contribution to our enjoyment was an attic studio which he rented in Penzance, one of those fantasy ideas which had half borne fact. In a moment of excitement Dennis had somehow committed himself to renting this large studio tucked down an alleyway off Chapel Street. I don't know quite what he had in mind - there was once, I think, some talk of using it for a film club. What in fact happened was that Dennis just went on renting the studio week after week, month after month, to no apparent purpose, and so gradually it drifted into almost general use. There were two or three old divans there, and a small electric point . . . during summer months all kinds of strange people might be found sleeping a night or two there. And of course it made an excellent place for a party. All it needed was a few candles, a fire, and some drink, and usually the atmosphere seemed to be created. I can remember many a gathering there though perhaps no event sticks more in my mind than an impromptu apache dance executed by Dennis McCarthy, art master of the local grammar school, with a dummy out of a women's-wear-shop window as companion. We nicknamed her Milly and for months after she stood sentinel at the entrance.

Throughout this first year at the Old Vicarage we had been desperately trying to stave off an almost inevitable disaster. It was all our own fault, I suppose, but that didn't help much. The fact was that in the desperation of our day-to-day living, by putting first things first and feeding our children before the building society, we had fallen greatly behind in our mortgage repayments on 16, Morrab Place. At first it had been a matter of a month or two, then four or five months, then even longer. Naturally the building society had been issuing some sharp reminders, but so far I had managed to keep them at arm's length (they were, after all, in Yorkshire). But now the arrears had really mounted up and were running into a year and even longer. Now and then we managed to make a payment, but in between another two or three months slipped by. Finally the building society got really tough and called in their mortgage, as they were entitled to do under the regulations.

Our only hope of salvaging something from the wreckage was to sell the house at a sum which after clearing the mortgage would leave us with a few hundred pounds capital. My word, how we tried, too! We advertised it up hill and down dale, in classy papers like *The Lady* and *Country Life* and in down-to-earth business-like papers such as *Dalton's Weekly*. We got plenty of inquiries, but sad to say nobody was able or willing to make an offer of anywhere near the price we needed which in itself was well below what we ourselves had paid. The fact was, as a smooth estate agent readily explained, that terrace houses were a little out of fashion. He didn't quite know what to advise. Perhaps.

'Perhaps' lasted a few more months and then the final chapter began. The building society announced its intention of exercising its rights to take over the house, and we were faced with the melancholy task of giving notice to our tenants and cutting off about a half of our income.

It was a curious experience. We felt rather like executioners, but we could not help ourselves. Indeed, already the house hardly seemed ours any longer. Several tenants were just casuals who had rented rooms through the local paper, and we had no feelings one way or another about them. But one or two, like Amy and Anthony Richards, had been with us for some years, and we felt in some way morally responsible for finding them new homes. We offered Amy the top room at the Old Vicarage and she was going to take this until on paying a visit she discovered it was haunted. Fortunately she managed to find a little cottage in Penzance.

With Anthony it was a different story. He meant well, of course. Yes, he really must find another place. Yes, time *was* getting short. He really would find somewhere.

The building society named a final day for our total evacuation. One by one the tenants departed, and we either removed the furniture to the Old Vicarage, or sold it off at rather ridiculous prices to local dealers.

But Anthony remained. There he was still installed in the ground floor flat, eating, sleeping, reclining on couches, clothes everywhere, no sign of any movement.

We began to call around anxiously.

'Any luck, Anthony, have you heard of anywhere. You won't forget... March 31st deadline.'

Immediately Anthony would look very worried and apologetic and mumble.

'Yes, I did hear there was a cottage at Newlyn, it's condemned or something, I might be able to get that.'

A night or two later we would ask eagerly:

'Did you get that cottage at Newlyn?'

Anthony would look most contrite: 'Er, well I've been busy, I haven't had a chance - but I must call there, tomorrow.'

Somehow we could never believe the inevitable would happen, but it did. March 31st arrived, a fine falsely happy sort of day, and still Anthony was installed at 16, Morrab Place. The rest of the house was an empty shell, echoing with mournful memories: but the ground floor saw Anthony at home for the day, resolutely eating his lunch. 'But Anthony you promised - '

'We've arranged for the furniture to be collected -'

'They'll be coming to cut off the gas -'

'Yes, and the electricity -'

Like a hunted man at bay Anthony went red in the face and brandished a knife and fork.

'I don't care - I can't deal with it now - I must have my lunch.'

Afterwards he calmed down and there then ensued an afternoon right out of a Chekhov play. Anthony's partner Len popped in, and one or two other friends, and we all sat around in Anthony's lounge sharing a bottle of wine.

Soon there was a loud knock at the door and I jumped to my feet.

'I'm afraid that'll be the electricity.'

It was too. Closely followed by the gas. Both armed with orders to cut off their respective supplies.

Fortunately there was a coal grate, and although Anthony had no coal there were one or two orange boxes around and we soon had a nice blaze going.

We were just settling down again and solving Anthony's immediate future by arranging that he should join Len at his new digs, when there came further arrivals. This time it was a dealer to take away Anthony's bed and the couch. He had hardly gone, when another dealer arrived for the chairs and tables. As each article of furniture went, so we manoeuvred about, one sitting on the window seat, one on a remaining chair, one on an upturned orange box. Meantime the lights were fading and so Len slipped out and came back with some candles. I think also somehow he managed

to obtain a second bottle of wine.

Then, with all the furniture gone, we all sat on the floor drinking wine by candle light, almost convulsed with a sort of gay hilarity over the bizarre situation. Maybe it was the wine, or maybe the cosy effect of the candle light and the fire, but as the evening wore on we became curiously exhilarated, and what was in a way a disastrous day for us, somehow momentarily became a slice of life's comic opera. We sat close together, a curiously charmed circle, each in turn remembering some facet of the turmoil of life that had filled the house in the past four years. I often remember that scene by the fire, it is a symbolic part perhaps of those golden years when life was often hard and desperately worrying, yet there was always this tremendous communal strength, so that at the very worst moment we could always raise a laugh. And perhaps that is the best way to confront these things.

Chapter Six

THE LIFE AND DEATH OF THE CORNISH REVIEW

'The bones of this land are not speechless', warns the poet, Frances Bellerby, of Cornwall. 'He who seeks to mirror this place should first learn their language.'

It was because I found so many people at work endeavouring in their various creative ways to 'mirror this place' that, after settling in Cornwall, I began to think seriously in terms of a publication which might serve their needs. The pottery of Bernard Leach, the paintings of Ben Nicholson, the sculpture of Sven Berlin, the printing of Guido Morris, the poetry of W. S. Graham, the autobiography of Jack R. Clemo, the scholarship of R. Morton Nance, Grand-Bard of the Cornish Gorsedd, the dialect stories of George Manning Sanders, the memories of A. L. Rowse, the travels of Anne Treneer, the sketches of Lady Vyvyan, the perceptive essays of R. Glyn Grylls - surely all these activities constituted a culture, a creative life, of which Cornwall might well be proud? Certainly I myself found it a fascinating aspect of Cornwall, the way in which artists of all kinds seemed to be (sometimes quite mysteriously) drawn down to this western tip of England's most westerly county. The hold which Cornwall exerts on the creative artist is difficult to illustrate. The easiest example is perhaps the sculptor; for here indeed is a sculptor's country. As Sven Berlin has said, Cornwall has a most peculiar influence on the unconscious mind of man. In his own case he was made to feel that he was so rooted in the Cornish landscape that to go and work in a city or some other area would so alter his vision that it might be impossible to work for a conceivable time. Peter Lanyon, a Cornish-born painter, once said about the north Cornish coast:

Here, in a small stretch of head-land, cove and Atlantic adventure, the most distant histories are near the surface as if the final convulsions of rock upheaval and cold incision, setting in a violent sandwich of strata, had directed the hide-and-seek of Celtic pattern.

Writers, as I can testify from my own experience, are equally inspired by the Cornish setting and atmosphere: it is difficult to travel about in Cornwall without being made acutely aware of the vast mystery of life, without being tantalized by haunting vistas of the past, and even hints of the supernatural.

Perhaps, on reflection, it was as well I lived on Trencrom Hill when I began to think about publishing a magazine. Somehow in such surroundings I was inspired to think only of the creative functions of such a magazine, all the interesting articles it could publish, the fascinating paintings it might reproduce, all the reviews and essays and stories and poems and other items which could reflect creative life in Cornwall. Up in the Penwith hills, or alternatively talking to eager painters at work in their studios, I was undoubtedly encouraged to look on the rosy side of such a venture. A more realistic Gallup poll among the average residents of Camborne, Falmouth, Truro, and a few other Cornish centres might have thrown a necessary cold douche on my optimism. That there was a real need for such a magazine I believed then, and indeed believe now; but of course to go blithely ahead on my own, using my own capital and just hoping for the best was asking for the trouble that I eventually got. I ought to have been warned by the knowledge that a whole half century had elapsed since the last ill-fated attempt to run such a magazine. And doubly warned by the significant fact that, although edited by no less a figure than 'Q', Sir Arthur Quiller-Couch himself; that magazine came to an untimely end after only a few issues.

Far from taking warning, I was simply mystified that no one had had the enterprise to start such a magazine during all those fifty years. Well, I was going to change all that. I was going to bring out the *Cornish Review* whose declared aim was, simply, 'to fulfil an obvious need - to provide a platform for discussing and analysing cultural activities in Cornwall, along with an outlet for new poetry and fiction by writers of Cornish descent or living in Cornwall'. What's more I would make it a 'proper job'-no half measures, but a magazine which any bookstall would be proud to display, whether in Penzance or St Austell, or the West End of London. A prospectus was drawn up and printed, and for night after night we would sit by the oil lamp in our cottage folding up these leaflets and inserting them in envelopes addressed to a whole variety of Cornwall lovers, both at home and farther afield (addresses culled from a variety of sources, one of the most helpful being the London Cornish Association). The magazine was to be published quarterly, price 2s 6d or 10s 8d, annually post free, and the contents of the first issue would total 96 pages, including 12 pages of photographs. We mailed out some 500 prospectuses and within a week or two had accumulated 200 annual subscriptions.

This was good - on its own small scale remarkably good - but of course not enough. Subscriptions are an important basis of any publishing venture, but in addition one simply must have a wide range of retail sales. Many new publications employ agencies to do this work for them, but of course this applies to a national sales coverage. The *Cornish Review* sales would be achieved almost entirely through bookshops in and around Cornwall, and if anyone was going to contact those bookshops it obviously, if only for economic reasons, had better be me. So I got an early dummy prepared by the printer, whipped up all my enthusiasm, climbed into the very old Austin Seven we ran at the time, and one memorable morning set off to sell the *Cornish Review*, ahead of publication day, to the shops which I naïvely assumed would receive it with open arms.

I suppose it can only have been a kind of sublime enthusiasm that carried me through what, in retrospect, I see as one of the most dismal journeys ever made by a misguided idealist. In the first place it hardly even occurred to me that anyone in Cornwall would not welcome a purely Cornish publication - least of all local booksellers. If only for its novelty value I imagined that the *Cornish Review* would be greeted warmly, given a sort of extra push as being a local, and so on. Indeed, in more luxurious moments, I often dreamed of whole windows filled with compelling displays of Cornwall's new and exciting magazine of the arts. Well, leave us our dreams.

Perhaps here I should explain that from the patriotic viewpoint, Cornwall is more of a continent than a county: that is, it is not so important that you are in Cornwall, what matters - drastically, irrevocably - is *what part* of Cornwall you come from. Thus, initially, on the first day of my personal sales campaign I was given a false kind of confidence, in that my first calls were essentially local ones. Living mid-way between St Ives and Penzance I naturally visited these towns first. In St Ives it was assumed to be a St Ives venture, and in Penzance a Penzance one, consequently the booksellers were at least a little interested. It is true that one of the largest bookshops in the West Country, noted for its specialization in Cornish books, required twenty minutes' earnest consideration before tentatively ordering six copies of this dubious new magazine, 'O.S., of course ...' (the book trade's favourite initials, a formula by which they only need to pay for copies they actually sell, even if they have them for months). Still, the orders quickly mounted up to several hundreds, and the next day I set off 'on the road' in the highest of spirits. These were somewhat dampened by a mistaken stop at Hayle and an exhausting search there for bookshops which simply did not exist. Never mind, I re-assembled my enthusiasm and advanced on Camborne and Redruth, Cornwall's largest urban area. Really I ought to have been warned by my experience of helping to start the Studio Theatre there some years previously. But then theatres are expensive and have to be supported regularly every week: the *Cornish Review* was merely coming out four times a year, and at only 2s. 6d, a time, surely...

Well, I won't differentiate between Camborne and Redruth, but the total orders from this area of more than 20,000 people amounted to 24 copies. In Falmouth and Trurot was better, but in Newquay - Cornwall's most commercially successful holiday resort, supposedly with an eye for new business (?) - I hit an all-time low, no orders at all. This record was equalled by Bodmin and Liskeard and Budte, and though I doggedly penetrated down the tortuous cliff hills of Port Isaac and Boscastle and, over on the south coast, Polperro and Fowey, the orders formed the thinnest and most anaemic of trickles. When I finally returned to the welcome remoteness of Trencrom after nearly a week of exploring Cornwall in all its facets I had indeed gained a greater understanding of the county's almost unbelievable insularity - but I had only obtained orders for the *Cornish Review* which, added to subscriptions, still fell short of 1,000. Since the cost of producing 1,000 copies of a 96-page review, including two dozen blocks, was going to be in the region of £200 and the income from selling 1,000, even allowing for full price in the case of 200 subscribers' copies, would hardly exceed £100, even the most elementary businessman would have scrapped the whole project. I suppose the trouble is I am just not an elementary business man, but I must admit even I hesitated. I never expected to make any real profit out of the *Cornish Review,* and indeed I was secretly quite prepared to lose a certain amount of my own money. After all, I told myself, I didn't smoke, many smokers I knew spent as much as £150 a year on cigarettes, surely I could look on it in those terms? (All wrong of course, but it helps to keep up morale.) But supposing the losses were much heavier than I expected, what would happen then

Fortunately I am so constituted that I can never look that far ahead. A few days up among the Penwith hills restored my Celtic buoyancy. Wasn't there a crying need for such a magazine Hadn't I already assembled a pile of excellent material, with the promise of many more manuscripts from authors, many of them very well known What about that fascinating series 'My World' by leading craftsmen The portraits of Cornish towns? The interviews with painters? The poetry anthologies? The reviews of art exhibitions. The account of the revival of the Cornish language? The history of the Cornish Gorsedd? The studies of Richard Trevithick and John Opie and 'Q' and Charles Lee and other famous figures of Cornish life! Much of this material was already on my desk. And then there were all those subscribers, who had rallied round so readily (not to mention those well-meaning friends in all spheres who, though unable to help financially, were constantly and even extravagantly urging me on). It was perhaps a sobering thought that even at this time similar magazines which had fostered art and literature in other Celtic countries - the *Welsh Review* and *Wales* in Wales, and the *Bell* in Eire - were in process of folding up (what's more, I knew this only too well). Surely then all the portents and omens were against going on with the *Cornish Review?* Of course they were. And how many times do we meekly obey those omens? Far fewer than we realize. Maybe it is something inherent in our human nature.

So I parcelled up the editorial contents of the first issue and posted them off to the printer and thus set into motion the processes which, in the Spring of 1949 offered to the world the first number of the *Cornish Review.* It was beautifully printed by Underhils of Plymouth, with an attractive green and white cover with the titling -lettered by Misomé Peile of St Ives - printed over an outline of the county of Cornwall. Among the varied contents were an outline of 'Cornish Culture' by R. Morton Nance, and of 'Cornish Drama' by P. A. Lanyon-Orgill, with some pertinent 'Reflections on the Cornish' by Lady Mander (R. Glyn Grylls of the old Cornish family of that name); a story by Lady Vyvyan, a study of 'Q' by E. W. Martin, poems by Jack Clemo, A. L. Rowse, Ronald Duncan, Frances Bellerby, Gladys Hunkin, and reproductions of paintings by Ben Nicholson, John Armstrong, John Park, Barbara Hepworth, Tom Early, Sven Berlin, W.

Barns-Graham and Alfred Wallis. At the rear of the magazine we printed reviews of books by authors in Cornwall, and of plays put on in the county, as well as comments on current art exhibitions: there were also, as I felt in a regional magazine they would be appreciated, very full biographical notes on contributors.

My experience with booksellers had made me a little wary as to the general reception of the *Review,* but fortunately here I was unduly cautious. It is a fact that I have had many years experience of editing a wide number of magazines so that, looking back now, I think it is fair to say that our first issue was a good one and, as the *Times Literary Supplement* commented, 'fully deserves the local support for which it appeals'. Still it was greatly heartening to receive so many congratulations, most of which are perhaps best summarized in a letter which Howard Spring wrote, from his lovely white house at Falmouth, and which we reproduced in our second issue:

It is fitting that this region should have a place for uttering its own voice, for it is a region of character and idiosyncrasy. Its people, and climate, and their interaction, have produced something easily distinguished from anything that will be found elsewhere; and this is true despite the levelling consequences of our day. So long as it remains true there will be a reason for a magazine like this, which seeks to make known what is peculiarly Cornish in writing, painting, sculpture and all that belongs to a native culture. The expression that is given to this need not spring out of the heart of the Cornish-born. Many who paint in Cornwall, and write in Cornwall, are not Cornish-born. Nevertheless, Cornwall speaks through them; and the thing in this magazine must be that the voice of Cornwall shall speak, through whatever mouth.

Mr Spring went on to say that it was a duty of Cornish men and women to support our new venture, and indeed in the general atmosphere of goodwill it was almost impossible not to discern a feeling of success and expansion. Never much of a pessimist, anyway, I gave myself up hook line and sinker to this heady wine of success. The *Cornish Review* would triumph over all hesitant booksellers, it would sweep the county - no, more than that, it would invade England too, soon it would be selling in London and other great cities, why, there might be no end to it. One bright and false morning, with the greatest unwisdom, I picked up the telephone and told the printer to reprint a further 1,000 copies. A day or two later, now completely in the clouds of cuckooland, I rang up again and said, 'Make that reprint 2,000'.

So in the end we printed 3,000 copies of the first issue of the Cornish Review: and the only comment really necessary on that piece of foolhardiness is that for several years after - during which we moved two or three times - wherever we went I had to lug them with me, those dozens and dozens of neat unopened parcels of new *Cornish Reviews.* Now and then some reader would order a single copy, to complete a set perhaps, and this would involve opening one of the neat parcels - a fatal move, as sooner or later the 50 or so copies would seem to get distributed about the home. Towards the end (of my patience) I remember that most of the parcels had split open, and anyway there was less space, and so I would spend hours trying to stack them up in higher and higher piles, none of which quite balanced, so that inevitably there was a crash and dozens of copies of that now unutterably familiar front cover lay splashed around. I can't think now why I kept them all that time, but in the end on discovering a second-hand bookseller in Mousehole who was glad to buy a few I developed a weekly habit of sidling in, saying: 'I just happen to have found a few more copies of this very rare first issue.' However, in the end even this source dried up, and the final ignominious end to that huge, and indeed largest ever edition of the Cornish Review was that I sold the remaining copies to a scrap merchant by the pound weight! I think it worked out at something like a farthing per 2s. 6d. copy.

So as I say the business end of the *Cornish Review* was woefully inadequate from the beginning. Strictly speaking we ought never to have come out at all, whereas in fact we did. What's more the magazine continued publication, sometimes almost flourishing, for nearly four years - during which time, never one to learn a lesson, I was even obsessed enough with my editorial mission to launch a sister venture, *The Cornish Library*, which offered in permanent book form a series of limited editions of work by writers and artists in Cornwall. The first four volumes announced were Paintings from Cornwall, reproductions of work by about thirty well-known artists; *Witchery of the West*, a recounting by Georgina Penny of some of the most famous Cornish legends; *Leaves from a Cornish Notebook, a* selection of essays by 'John Penwith' of the Cornishman; and *The Cornish Renaissance, a* critical study of Cornish literature by E. W. Martin. The painting book was useful because it pinpointed the fascinating break-through of the abstract movement now so prevalent in Cornwall; however, probably the most interesting of the books would have been *The Cornish Renaissance* - unfortunately Ernest never quite got around to writing it, and in any case I should never have quite got around to publishing it, since by then the Library, like the *Review,* had come to an untimely end. I always felt it would have made a fascinating study, for there are very nearly as many writers working in Cornwall as there are painters (if one was to make the criterion of measurement publication or sale, then more writers!). Only a small proportion of these writers are Cornish-born, but they make an interesting group, ranging from A. L. Rowse, author of that fine autobiography, *A Cornish Childhood*, and also well known for his many studies of Elizabethan England, to young poets of such different but impressive achievement as Jack R. Clemo, author of *Wilding Graft* and *Confessions of a Rebel,* who has lived all his life in St Stephen's, a remote clay mining hamlet near St Austell, and Charles Causley, a schoolmaster at Launceston, whose poetry, with its Kiplingesque lilt and expert use of colloquialisms, has a ready appeal to the mass public - as witness the large sale of his naval poems, *Farewell Aggie Weston.* Then there's Anne Treneer and R. Glyn Grylls and Terence Tiller and Ronald Duncan and Geoffrey Grigson and J. C. Trewin and Ronald Bottrall and Frank Baines . . . . Oh, yes, the Cornish writers are a formidable bunch, even if much more loosely linked than their Welsh or Irish counterparts. But what is equally interesting is how Cornwall has drawn so many other fine writers, many of whom have paid a visit and stayed a lifetime. One thinks of the Scottish poet, W. S. Graham, whose striking poems are impregnated with Cornish images: of best-selling authors like Daphne du Maurier or Howard Spring, Winston Graham and Walter Greenwood, all of them then living in Cornwall, many of whose books make the fullest use of Cornish background and characterization; or of more scholarly writers like Phyllis Bottome, F. B. Halliday, Wallace Nicholls, Ruth Manning-Sanders, and others like them who have found true creative inspiration in Cornwall.

No doubt it was the knowledge that as an editor I could draw on such a strong supply of literary talent which encouraged me to continue with the *Cornish Review,* after the smoke had cleared and revealed the financial chaos ensuing from that first exciting, disastrous publication. Among future contributions already lined up were such articles as, 'Planning a future Cornwall', by H. J. W. Heck, the County Planning Officer; 'Ben Nicholson' by J. P. Hodin; 'My World as a Potter', by Bernard Leach; 'Early Cornish Railways', by David St John Thomas; 'John Opie', by J. W. Scobell Armstrong; 'The Face of Penwith' by Peter Lanyon; 'Cornish Wrestling', by Tregonning Hooper; and a host of first-class poems and stories and reproductions.

As a writer myself I held firmly to the principle that contributors must receive payment, and although our average was small enough, about three guineas for an article or story, and half a guinea for a poem, this did not help the financial situation. Already money that I earned by my own writing was having to be poured into one of the innumerable breaches, to keep things going. Already we were involved in financial difficulties at home. At the same time manuscripts were coming in with almost every post, and also - at that stage even more welcome letters from people not only in Cornwall, nor even just in England, but in Africa, South America, North America, Canada, New Zealand, Australia, everywhere, indeed, where a Cousin Jack (or his female equivalent) might be found. They were warm and friendly and encouraging, those letters, many of which enclosed subscriptions as a present to friends, and they always put new hope into me. I always felt that if somehow 1 could have got in touch with all the people who loved Cornwall but were exiles, then the *Cornish Review* would never have had to close down.

We carried out a lot of circularizing, but as we began planning the second issue, wondering how on earth we could try to catch up on the heavy financial loss so far, we had to think of something immediate and more effective: and so I began on yet another new career, touting for advertisements. I use the word touting in no superior tone, but as the most accurate description of what now took place. Nobody it seemed (how I was reminded of those booksellers!) wanted to advertise in the *Cornish Review* - and frankly I could not really see why they should, except out of a spirit of philanthropy. And of course this is precisely why in the end many of them did. They felt a certain sympathy for this lonesome, doomed venture. Yes, perhaps it wasn't a bad idea to have a cultural magazine...all right, put us down for a quarter page. Since all my advertising rates were far too low this gesture was fairly easy to make (I think a quarter page originally was a mere 30s.). However, slowly, laboriously, at the cost of a physical and psychological effort quite out of proportion to the results, I began to collect a few advertisements from local tradesmen and other organizations.

Then, thank goodness, Arthur Caddick came into the picture. Known sometimes as the Poet Laureate of Nancledra, Caddick - who looks like a Shakespearean actor (he also has the full-blooded booming voice of one) - is best known as a writer of comic verse, several collections of which have been published. I was publishing some of his work anyway, but he was sincerely anxious to be of practical assistance as well, and he suggested that he took on the job of collecting advertisements. So one day, armed with some specimens of our first issue, Caddick set off to beard the business men of Penzance in their offices (I, so far, having only weakly covered St Ives). What's more, at the end of the day he re-appeared somewhat bleary eyed but waving a pile of papers triumphantly. 'I've sold you five pages - and more to come!'

In the end between us we raised about twenty pages of advertising for the second number of the *Cornish Review*: about the largest amount of advertising, had we but known it, we were ever to publish in one issue. Caddick continued collecting local advertisements for several more issues, often succeeding - I imagine by an ingenious mixture of oral hypnotism, Shakespearean grandeur, outrageous flattery and sheer downright bullying - where the more conventional approach would have failed. He was particularly good at impressing hotel-keepers and publicans although, as a single call might lead to a very convivial 'session', this can hardly be described as good economics. Some years later, on his own account, Arthur Caddick conceived the idea of an annual publication about the pubs of Cornwall, designed to interest the holiday-makers. It was called *A Hundred Doors are Open,* and represented the fruits of a series of expeditions down the highways and byways of Cornwall - a monumental saga of one-man enterprise if ever there was one! Moreover a saga repeated once yearly. I love to think of the alarmed looks on various publican's faces as from afar they heard the vast booming of Caddick's voice, probably declaiming one of his latest extremely pungent satirical poems.

My own advertising career followed a more cowardly approach. It was just not in me to beard a business lion in his den and convince him, against both his and my own better judgment, that he should pay out good money to advertise in a publication with such a small readership as the *Cornish Review.* On the other hand I am very good at writing persuasive letters. Face to face I am inclined to be mild and self-effacing, and certainly do not assert myself nearly enough: behind the screen of the postal services I become uninhibited, daring, powerful and even aggressive - all basic necessities for an advertising man. Thus, leaving local 'face to face' contacts to Caddick, I ventured farther afield. I composed cunning epistles seeking to persuade publishers in London that they should advertise their West

Country books in our Review and ditto to any other business concern in London with the remotest connexions with Cornwall. I also focused these verbal powers of persuasion on a variety of unusual approaches in the county itself - in this way enticing such unlikely advertisers as a shop buying and selling old magic lanterns, a garden designer, a multi-spring mattress maker, a manure firm, a maker of ivory miniatures, a fabric printer and an Irish Catholic Association.

So between us Caddick and I furnished about £100 worth of advertising for the second number of the *Cornish Review*, and thus set things momentarily on a more even keel. It was, I flattered myself, a good meaty issue, including Bernard Leach's fascinating account of his life's work, a study of Richard Trevithick by Hamilton Jenkin and of Charles Lee by H. J. Willmott, a memory of the great Western Rebellion of 1549 by Ashley Rowe and an article by Ivor Thomas, 'County or Country?' which I had commissioned especially with a view to provoking some controversy. It was, however, an item in a small section of the paper at the very end, Readers' Forum, which really caused a sensation up and down the length and breadth of Cornwall. This was a letter from Sydney Horler, the well-known thriller writer, who happened to live at Bude in North Cornwall:

> Sir:
> *Pick up any book about Cornwall, and you'll find the writer expatiating about the lovely coast scenery, the different points of interest, etc., whilst remaining very reticent about the natives. I have lived among the Cornish - the Bude variety in particular for years now, on and off, and I have been appalled by what I have discovered in the local character. I have found a certain class to be treacherous, two-faced, sly, deceitful, flagrant humbugs (more especially when they profess themselves deeply religious, as many of them do) and altogether undesirable. In fact, in sheer self-defence, I now refuse to have anything to do with the 'locals', and if newcomers to the county take my advice they will adopt the same precaution. If they don't, they will inevitably learn the same bitter lesson as myself.*
>
> *What is the reason for this deplorable anti-social behaviour? The principal cause, I believe, is that the Cornish, a primitive people at the best, cut off for centuries from the rest of the country, have always hated the intrusion of anyone from outside - the 'foreigner', as they call him. They like his money, but they keenly resent his physical presence. And the kinder and more generous he is on arrival, the more they will hate and fleece him. This is the stark truth. Perhaps being a very backward, illiterate and ignorant people, they develop a strong sense of inferiority when they come into contact with anyone of a different and better type; but the fact remains that the 'foreigner' is only safe if he leaves them strictly alone.*
>
> *I have actually heard Cornishmen boast that their forebears lured ships on to the rocks by false lights; and their present actions are*

influenced, no doubt, by what is in their very blood. A man who should know (he served in the intelligence Service during both wars) assured me that German submarines were refuelled in coves along the South and North Cornish coasts in 1914 - 18, and that the crews were allowed to come ashore and mingle freely with the natives. After living in Cornwall, I can well believe it: in spite of the crowded chapels - or, perhaps, because of them - there is more farmyard immorality in Cornwall than in any other part of England. Many of the stories I could tell you would be judged incredible by any ordinary standards.

Perhaps this sexual lust can be partially explained by the strange mixtures of blood in the Cornish; the frenzied chapel goer will deny it at the top of his voice, but in spite of the strenuous attempts to hush it up, there is undoubtedly a lot of foreign blood among the natives; you can see men in Newlyn and other places standing at street corners, unshaved and wearing filthy trousers, who are pure Iberian, and who might have stepped out of a picture by Goya. This may account also for the Cornishman's indolence, carelessness, and general shiftiness in some measure, at least; although the worst kind of Cornishman would be a natural rascal, I am afraid, in any case.

Sydney Horler

Such a letter speaks for itself, it is pretty obviously exaggerated and written in anger by someone who, for one reason or another, hasn't hit it off with his neighbours. Of course it contains within it sufficient half truths to make the wounds hurt. At least I can only assume this was the reason for the extraordinary aftermath! There was, literally, an explosion. First of all the West Country newspapers seized on what they spied as a good story, printing parts of the letter, and interviews first with Horler and then with others attacking him. The story was taken upon the radio, and in Sunday and weekly newspapers. After a few days, Sydney Horler, whom incidentally I never met, rang me up to say that he had received two threatening telephone calls. Meanwhile, letters poured in, both to papers like the *Western Morning News* and to myself. In the next issue I printed a selection of them. One was from a St Ives furniture firm cancelling future advertising, and the general tone of all the letters was - the sooner Sydney Horler leaves Cornwall, the better it will be for everyone else. (In fact soon afterwards Mr Horler did leave the county, and subsequently I read of his death.) The last outward manifestation of the controversy which I witnessed was a highly emotional burning of an effigy of Sydney Horier at a huge Guy Fawkes' bonfire held at Newlyn and attended by thousands of people.

Sydney Horler's letter in our second issue certainly caught the public eye: but it was an item which in fact had literally to be cut out of our fourth issue which involved us in the greatest instance of national publicity. At this time the ancient art of mead making had been revived at Gulval, near Penzance, by a new enterprise, Mead Makers Ltd. The company seemed to have large financial resources, various well-known names figuring among the directors and shareholders, and under the leadership of the chairman, Lt.-Col. Gayre, who had made a study of mead and its history, the company had big marketing plans for selling mead both in Britain and abroad. As part of the general publicity, the company had opened its own Mead Hall, where exotic meals were served by liveried waiters, each course accompanied by the appropriate type of mead. As another part of the publicity there had been introduced an elaborate 'blessing of the mead' ceremony, conducted by a local canon. In addition Colonel Gayre had written and published a history of mead, as well as a number of booklets, all of which were expertly distributed in the locality, also to visitors and farther afield.

Whatever the qualities of mead itself, there did seem, to say the least, an element of pomposity about the way it was being put over to the public. When, therefore, Arthur Caddick sent me in a wickedly amusing take-off poem, entitled 'The Makers of Woad', I decided to publish it in the next issue of the *Review*. It was funny, it was clever, and it was very good verse, and surely not really harmful. As it happened the *Cornish Review* public were never given the opportunity to judge. Somehow Colonel Gayre and his friends got to hear that the poem was being published and, without bothering to approach me, the editor, went straight to our printers at Plymouth and thoroughly alarmed them - so much so that just as I was anxiously awaiting delivery of the issue I received a long-distance phone call from the printers stating that in view of a threat to sue if they printed the poem, they felt unable to complete publishing the issue as it stood. I protested and argued, appealed to their sense of morality, liberty of conscience, etc . . . . but all to no avail. I was faced with an ultimatum: and at this very last minute, with the issue in print and everyone waiting for it - plus the fact of an uneasy suspicion that if an experienced printer thought the poem was libellous, may be it was - I could see no alternative but to agree to the printers' suggestion. A day or so later the *Cornish Review* was on sale with the sheet containing pages 19 and 20 conspicuously absent, and obviously cut out by hand. Meantime the line still evident in the contents list, ' "The Makers of Woad" by Arthur Caddick,' raised an intriguing query.

I had, of course, told Caddick what I had been forced to agree to, and he was naturally upset. When, however, he roared out that he would take the Mead Makers to court I did not altogether take him seriously. I was forgetting that in his youth Caddick had studied for the Law and had just missed taking silk as a barrister. He knew all the ins and outs of legal procedure and before long he had come up with his trump card. He would take out an action against Colonel Gayre and the mead company for conspiring to damage his reputation as a professional poet.

'It's plain as a pikestaff, dear boy!. boomed out Caddick. 'Look at this issue of the *Review,* appearing with my poem obviously cut out - what on earth is the average reader going to think? He's going to assume that this fellow Caddick must be so bad at his job that the editor had to leave out his poem at the last moment. But it isn't like that at all is it. It's Colonel Gayre who has unreasonably brought pressure to bear and by so doing damaged my professional reputation.'

For a long time the whole matter bordered on something of a joke, but gradually it became apparent that Caddick was in deadly earnest. Papers were served, writs issued, witnesses summoned, the whole paraphernalia. Caddick announced that he would conduct his own case, and, by now somewhat alarmed I fancy, the mead company briefed a leading West Country barrister. It had been hoped, at least by the Caddick faction, that the case would be tried by Judge Scobell Armstrong, judge of the Cornwall County Circuit for many years and nationally renowned for his witticisms and somewhat unconventional behaviour. Before it could take place however, the judge's retirement was announced, and the mead case was finally heard by Judge Rawlins. As it transpired, this represented no loss, and the judge's urbane handling of a most unusual and even unorthodox trial was a pleasure to behold.

Needless to say the case tickled the public fancy, and when finally it was held at Penzance County Court the national newspapers were well represented. So, too, were the local artists, both as legal witnesses, and as moral support for Caddick. The star performer was Caddick himself, making an auspicious and dramatic start to the day's events by standing up and reading out aloud the whole of his poem - so that it then became legal for any of the national newspapers to reprint it in their reports of the case. (Many of them did just this, and so 'The Makers of Woad' received a thousand times greater publicity than it could ever have obtained confined to the pages of the *Cornish Review*.) I can still remember the hilarity of that episode, Caddick standing up and uttering the verses in his booming voice, while all around we strove to control ourselves, sometimes bursting into laughter - and in their corner the representatives of the mead company endeavoured to look stern and unamused.

Evidently, though, they were not entirely unaffected for though the case was adjourned for lunch while I was being cross-examined, when we re-assembled in the afternoon there was a great deal of whispering and consultation, and then came an announcement welcomed all round. A settlement had been reached, said Judge Rawlins, smiling broadly to indicate his approval. Mr Caddick would withdraw his case, while the mead company for their part, as a gesture, had agreed to commission Mr Caddick to write for them an official Mead Drinking Song. I can't remember the more exact details, but I do know that we all looked on it as a moral victory for Caddick - had not the judge congratulated the plaintiff on the manner in which he handled his case - and we all went off to celebrate. But not in mead!

Such episodes, amusing as they were, though they certainly represented a great deal of useful free publicity for the *Cornish Review*, had little ultimate effect on the magazine's career. Or if they did it was an unfortunate one. Already I had made my own cross, had I but known it, by determining to bring out a literary magazine which set out resolutely to deal with cultural activities both among Cornish and people living in Cornwall. 'Approximately one third only of your contributors are Cornish', wrote one reader angrily. 'Please give us a *Cornish Review* and not a review of the Cornish by a "passel of arty foreigners".' This is a parochial attitude with which anyone who lives for any period of time in the county becomes all too familiar. Its requirements are adequately met by the local newspapers, where all the minute trivia of local life is duly recorded. My own experiences with theatre companies, and in other spheres, had proved to me - and my experience with the *Review* alas, was to confirm this - that culture in Cornwall, while not quite a dirty word, needed a good deal of propaganda behind it merely to make it acceptable, let alone popular. This was one of the several reasons why, admittedly, we did concentrate on artistic activities in the county, whether in the spheres of painting, drama, or literature. (I must in passing point out that we printed numerous non-arty articles on such subjects as the Camborne School of Mines, Porthcurno Cable Station, Cornish Churches, Cornwall's Flower Industry, Cornish Language, and Cornish Nationalism.)

In focusing, in particular, upon the work of artists in Cornwall we were, of course, fortunate in the richness of our material. There can be few places in the world, let alone Britain, where so many professional painters live and work and earn their living (as well as reputation) as in the small peninsula of West Penwith. Looking through various numbers of the *Cornish Review* I see that we reproduced painting and sculpture by Ben Nicholson, Barbara Hepworth, Peter Lanyon, Bryan Wynter, John Armstrong, John Park, Dod Procter, Lamorna Birch, Mary Jewells, Charles Pears, W. Barns-Graham, Sven Berlin, Denis Mitchell, Hyman Segal, Leonard Fuller, Bernard Ninnes, among others. With our fourth issue I introduced a system of reproducing a woodcut or lino drawing on our front cover, and this also reflected the versatile talent abounding in West Cornwall. Art in fact was and is as commonplace a part of everyday life as, say, motor car production is in Birmingham or Coventry. This has many good effects. For instance wherever you go in West Cornwall you are quite likely to come across original paintings adorning the walls of pubs and cafés and hotels - but there are also less happy by-products. An example of this was provided in St Ives at the time when the *Cornish Review* functioned, when the local traditional and abstract artists, after having been at loggerheads for years, finally came to open warfare and set up two rival societies. I was sympathetic to the new group, the Penwith Society of Artists in Cornwall, which in general sought to take a more progressive view of art and life, and for years I was a lay member. But after a while of watching endless committee wrangles and internal disputes - often over the most petty and hair-splitting points I began to wish that painters would emulate writers, and get on with their own work rather than waste so much time in bickering.

Nevertheless, individually, I have great admiration for a number of painters in Cornwall, and like to think that we helped them in some way by publishing their *work* (not their personal poses!) in the *Cornish Review*.

Some of them showed their appreciation, anyway, when as a last effort to keep the good ship *Cornish Review* from foundering, I hit on the idea of holding a Mock Auction. By one of those ironic twists of fate this was held in the long bottom room of St Christopher's, at that time a St Ives guest house, now our own home. I had a slight suspicion that we were not really legally entitled to run a public auction, but thought it wiser never to inquire at the time. Legal or otherwise, it proved a most entertaining experience. Previously I wrote round to a list of writers and, painters who had contributed work to the *Review* in the past. Would they be willing to contribute a signed copy of an example of their work, to be put up for sale at a Mock Auction in aid of the *Cornish Review* ? I can't think why I used the term 'mock', unless it was to salve my conscience about the regulations, for the fact was we were in dire straits financially.

By now we had published seven issues and while subscriptions had kept up encouragingly among the faithful, other sales had remained fairly static. It had become quite clear that the only way to maintain such a magazine was by running it as economically as possible, and being satisfied with a small but steady circulation of about 1,000 copies per issue, possibly increasing the price to 3s 6d. or even 5s. My problem was to find a way of clearing off many hundreds of pounds of debts incurred on the earlier numbers. If we could have done this then I am pretty sure we could have kept the *Review* going to this day. I used to dream of some wealthy Cornishman suddenly appearing, pulling out a cheque book and saying: 'Here, will this put you straight!' Alas, life is never like that. As the next best thing at one stage I launched a Goodwill Fund, which was contributed to by many eminent Cornish men and women, and lovers of Cornwall. In all we raised over £150, but this was not nearly enough, and so we came to the auction which, as I have indicated, was far from mock, but in deadly earnest.

It was finally held on a Saturday afternoon. Word must have got round about possible bargains, for I fancy there must have been nearly two hundred people there by the time I rose to introduce the main speaker and opener, Winston Graham. Mr Graham delivered a short but fighting speech on behalf of such enterprises as the *Review* and then made way for the main protagonist, the very uninstitutional auctioneer Arthur Caddick. Time blurs exact memories of the occasion, but I have a strong recollection of Caddick working desperately hard to liven up the bidding and of a curiously apathetic audience showing a surprising reluctance to enter into the fun of things. After all, the artists had freely given their pictures and sketches to help a good cause, just as authors had in many cases had to buy and sign a copy of their own books to give. Surely the sort of public that came to such a ceremony would be well-wishers, ready if anything to over-bid rather than under-bid? One would have thought so; but the event proved different. Whether it was the native Cornish eye for a bargain or what, the fact is that few of the paintings and sketches fetched more than a pound or so, and practically all the books, even signed by such names as Winston Graham, Howard Spring and Jack Clemo, etc., went at about half their published price. Only some of the crafts fetched even their normal price . . . I think the best sale of the day was a small table by Robin Nance. When all expenses, including advertising, had been met, the total profit was about £37. It should have been at least three times that figure.

This was in many ways the final blow. With the lack of a private (or indeed public) backer, the failure of our various efforts to raise capital in other ways, and finally this further confirmation of the very limited amount of genuine support for the *Review,* it became literally impossible for me to continue indulging in such an expensive pastime. I decided, as I put it in my last editorial, to go down with flags flying, and I like to think that the tenth and final issue of the *Cornish Review,* with contributions by Jack Clemo, A. L. Rowse, W. S. Graham, Norman Levine, Richard Gendall, Charles Causley, Arthur Caddick, Daniel Trevose, Gladys Hunkin, and others, was one of our very best. For myself I said very little in my brief editorial: I think everything was pungently summed up in the following 'Funeral Lines for the *Cornish Review'* by Arthur Caddick:

> *O Printers' error on a mammoth scale,*
> *At sight of whom the local bank clerks pale,*
> *O watcher of the skies for rains of pennies*
> *From heavenly advertisers, Denys!*
>
> *Attend me now, I have a tear to shed*
> *Before your paper joins the silent dead*
> *And you become, in solemn mourning hue,*
> *Ex.-Editor, Ex-Comish, Ex-Review!*
>
> *I hear low moaning rise round Carbis Bay*
> *Where highbrows weep for what has passed away,*
> *(And might one just dispassionately hint*
> *Some mourn their last, lone chance of seeing print?)*
>
> *I hear some craftsman, at Trebogus Cove,*
> *Where soulful, simple, soapless creatures rove,*
> *Exclaim: 'It's bust, and I've just written Baker*
> *"My Lonely Life as Fancy-Doodle Maker"!'*
>
> *In fact, dear Denys, it is weeks and weeks*
> *Since misery laid low so many freaks.*
> *Yet though exotic grief attends this funeral,*
> *Far odder persons will not weep at all.*
>
> *From Penzance Guildhall fat relief is rising:*
> *'We needn't now go on not advertising!*
> *We needn't now refuse to pay for space*
> *When third-class Shakespeare Festivals take place!'*

Ditto the civic feeling in St Ives:
'We give our help to anything that thrives,
We bless success, but struggling papers, no!
Let Art attract the tourists' cash or go!'

With luke-warm bookshops it is much the same:
'The paper's dead? . . . I didn't catch the name.
Cornish Review ? That local thing? . . . Ah, quite!
The comic postcards, madam? On your right!'

So here's the crux, the one essential clue
To this quick dying of your young Review -
Its friends, the artists, had no cash to spare
And those who should have helped it didn't care.

Chapter Seven

THE DREAM AND THE REALITY

During our third winter at the Old Vicarage I worked very hard on a new novel, *A Journey with Love*. I have always been fascinated by the varying relationships between men and women. Now I took the situation of a happily married couple, sexually in tune, and how they coped with life when the husband was rendered impotent by a boating accident. At the same time I used the opportunity to set the book in the Cornwall I had come to know and love so much; and, by making the man a painter, to dwell on the subsidiary problems of the artist at work in Cornwall.

In fact the book was really as much about Cornwall's strange influence on artists living there as it was about Martin and Lesley. I tried to combine the two threads, to inter-weave them. There is for instance a scene where Martin takes Lesley to stand on top of Trencrom Hill and they look around to where the coast-line curls out 'like reptile teeth biting into the sea'. The very land, says Martin, seems alive, to writhe with sensual movements:

Lesley nodded. She knew what he meant. Ever since she had come to Cornwall she had been vibrantly aware of herself and her body. It was something more than the natural awakening of their love, and desire; something reactive in the very land and atmosphere to which she felt the urge to respond. Sometimes, walking alone among the cliffs, she felt impelled by a strong desire to take off her clothes, to feel the sun and the wind upon her naked, living flesh. And when she did so she felt an exquisite sensation of well-being, as if in her nakedness she became part of the wind and the sun and the cool air, of all the elements; and part of the land, too. She would lie down on the green cool turf, stretching out her limbs, running her hands gently over her flesh, imagining that Martin was there too, like a lover born out of the wind; imagining that they were his hands that fondled and caressed; closing her eyes before the sun's beating heat and giving herself up to strange and erotic thoughts and dreams, in which Martin and the wind, the sea and the jagged rocks were all interwoven and confused.

Later in the book Martin begins to mix with fellow painters and to become conscious that his future as a painter is tied up with the land around him into which he has so determinedly rooted himself:

Three of these painters, in particular, interested Martin. One was a man who saw Cornwall starkly, vividly, in splashes of garish almost distorted colour, who almost hacked his way through the oils: his paintings were bright and startling and somehow communicated the land's curious virility and power - but mainly through colour. Another was more of a draughtsman, a man of curiously detached vision, sometimes appearing remote from human relationships, yet intensely observant. He, it seemed, saw Cornwall in terms of birds and mammals, in great monolithic creatures of the past - as if when he looked around he saw the gaunt bones and effigies hanging shadow-like upon the surface of the land. So when this man drew buildings and silhouettes, cliffs and fields, or even an entire fishing port, these strange birds and other preying creatures hovered around - so strongly that even if they were not specifically drawn in, their presence was somehow felt. And in the same way, everything that was drawn, houses and shapes, even the general lie of the land, took on a strange, almost sinister element of humanity.

But the third painter - in Martin's view a synthesis of the other two - he most of all seemed to have achieved discovery, exploration, originality. Perhaps this was because he alone of the group was also Cornish, understanding instinctively much that baffled and confused the outsider. He used colour as harshly as the first painter, though not so brightly, and he had the same conception of birds and skeleton-like life imposed on the land as the second painter, but he combined and added to these approaches a strange subterranean viewpoint of Cornwall. His favourite paintings were of under the land, as if exposing huge chunks of what was hidden by rocks and weeds and earth. And in his weird, swirling drawings, never quite clearly defined, yet always disturbingly suggestive, he somehow captured, like raindrops in the sun, a fleeting moment of revelation.

In Cornwall, this painter had once said, sea and land answered the deep roots of man, and presented him with a face. Yes, thought Martin, in Cornwall the land is man's image, in all his complexity and mystery. He began to play with this conception, and gradually he caught glimpses of exciting developments and discoveries that might happen with his own work.

I have quoted these extracts from *A Journey with Love* because they reflect my own feelings about artists at work in Cornwall. In writing this present book, indeed, I am constantly torn between the two tasks - to write about my life in Cornwall, and to write about Cornwall in my life. Fortunately the one task does not necessarily cancel out the other, but it is sometimes difficult to be sure I am drawing the right balance. Because writers and artists in Cornwall are frequently obsessed with poverty or difficult living conditions (equally because often they are seen to be drinking in pubs or cavorting at parties) this does not mean that therefore the other side of their life does not go on. They, perhaps more acutely than many others, are forever sensible of the hidden mysteries. As Richard G. Jenkin, a Cornish poet wrote:

'I see in dreams the lost land of Langarrow
Sleeping under silent sandy waves;
In every house and every roadway narrow
The dry bones stir in their unquiet graves...'

This vision, this compulsion on the imagination, confronts every sincere artist in Cornwall. It is reflected in the carving of Sven Berlin or the painting of Peter Lanyon, in the sculpture of Barbara Hepworth or the pottery of Bernard Leach, in the poetry of Jack Clemo or the novels of Frank Baker, in the autobiographical works of Leo Walmsley or Frank Baines.

But then, conversely, it would be foolish for some visitor from another planet who first hears some beautiful lines of poetry, say by W. S. Graham:

> 'What ship cry falls The holy families of foam
> Fall into wilderness and "over the jasper sea"
> The gulls wade into silence. What deep sea saint
> Whispered this keel out of its element?'

to assume that the poet spends his whole life staring at the sea, or marvelling at the Cornish landscape. The fact is that like many poets, Sydney Graham is a sociable being, a singer of songs in pubs and in the right mood a dancer of Scottish jigs at parties.

In Cornwall there exists a large, matured yet loosely knit community of writers, artists, craftsmen, and other rebels against the conformity of society. They came to Cornwall for a variety of reasons. Some, like myself, because they were drawn in some intuitive rather mysterious way, others like our friend Len Missen because they suddenly wanted to get as far away from London and civilization as possible; still others for the more practical reason that they thought it might be cheaper to live in some remote cottage, as well as helpful for getting on with their work. Most of the people I have in mind are relatively poor, some have had exceedingly difficult times, especially those with families. Some are dressed fairly normally, others flamboyant in full bohemian regalia. Not all by any means extend the subtle unity of creative purpose to personal friendship, there are the normal likes and dislikes, petty feuds and so on - yet even so I think the ranks would close if necessary.

For one reason or another we have all made our protest against the deadening lifeless standardization of civilization, we have tuned away from those office jobs, those factory lines, those executive positions, and a hundred and one other cypher jobs that are simply part of the capitalist pattern of nothingness. And what is equally important - in Cornwall we have found the one place which, perhaps because of its own strange background of eccentricity, is able to absorb us *naturally*. For it is a curious fact, sometimes it almost seems unbelievable, yet in some strange way the Cornish seem able to respect the sincere artist and craftsman out of a kind of instinct. No one is quicker to see through the fraud and the charlatan: no one more deeply sensitive to the artist of real integrity.

When I had finished *A Journey with Love* I naturally hoped to have it published in Britain, and indeed the first reader to vet it officially - Malcolm Elwin - put in an enthusiastic report and urged his firm to publish it. Eventually, however, they decided against. So, alas, did publisher after publisher, large and small, many of them with a suspicious lack of comment. Finally I took up the matter with a friend, the late L. A. G. Strong the novelist, and also a director of a large firm of publishers. He told me quite bluntly that so long as the book had a number of frank passages about sex it was unlikely to be published in Britain. He quite appreciated that it was relevant to the theme to describe physical passion, as a contrast to the later situation - nevertheless he was advised that if the book was published certain sentences had only to be taken out of their context for a prosecution case to succeed. Later Dorothea Benson, formerly my publishing manager, now running a literary agency, assured me that no publisher would dare touch it. I am afraid to date she has been right, though perhaps the *Lady Chatterley's Lover* case may clear the air for serious novels around a sexual theme.

This reception in my own country, or lack of it, was all the more exasperating by contrast with the book's experience in America. There Samuel Roth at once accepted it for publication and brought it out with a most tasteful cover, printing it word for word as I wrote it. When it appeared a critic said: 'We believe that this is the first real love story produced in English for at least thirty years. Only wars and horrors bloom without effort. But just as love springs up between two people, in its unlikely and beautiful way, so has a perfect love novel sprung up from the unlikely and beautiful land of Cornwall . . . *A Journey with Love* is a truly three-dimensional love story of two people which is so natural in its simplicity that it is as much a manifestation of the universal powers of the sun and the sky as the waves pounding upon the shores of humanity, as of the wavering destiny of a marriage that is of the mind as well as the body.' Subsequently the book was reprinted in a paper back edition, Crest Books, that sold all over America and Canada in an edition of 100,000 or more. At no time was there any attempt to suggest that the book was pornographic, or in anyway other than I meant it to be - a serious love story.

If for once I blow the trumpet about one of my books, it is for two reasons. One is the obvious and as I say exasperating one - that a book which had two editions in America, one of them running into 100,000 copies, would at least seem worthy of seeing the light of day in Britain, where it was written. The other reason unfortunately had an even greater significance for us at the time; following the loss of our only regular weekly income from Morrab Place our financial position had become alarming. It would therefore have made all the difference in the world to myself and my family if I could have received the advance of, say £100 to £150, which would have come to me if the book had been taken by an English publisher. What made it worse was that each time I sent the book out - and remember, I believed quite honestly that it was the best book I had written, and I had had many published before - I could hardly believe that it would not be accepted. This state of mind in itself was distracting to other work.

Altogether though every now and then I sold the odd short story and article, we embarked on a very hazardous time. Saturday mornings were now approached not with hope but with fear, for we knew we had to have at least two pounds to see the family through the week-end. Sometimes one of my own payments would come through and the situation was saved, but only too often the dread that the post contained no more than bills and returned manuscripts. Then indeed my writer's imagination had to work fast. If there was no money in the bank, and our friends were in much the same state of financial depression, there was only one possible course left, and that was to sell something. In London, and indeed in most large centres, there exist pawnshops to cater for just such emergencies. In Cornwall, officially, there are no pawnshops, and the best we could find in Penzance was a tiny shop near the Post Office where whole suits would be bought for ridiculous sums like seven shillings and sixpence, or a second-hand shop in Chapel Street where old Mr White might give a few shillings for twenty-four gramophone records, or a heap of old books. Later I found another gift shop which provided a curious and unexpected market for old copies of the *Cornish Review* and odd pieces of pottery and other ornaments.

Looking back, a picture of a typical Saturday morning of this period can be seen, I suppose, as a tragi-comic epic. First we would embark on a frantic search around the old Vicarage for anything sellable (children excluded). If it was a real emergency then I, personally, would be quite ruthless - treasured books, old pictures, family ornaments, all would go by the board. In this way I not only disposed of many excellent novels of my own, by Graham Greene, Evelyn Waugh, Henry Miller, Aldous Huxley, etc. but also, accidentally, a few of my wife's books (a mishap for which I have never been quite forgiven). Having found enough articles, we would stuff them into the back of the car, followed by the six children all hungry and hopeful for their pocket money, and off we would set. At least we would if there was enough petrol to get us to Penzance. If there wasn't and we had not enough money to get some, we would have to collect some of Donald's rent in advance, always assuming he wasn't in the same financially forlorn state as ourselves. If there was no money and no petrol, then in extremis the family would have to get out and literally push the car about a quarter of a mile to a point where it was possible to free-wheel into Marazion where there was a garage which would supply petrol on credit.

On arrival at Penzance we would have to start the round of the hock shops, a case of the family waiting with fingers crossed while I furtively staggered in carrying my load of books and records and so forth. Sometimes I might emerge beaming with a handful of notes, but often I would come out with a hang-dog look, perhaps still carrying a pile of rejected goods, and the whole business would have to be tried again at another shop. Somehow we always seemed to manage to raise enough money, at least to buy the basic week-end food, give the children their pocket money and five bob to get some fish and chips, and a few shillings over to enable us to retire to meet our friends for a mid-day drink at the old 'St John's House'. By the time we reached this last establishment we were often emotionally exhausted, and I suppose this often showed. I shall never forget one morning we went in and said rather mournfully: 'It'll have to be half a bitter each today'. A quiet lady in a tweed coat who had been sitting in the corner suddenly beckoned Jess over and asked if she could have a word with her outside. When she got Jess out she said: 'I often see you in here and admire your good spirits. I don't like to see you in difficulties. Would you mind accepting this? - and into my wife's hand she pressed a pound note. It was one of the very sweet spontaneous gestures which I only wish everyone, including myself, could more often bring themselves to make - the world would be a much better place if we could.

I find it difficult to convey the full sense of what it means to live in this fashion. It is a life very peculiar to one class of people, the self-employed class with no fixed or regular income - and in particular the artistic worker whose temperament usually enhances the difficulties by being unable to acclimatize itself to any attempt to regularize life into a routine. For instance, during the period I am writing about we were often forced to run up bills with tradesmen, simply because they could only be paid when my own very irregular payments arrived. Often these debts would reach £50 or more. So there we would be one day having to scuttle down back streets of Penzance to avoid catching the eye of one of our creditors in Market Jew Street - the next day, the bills would have been paid and we would be celebrating with a night out, or perhaps by treating ourselves to a luxury, a new dress for Jess or perhaps some new books for me. Bank managers and other exponents of orthodoxy could never understand this going from one extreme to another, they were constantly urging thrift and planning and regular saving and putting money aside for the future . . . not able to comprehend that when one lives under constant strain the only way to bear it is to have the occasional outburst. The strain to which I refer, of course, is basically the knowledge that at all costs six young children must be fed and clothed and kept alive, as well as ourselves. Say what you like, this is an awesome prospect, especially when you have just lost one of your main sources of income and you know your next editorial cheque isn't due perhaps for three weeks.

During this trying period I embarked on another scheme for raising money. One day a strange little man who had once had a room at Morrab Place, Mr W., came out to the Old Vicarage and after a lot of beating around the bush put up an odd proposition. He had noticed, he said, that we had a lot of dead trees around, as well as many standing that could no doubt be cut down. Well, he could guarantee a regular sale for fire-wood logs - supposing he and I went into partnership? He would come and cut up the logs, and I would help him deliver them to houses from where he had got orders. We would split the money fifty-fifty.

By now I was so desperate about money that I was ready to grasp at any straw in the wind. Besides I had already had experience of how wood can bring in cash. Accordingly every day little Mr W. came out with a saw and worked away cutting up logs. From somewhere we procured a lot of old potato sacks and filled them up with logs. After two or three days of this we loaded the car up with sacks, and set off. People often say,

but didn't you feel rather humiliated? I don't think so, because both with the hocking of old books and now the selling of logs, I always saw these things as an adventure. Mind you I was a bit taken aback, after we began driving slowly up and down one or two quiet back streets of Penzance, to realize that Mr W. had been exaggerating when he implied that he had orders waiting. What he was now doing was hawking the wood from door to door, hoping to sell it on the spot. In fact, logs being in demand, we usually did manage to get rid of our loads. After I had paid for the petrol, calculated the hours of my time wasted, apart from the physical fatigue carrying heavy sacks up and down garden paths, it began to seem to me that the 10s. or 12s 6d which I was left with after a day was hardly worth the candle. However we carried on the venture until one day, in pouring rain, I staggered up to a back door to deliver a couple of sacks - and found myself being paid by my assistant bank manager! Somehow this seemed to put things into perspective: I decided I had better get on with some more writing.

When I finished my new novel our friend Biddy came over and Jess and I took a few days break to attend the annual conference of the West Country Writers' Association. This organization was started, largely through efforts of Waveney Girvan, then chairman of Westaway Books, to bring together a large number of authors who lived or were connected with the West Country. At one time I used to think perhaps the Association might do some useful work on behalf of authors' professional interests, but most members have now come to accept it as a social affair and no more and even as such it makes a useful contribution. It is always stimulating to meet one's fellow authors, and one of the happy customs of the Association is to hold its gathering in a different West Country centre each year. Very often the particular corporation or council feels honoured to be so selected and provides a much appreciated mayoral banquet: in this way we have wined and dined most pleasantly at Bath, Bristol, Torquay, Weymouth, Taunton, and other centres. While there is a tendency to visit the most beautiful centres - especially when like Bath they are unusually lavish with their banquets! - forays to smaller towns are now being made and most enjoyable they are too. Only recently the conference was held at Barnstaple, that warm, thriving little Devonshire community where, curiously enough, the Association had one of their best ever attendances, of about seventy. As Ronald Duncan, the poet and playwright, declared open a book exhibition at the local Smith's, I could not help being amused to look around and observe that in that very small branch bookshop there stood a bevy of best-sellers such as Barnstaple never has seen or perhaps will see all together again.

Some very good speeches have been made at the W.C.A. conferences, notably by such guest speakers as Compton Mackenzie and J. B. Priestley, and of course by our good friend Henry Williamson. As readers of some of his autobiographical books may surmise, Henry has a lively sense of fun, and he is a great practical joker at the W.C.A. conferences. Members are all somewhat gravely handed name badges to wear on arrival, and it sometimes requires great skill quietly to decipher the name on someone's badge while you engage him in conversation. Henry's badge, however, was just as likely to be the cap of a milk bottle or an advertisement for a detergent - thus quietly pricking the bubble of pomposity. I shall never forget another occasion when I was visiting Henry at his caravan home at Georgeham in Devon, when a rather literary-conscious writer was with us in the local pub, discussing a stream of famous names. Henry suddenly broke across this critical discussion by nodding at a complete stranger sitting in the far corner. 'Know who that is - it's Graham Greene.' Our companion pricked up his ears. '*The* Graham Greene?' 'Yes.' Henry looked dramatically conspiratorial and bent forward and whispered. 'He's down here incognito - nobody else knows of course.' So deadpan was Henry in this performance that I have never been sure to this day whether our companion realized that 'Graham Greene' was in fact a local farm labourer.

Behind this sense of fun, of course, Henry Williamson is a serious and sensitive artist. More than thirty years have elapsed since he won the coveted Hawthornden prize with his nature book *Tarka the Otter,* and with the £100 cash award bought a field on a hill above Georgeham, a remote village in North Devon. Though still famous for *Tarka,* and the sequel *Solar the Salmon,* he believes his real mission as a writer has been to recreate the almost forgotten world of 1914 -18 a world to be found in precise and loving detail in his now famous epic series of novels under the corporate title of *A Chronicle of Ancient Sunlight.* Most of these books have been written in the same wooden chalet in that Georgeham field.

It would be difficult, I think, for anyone to meet this still very fit white-haired upright man in his mid-sixties, with the clear eyes and sun-tanned complexion of a man ten years younger, and not discern a quality of creative energy and determination quite out of the ordinary. Here is a writer of tremendous integrity and self-discipline, a man who has been buffeted by small-minded critics but who is recognized by the best of his profession as one of our greatest living authors.

At conferences such as the West Country Writers' Association one runs the whole gamut of authorship - from the elderly absent-minded professor type to the slick journalist, from the dear doddering old lady poetess to the spritely young lady novelist, from the hard-bitten best-seller to the simpering over-shy published-at-her-own-expense beginner. Personally I cannot help being drawn to essentially professional authors, and I have a fatal tendency to see the comic side of the more pretentious - a tendency shared, for instance, by Charles Causley, the Cornish poet and schoolmaster whose lively sense of humour about such matters is a mixed blessing to have beside one when sitting through some pompous speech. Charles is one of a number of writers working in Cornwall with whom my work with the *Cornish Review* brought welcome contact. Ernest Martin, who has written many fascinating studies of rural life as well as critical biographies of writers, is another; though to be strictly accurate his isolated home at Black Torrington is just over the Devon border. Two delightful Cornish lady authors are Lady Vyvyan, an indefatigable traveller from her ancient home at Trelowarren near Helston, and Ann Treneer, author of those delightful intimate studies of everyday Cornish life, *Schoolhouse in the Wind* and *Cornish Years*. Then there is R. Glyn Grylls (Lady Mander) who apart from her own excellent biographies of past literary figures such as Mary Shelley has taken a particular interest in the Cornish modern art movement: for the first issue of the *Cornish Review* she wrote one of the most perceptive articles I have ever read about her fellow Cornish, full of such pearls of wisdom as: 'The Cornish have colour enough to turn the spectacles of most onlookers pink but it is not fast to light', and 'The impulsiveness that goes as far as magnanimity does not sustain generosity', and 'their devotion, loyal to fanaticism, has no fidelity'. Winston Graham, who walks across the sands of Perranporth to write his novels in a lonely wooden chalet far from distraction, and Howard Spring, who by contrast turns from the lovely garden of his white house at Falmouth to do his thousand words a day at a simple writing desk before a blank wall, are two famous novelists whose company I have found charming; a third, until recently living at St Ives, was Phyllis Bottome, white-haired and gracious, a fine novelist and, like Lady Mander, a great encourager of the Cornish art movement.

Brief though they were I always found these gatherings of West Country writers invigorating, a welcome reminder that one is not alone in pursuing what is essentially a lonely craft. Sometimes, too, there ensued rewarding friendships - Henry Williamson was one such example. Another writer of Henry's generation and one not unlike him in style and subject, was Leo Walmsley. There must be many thousands who have read his delightful

Love in the Sun, and his interesting autobiography *So Many Loves.* Few writers have managed so simply and tenderly to capture the everyday life of a family living and working in Cornwall. Now Leo is back 'up a creek' near Fowey living a life not unlike that described so romantically in *Love in the Sun.*

One of our most delightful encounters with West Country writers who attended the conferences was with the late W. Gore Allen - an author very close to myself, in that for two or three decades he too had struggled to make a living by writing while somehow maintaining a large family. In my case the setting had been Cornwall, in his case Devon, where in the market town of Tiverton he was very well known, among other works, for editing the *Devon Journal,* a monthly county paper. Gore Allen once wrote for the *Cornish Review* a powerful article, 'A Frontier in Dumnonia', in which he commented: 'Whenever I cross the Tamar, journeying either East or West, I am surprised afresh that one of the world's least penetrable frontiers should be made evident by so small a width of water' - and went on to make the interesting point that Cornish society has achieved a broad equality with no class distributing culture or employment and no ther class merely accepting these benefits at its hands. 'The fact is, by contrast, the Devonians do not relish an eccentric; they prefer that there should be a few human types, each easily depicted and every man yielding to classification within them.'

Well, the Devonians must have made an exception for dear Gore Allen! When he came to stay a few days with us at the Old Vicarage we warmed to his ebullient convivial personality, erudite and yet full of mischievousness. With me, he saw the full comi-tragic aspect of the free-lance writer's life, and the irony, for instance, of the fact that although a much respected Justice of the Peace at Tiverton, he had only staved off bankruptcy by inviting all his creditors round for a drink and mellowing them into a creditors' agreement!

Gore Allen had a delightful wit, a wry way of recounting stories both for and against himself, that was very endearing. In retrospect I sometimes wonder if there is a common quality which links many writers to whom I have personally been drawn - this sense of humour, a delight in pricking the bubbles of pomposity, coupled with an inevitable integrity in their own work. But of course this is not a quality restricted to writers. It was present pre-eminently in our friend Len Missen, who might well have been a writer but chose painting instead. In general, though, I have found painters more addicted to pomposity than a sense of humour; more's the pity since I live surrounded by painters.

Another writer whom we took to very much when he came to the Old Vicarage was Frank Baker, perhaps best known as the author of *Miss Hargreaves,* a delightful novel which has subsequently been made into a play with Margaret Rutherford in the name part. In fact *Miss Hargreaves is* only one of about a dozen novels which Frank Baker has written, many of them set in Cornwall - one or two, such as *Embers* and *The Downs So Free,* touching most perceptively on the strange eccentricity of life in Cornwall. For many years he lived at Mevagissey but he grew up at Goldisthney, which explains why we weren't altogether surprised when one day he knocked at the door and said: 'I've got some bottles of beer - would you like to help me drink them?' We were delighted to see him, for we knew that he had once been organist at St Hilary Church at the time when Bernard Walke was vicar, and Frank was able to tell us some fascinating stories of those days. He himself seemed to be drifting farther and farther from Cornwall, and now I think lives in London, but he retained a great admiration for Walke. Almost his last words were to urge us to read the latter's *Twenty Years at St Hilary,* a minor classic of its kind.

I never knew Bernard Walke, but he was obviously an outstanding man, for during his time at St Hilary he attracted followers from all walks, writers and artists, as well as local farm people and miners, all equally drawn by his obvious sincerity. He seems to have been what so few so-called spiritual leaders are - a true lover of his neighbours, a consistent advocate of turning the other cheek (he was a pacifist, which I only wish all clerics and other supporters of the H-bomb could have the humility to be). While vicar of St Hilary, Walke enlisted the aid of his many artist friends - Dod and Ernest Procter, Harold and Laura Knight, Norman Garstin, Joan Manning Sanders - to paint murals and panels in the church. It was also used by the B.B.C. for broadcasting an annual Christmas Nativity Play. In his book Walke gives a simple but moving account of how this came to be arranged through the interest of the producer Wilson Young; how the church was filled with batteries and the broadcasting apparatus and he feared that perhaps the atmosphere of devotion would be lost; but how, in the end all was well. After the first broadcast a message came through from Sir John Reith, then Director General, saying that Ramsay Macdonald had been dining with him and they had listened to the play together and wished to thank the players for their beautiful presentation of the Nativity.

During Walke's ministry his controversial actions often displeased people. On one occasion he was locked out of the church by a group of Kensitites, who smashed various ornaments and tore down the canopies.

As successors to Bernard Walke in the inhabitance of the Old Vicarage - not I hasten to say in the incumbency of the church! - we naturally felt a kind of link with him and his period there. I am myself what would be called an agnostic, that is, I cannot subscribe to the conventional and surely outworn Christian church dogma. Discounting the very efficient public relations job done by the Bible I cannot see any basic difference between Jesus Christ and, say, Gandhi. Both were great prophets and spiritual leaders - so were Mohammed and Jeremiah and Buddha. I find it a little distasteful to suppose that we must all be treated as children, imagining some benign father figure hovering up in the sky, a little way beyond the highest flying air liner (though perhaps within startled reach of the first space man). I am not scientifically inclined, or disposed, but I am quite ready to believe the evolution of humanity has been a thoroughly practical and physical affair evolving from one level of matter to another. What I do feel, however, is that perhaps in a way we make our own kind of God, that in the process of our living every one of us in some degree makes a minute contribution to a kind of sum total of humanity - and that, a kind of being, or even at most, a haunting memory of past, is carried on, to be inherited and absorbed and enlarged by future generations.

From what I can learn of Bernard Walke I feel that, apart from ecclesiastical matters, we might well have had much in common. I think he might have liked to think of the Vicarage still being used as a centre of creative activity, and especially as the publishing headquarters of the *Cornish Review*. Indeed I have no doubt he would have been a regular contributor. Above all he seems to have loved life and laughter, to have admired people who seek in a world of destruction to create beauty - here we should have met in agreement. Indeed, when I read of some of the dinner parties which Walke used to hold at the Vicarage, attended by many writers and artists, I think he might well have felt much at home at some of the similar gatherings that took place there in our time. I wish, indeed, he could have attended our one big party of the year, which was always held on Boxing Night.

At Christmas time we always had the whole house decorated with streamers and holly and mistletoe, and there were always children and friends around for the Christmas festivities, so Boxing Night made a wonderful winding-up to the annual celebrations. We used to send postcards off to all our friends in St Ives, Zennor, Sennen, Mousehole, Newlyn, Lamorna, Penzance, Helston, Porthleven, and sometimes, hopefully, to London. Probably we would ask about sixty, but in the end there were often more like a hundred when the great night arrived. Because we lived in a fairly remote spot and people had to make a special journey I am inclined to think that this very fact contributed something extra to the spirit of these Boxing Night parties. Altogether I think we had five at the Old Vicarage, and from them all I have a composite memory of the long line of cars drawing up in the drive, of lights blazing everywhere, and of the 25-foot-long sitting room, with its huge glittering Christmas tree at one end and a roaring log fire at the other, suddenly crowded with what, to us, seemed like half the population of West Cornwall. Perhaps of all these parties the one that sticks most in my mind is when, for a change, we decided that everyone should come dressed up as the title of a book or a film or play. The entrance hail of the Old Vicarage may have seen some strange sights - Bernard Walke tells an amusing story of how his donkey got wedged there - but I doubt if ever before it has welcomed four walking editions of *Under Milk Wood*, three *Mine Own Executioners*, two (identical) *Forever Amber* (traffic lights), and a few extremely odd versions of *Three Men in a Boat*, *The Naked and the Dead*, and *All Passion Spent*. That night the party went with a real swing. There was a rum punch that positively flowed, as well as a barrel of strong Cornish beer, and plenty of music. We pushed back the furniture and turned up the carpet and soon all these fantasy figures were wildly dancing. Before long the dancing and the good

spirits spilled out of the dining-room into the landing, into my study, into the kitchen, and indeed all over the house. The children, peeping excitedly over the bannister, must have seen bizarre sights they will long remember. Some time after midnight Donald Swan insisted that the party migrate temporarily to his studio, whereupon six hefty painters took hold of our piano and bodily carried it across the drive, and through a narrow archway, finally dumping it in the centre of Donald's studio. There the party continued with an inspired dance of the Conga, until at some stage the piano was heaved back to the house again. It was the kind of wild, merry party which I fancy the general public imagine artists embark on every other night - but of course they don't. Just now and then!

Some time in the early hours of the morning the cars began to drive away to their various and sometimes very distant corners of Cornwall: and a few of us were left to make coffee and fried eggs and survey the rather sad remnants of a party we were not likely to forget.

Chapter Eight

A POTTER AND HER HELPS

Our years at the Old Vicarage began to slip by with astounding regularity. This, I suppose, is the effect of a large family existence. No sooner is Christmas over than it is soon time for Gill's birthday, and a month after that Genevieve's, and soon after that Martin's, and then Demelza's and Jane's and Stephen's and mine and Jess's - my head reels to think of all the presents and birthday cakes and candles. As we could neither financially afford, nor physically cope with, six separate large children's parties we evolved a system of a small birthday tea for each child on the appropriate day, and one enormous combined children's party each year, usually during the Christmas holidays. Each child was allowed to invite six friends, but of course there were always somehow more than that. Sometimes we would manage to press-gang one of our friends into service as an entertainer, perhaps an amateur juggler or ventriloquist, but in general the children's party involved a wearying sequence of musical bumps, musical chairs, postman's knock, kippers - the whole exhausting lot. Still it did not seem a bad system (until later on in our family life, when, thinking we were being clever, we decided to have two parties, one for the younger children from three till six o'clock, and the other for the teen-age element from five to nine o'clock, the two elements merging for a combined tea at five. It was all very well in theory, a nice neat subdivision of different age-groups and so forth. But of course what happened in practice was exactly what the most experienced, disillusioned and cynical student of child psychology would predict. At least half the small children just never went but stayed on to turn the teen-age party into a minor riot - while the teen-agers for their part stayed on two hours longer than we expected, retiring somewhat alarmingly to a very darkened corner of the room and playing giggly games with names like Hyde Park Corner, which we had never heard of but which were apparently based on kissing and sniggering. Little wonder that after the first of these occasions I went down the next day with pneumonia!)

Sometimes, in writing this book, I wonder if I should write more about the children. Naturally the name of each one is sufficient to bring a flood of memories - Martin in his anti-washing period having to be held bodily in the bath still wearing the under-clothes he had refused to take off - Gill, having stayed out against orders, climbing over the rooftops and quietly getting into her bedroom window to find her mother sitting patiently by the bed - Jane, with a genius for accidents, treading on the only adder in West Cornwall during a perfectly ordinary afternoon outing - Stephen, at the age of about 5 saying very seriously to our friend Len, 'When I grow up I'm going to be a typewriter' - Demelza grimly singing badly off-key the entire verses of Jerusalem - and little Genevieve, looking like an angel, acting the part of Goldiocks in a home-made version of the Three Bears. These are just the more lighthearted memories - conversely there are more alarming moments: the time Martin put his arm through a plate glass window and cut an artery, the time Demelza groaned all night with a stomach-ache and was rushed to hospital and operated on for appendicitis, the time Stephen had his tonsils out . . . . The intricate and delicate shades of family life are incommunicable to anyone who has not known them; and it is superfluous to outline them to those that have. Jess was one of five sisters, and is well versed in the ploys of inter-family strife, As an only son I came to it virgin-like and comparatively innocent. Now I am like the old lion retired to lick his wounds. The best I can say is 'Well, it's all experience', for children and parents. I do not advocate large families. The ideal, I would say, is a boy and a girl, close together in ages. A family that consists of two adults and two children is still a mobile unit - it can travel anywhere and do anything together. Anything over that becomes an expedition with all the operational planning that such a word suggests. On the other hand one of the good things about large families is that, willy nilly, children learn to become more independent. It puzzles me sometimes why we parents bother at all about our ungrateful self-willed, mutton headed, go-their-own-way, brood who as soon as they have got their wings will fly off and never quite come back again. What is the point of it all? And then, of course, I receive my answer in one of those fleeting but illuminating moments when Jess and I catch one of the children in some revealing pose or expression, perhaps the way the head is held to one side or the eager glisten of a pair of big brown eyes - and our hearts fill with tenderness as perhaps we see something of ourselves, and something rather wonderful beyond ourselves.

All the same I am rather dubious about people who write jolly gossipy books about their children. For one thing I can't believe that the children like it very much-for another, I can't help wondering if the parents are being altogether honest. In my own experience, parents who really have to cope with their children are far too exhausted, mentally and physically, to *bear* to use up their precious off-duty hours in writing about the little horrors. When I wrote a comic book *How to be a Parent* many people assumed it would be illustrated with actual examples from our own family life. Did they but know it probably was - but not in the conventional direct way they might expect. Probably I could go through the book, which is written humorously in the form of general advice on parenthood, and point to paragraph after paragraph and say 'Hmmmm, yes that was after Stephen broke the windows', or 'Ah, that was because I remembered Gill doing so and so' . . . . The fact is, I suppose I couldn't bear to relive those particular incidents directly, some defence mechanism made me reduce them to a sort of detailed generalization. And of course, knowing my children, one or other, or more likely the combined horde led by Martin, would have sued me for libel or slander.

However, the point is that despite all these problems our children have survived us and we have survived our children, and still the twain do meet once a week for Sunday lunch. The rest of the time, somehow, we manage to a large extent to lead fairly separate lives; though of course at the time I am writing about, at St Hilary, we were much more necessary as bulwarks to lean on, comforters in distress, hands in the pocket for a penny for the sweetshop. And I suppose, really we rather enjoyed it.

At the same time we were glad to have our occasional escape, usually a trip into nearby Penzance, which was still our main shopping centre. Also it was here that we could always find our two greatest friends, Len and Anthony, working away at their small pottery premises. Here we were always sure of a gay welcome and some fascinating talks, especially with Len, whose mind and wit sparkled in all kinds of directions. He was a man who fascinated both Jess and me by a kind of golden quality of promise which, had we but known it, was full of tragic irony. Len's trouble was that he had never quite fulfilled himself, in life, in love, or even in work - and yet potentially, or even in his failure, he was worth a dozen other apparent successes. I find it literally impossible here to capture his qualities in words, and yet the word was the very measure of his qualities - but it was the spoken word, his spoken word. He had a way of talking, of lighting up people's characteristics, of bringing situations vividly to reality before your very eyes. He could sometimes be cruel, but more often than not it was the accident of being too wise and honest. Sometimes this cruelty would be directed at Anthony, whose muddled way of living, and of handling his relationships with people, did not meet with Len's approval. Having passed through an unhappy marriage himself Len wanted very much to learn from his mistakes. Though outwardly he seemed gay and flirtatious, underneath he was desperately anxious to find a new permanent relationship, for which he now seemed very well suited. It must have seemed ironic to him that whereas he failed in his quest, Anthony, without any of Len's heart searchings, muddled his way through to a happy second marriage.

Yet with all the differences Len and Anthony got on very well, and so did their pottery. We, for our part, spent so much time sitting in that tiny workroom that Jess, at least, became fascinated in the craft itself Eventually she decided to do something practical about her interest by becoming a student at Penzance Art School, under Bernard Leach's son, Michael, the pottery instructor there. Jess is a very physical type of person, loving dancing and swimming, and it was partly the physical nature of pottery, handling the clay and coaxing it into existence by physical craft, that appealed to her. But she had also spent some years as a chemist, and the more technical side of pottery was also therefore of special interest.

This was important because all too often hopeful potters have one or other of these interests, but not both. While the art of throwing is the basis of pottery, the art of glazing contributes much to the finished pots.

For several months Jess attended the Art School regularly and she soon began to develop into quite a skilful potter. Sometimes she brought back pots which she had made, and the sideboards of our home glowed with new colours and shapes. Friends of ours who saw these would ask hopefully: 'I say, can you make us some'

Sometimes Jess was able to do this at the Art School, but the trouble there, apart from queuing for the wheel, was that kiln firings were few and far between. Soon it was obvious that Jess was feeling rather frustrated as a potter.

One day I said casually:

'Why don't you get a wheel and a kiln of your own Then you could make pots to your heart's content. I mean, there's plenty of room out here.'

Looking back Jess always declared that she had no idea what she was letting herself in for. Be that as it may, we scraped together about £15 to buy a fairly cheap but reliable kiln wheel, and ordered a couple of hundredweight of clay, and began to set up a spare room at the Old Vicarage as a pottery workshop. The one remaining item, an electric

kiln, could well have run into £100 or more up till a year or so previously; but David Leach, Bernard Leach's elder son, had now patented a cheaper studio kiln which worked out at about £60, and which we knew to be very good. At last, after some hesitation, we borrowed the £60 as a business loan from Jess's mother, and ordered the kiln.

In the meantime, we had a wheel and some clay: Jess might as well throw some pots. And then, since we had to wait for our electric kiln what about doing what the old time potters did, and building a brick kiln of our

own in the garden?

Why not, indeed? With Donald as a learned adviser (he had done pottery at one time in his student days) we chose a clearing in the grounds and collected some of the bricks and blocks that always seemed to be lying about among the outhouses. It was all rather amateurish no doubt, but finally we had a sort of Heath Robinsonish affair which was enormous on the outside but contained at its heart a tiny chamber about twelve inches square. Into this we placed several of the pots Jess had thrown, packed the kiln tight shut with bricks and clay, and then set to work gathering immense quantities of shavings and branches and twigs and small logs to burn in the fireplace under the chamber. We kept the fire raging for hour after hour long into the night, and then stoked it as high as possible before going to bed about two in the morning. Alas the next evening, when we opened the kiln, everything inside was a dull disappointing lifeless black. Something, as the newcomer to pottery is constantly having to say, had gone wrong.

We had one or two further goes at this out-door kiln and may have improved on those first efforts, but fortunately soon after the new kiln arrived. In the meantime we had also experimented with digging up our own clay, for we discovered that the grounds of St Hilary ran over a bed of yellow clay, similar to the St Erth clay a few miles away. The trouble with making your own clay is that there is far more to it than just digging up the raw material. What you dig up has to be sieved and washed, and every kind of impurity removed. In the long run most potters save their precious man hours by buying clay which has already been through these processes, and is plastic and pliable and ready for immediate use.

It was an exciting day for us when Paul Weychan finally drove up our drive carrying our new kiln in the back of his estate car. Until that day, I suppose, we still thought of Jess's pottery as a kind of hobby. But once the kiln was installed and connected up and Jess's row of drying pots were packed in for the first biscuit firing, there was a subtle change in our attitude. After all, Cornwall was famous for its pottery - here was a commodity which was very much in demand, especially in the holiday seasons. Already several of our friends had given Jess orders for tea sets, and so forth. Supposing we were to extend this development? What about pottery not only for pleasure, but profit?

When I put forward the idea to Jess, I don't think she took me entirely seriously. But she agreed to make a range of samples, and I rashly promised to take them round the pottery shops of Cornwall to see if I could get any orders.

By this time the old Rover had gone the way of many old cars. In its place we had the second old London taxicab in Cornwall. The first belonged to Mary John, wife of Augustus John's eldest son, Caspar, now First Lord of the Admiralty. Indeed it was having a ride in Mary's that introduced me to the delights of the London cabs, and when she told me that the taxi company sold them off fifty at a time each year, I determined to investigate. On our next trip to London we visited the depot at Brixton, and there sure enough they stood in rows awaiting purchasers. At this time Jess had recently become the somewhat nervous owner of a new motor-cycle, purchaed as a sort of symbol of independence. Although she had bravely learned to use the bike and made one famous trip to a sister at Wolverhampton the truth was she was secretly rather afraid of the infernal machine. So when we had the chance of buying a taxi she sportingly, but perhaps not unhappily, agreed to sell her bike towards the cost of £70.

So now we rode the Cornish lanes neither in a buzzing little Austin Seven with a map of Cornwall painted on the side, nor in a sedate yet nippy old Rover, but in a squat, solid, ungainly and surely unforgettable vehicle labelled BUC 497, a 1935 Austin taxi. Even to write about her now, the dear old thing, brings back a flood of happy memories. She was absolutely ideal for a large family like ours. The children piled in the back while Jess and I huddled in the front with oh, blessed relief ! - glass panels cutting us off from the din at the rear. Misshapen as she might be, compared to more modern cars, BUC 497 could go anywhere - up the steepest hill, across muddy fields, through water fords - she was as tough as she looked. With her heavy body she could not exactly be called a racer, but she could chug along at a steady fifty, and we made at least a dozen trips to London and back, seldom taking longer than nine hours for the 280 miles. One of the delights of an old taxi is the roominess; if we wanted a picnic by the sea and it was raining we just relaxed in the back, as if at a dining room table. If on the other hand the sunshine blazed, then down came the folding leather roof and the passengers sunbathed and felt the wind on their face. Goodness knows how many children we sometimes carried, other people's as well as our own. I think we once had nine adults in the back and went up Newlyn Hill. She was indeed a gallant old lady who served us well and truly for five years before meeting the unexpected end of being stolen from a line of parked cats in Queensgate, Kensington.

Now, as I set off 'on the road' with my pottery samples I could not help reflecting that no commercial traveller ever arrived at his customers in a more extraordinary vehicle.

Working rather naïvely on the principle that the biggest and busiest Cornish holiday resort was the place for a good order, I drove the thirty miles or so across to Newquay. I had no pre-conceived ideas, and accordingly stopped at the first shop which exhibited pottery in its window. This, it transpired later, was rather a mistake, since it was very much a Gifte Shoppe type of place with corresponding bad taste, and the sort of pottery it requited would be cheap and nasty. The manager looked doubtful when he saw the samples, but I was so eager to get orders that when he diffidently said could we supply ash-trays with a drawing of Newquay Harbour on them I said 'Yes' without any hesitation. After that he mellowed, and in the end I staggered out of the shop somewhat shaken with an order for about £30 worth of Jess's pottery!

I was so excited that I went and rang up the master potter, whose reaction, though excited, included a helpless squeal.

'I can't draw Newquay Harbour!'

'That's all right', I said soothingly. 'Donald. . .'

I suppose in a way that's how Donald got roped into the St Hilary Pottery. For as with greater confidence I went round other Cornish resorts and pulled in still further orders, I noticed that most of them were for decorated ware. Donald had in fact drawn a few fishing boat motifs in copper (black) on the gold glazed sample pots, but I don't suppose at that stage he had envisaged becoming part of a production conveyor belt system.

Something like that, as the orders came merrily in, is what happened. It was certainly one of the oddest partnerships I have come across. Jess, all eager to build up her new business, would arise early and perhaps be busily throwing pots by ten o'clock in the morning. Donald, by contrast, was not only a late riser, but took hours to acclimatize himself to the fact that he had risen - consequently he would often make his first appearance in the pottery at about four o'clock in the afternoon. By that time Jess was packing up in order to go and make the children's tea. There was usually plenty of work for Donald to do, and indeed he worked long hours, often until nearly midnight - decorating not just one pot, but row after row of beer mugs, coffee mugs, and so forth. He undoubtedly worked very hard, at his own peculiar hours, but in the long run Jess found it an impossibly impractical arrangement if only because she and Donald were seldom in the pottery at the same time. Whenever this happy event did occur, they used to work together in almost perfect unison, for both were quick and efficient. They made quite a picture, Donald in jeans and an old jersey that I don't remember ever seeing off him -and Jess, because of the heat of the room often working in her brassiere and pants. One day the local vicar brought some visitors to 'inspect' this new local industry. I don't think he ever quite recovered from the shock.

In those days of course, the St Hilary Pottery was still in what might be called the experimental stage, and the working partners were inclined to get a little flustered by any kind of special order. On one occasion a well meaning R.A.F. sergeant from the camp at Sennen came over and ordered a set of drinking mugs as a farewell present for a comrade. They had some special design on, which was executed beautifully, but they had to be ready by a certain date. Unfortunately I had been deputized to switch the kiln off late the previous evening, and somehow I had forgotten - until I woke up in a cold sweat in the middle of the night and rushed to do so. Thus I knew that the mugs must have been ruined. I am afraid when I heard the jeep coming down the drive that afternoon I committed an atrocious act of gross cowardice: quietly I went off for a walk on St Hilary burrows and didn't come back until I heard the jeep roar off again, a positive note of distrust in its exhaust.

Soon after I caused a somewhat wasteful diversion of talents when, smarting a little at the idea of shops pocketing 50 per cent. of our price, I became obsessed with the idea of trying to make something which could be sold direct by post. I had made acquaintance with that bizarre magazine *Exchange and Mart,* through whose agonizingly small-type pages I sometimes feel half the trading business of Britain is conducted. I noticed that there were innumerable advertisements there for all kinds of gift items, and I hit on the idea of advertising a pottery Celtic Cross, to be called the St Hilary Cross. Full of enthusiasm I persuaded Jess to spend a lot of time making moulds, after Donald had done a Celtic Cross design. Meantime I had 500 cards printed, bought some elastic bands, and then the lot of us spent weary evenings either stamping out Celtic Crosses in the moulds, or trimming them, or, after they had been fired, making holes in the cards and tying them on with elastic bands. For a while each time we opened the kiln it was like looking into a cemetery! Anyway, in due course a cunningly worded advertisement appeared in *Exchange and Mart*, and we sat back and waited for the avalanche of orders. There were . . . *three*! At 2s. 6d. a time this barely covered the cost of the advertisement, let alone the printing of the cards, and the scheme was abruptly dropped. For months afterwards I would come across forlorn little pottery crosses in the grounds where Stephen or Demelza had dropped them after using them in some game.

Needless to say those early days, like those of any new business, were full of mishaps of one sort and another. In subsequent years Jess has become an established studio potter, and indeed is the co-author of *The Pottery Book,* a recognized text-book on the craft: and now she has developed a beautiful tin glaze range of pottery which is very much in demand both in Cornwall and London. But at the beginning she had to find out by endless and sometimes disheartening experiences. All potters go through a period where things go wrong: pots blow up in biscuiting, they are under-fired or over-fired, glaze creeps or jumps or crawls, and so on. Sometimes this was not always immediately apparent. I shall never forget the day Donald and I took a delivery to a dear old lady who had a shop at St Austell at the time. Even while we were still placing the pots down on the counter there were a series of plinging noises and slithers of fine glaze popped about on to the counter. The sweet old thing knew we were comparative novices, trying to do our best, and she whispered confidentially, 'Don't worry, I'll touch them up with a bit of black paint and no one will ever know.'

Gradually the St Hilary Pottery range became evolved. Today it is mainly a double glaze type, but then it was largely pictorial, boat motifs merging into the glaze, specific designs on plates and so forth. When, therefore, Donald decided to return to his portrait painting Jess not only had to find a replacement who would keep more normal hours - but also one who could paint boats and views on pots. Such a man was another friend of ours, Bill Pickard, who had worked for a time at the Lamorna Pottery, and in addition to his artistic ability knew a great deal about the laboratory side of pottery making.

No greater contrast to Donald could possibly be imagined. Day after, though he lived at Mousehole and had to catch two buses, Bill would arrive at the pottery at precisely 9.20a.m., and equally precisely he would leave at 4.20p.m. Where Donald would toss off his pictures and drawings

in what seemed literally a few moments, Bill worked painstakingly and thoroughly, every line carefully considered and correctly executed. As a result the rate of production was considerably slowed down.

This did not matter greatly with smaller orders, but I can remember how our agitation grew in the matter of our fabulous, biggest-ever order for Clovelly (ever after referred to as 'the Donkey order'). My fault really, but when I called on a shop half way down the steep hill of Clovelly, I blithely promised we would supply every pot decorated with a drawing of the famous Clovelly donkey. I imagine that Donald would have evolved a highly simplified donkey in order to save production time: but by the time we came to execute the order it was Bill who was doing the decorating, and he proceeded to draw his donkeys as methodically as anything else. The result was that on the coloured plates that had been ordered he produced real works of art that were worth treble what we were paid - and on the smaller cheaper items, the amount of time he devoted was like losing money.

Poor Bill! Near the end he was having nightmares about donkeys. Donkeys, donkeys, everywhere...When the order was at last ready I took Bill and his wife Biddy along with me, and of course almost the first thing we saw was - the inevitable Clovelly donkey. Only it was tethered in a field and not 'in operation'. We were told that a jeep has now replaced the four-footed conveyance. Unfortunately on that day there was neither jeep nor donkey and we were faced with the task of carrying several hundredweight containers of pottery across a field and down the cobbled streets of Clovelly (no cars are allowed in the village). If it had been uphill it would have killed us, but as it was down-hill and untold wealth awaited us (we hoped) at the end of our journey, we managed to complete our delivery. Then of course we stood absolutely trembling for fear the shopkeeper should inform us casually that he would send payment at the end of the month. Fortunately he paid in cash there and then, handing out seventy-six pound notes! If we had staggered under the weight of those containers going down we now positively bounded up the cobbled street in sheer exhilaration.

That was an exceptional order, of course; most of the orders I got were for £10 to £15, and as they involved two trips, one to get the order, the other to deliver the goods, it is doubtful if they were exactly economic. On the other hand they afforded an excuse for constant trips up and down Cornwall - we supplied shops in Newquay, Padstow, Polzeath, Port Isaac, Tintagel, and Boscastle up the north coast, and Mullion, Coverack, Falmouth, St Mawes, Porthscatho, Mevagissey, Fowey, and Polperro up the north coast. What with selling copies of the *Cornish Review*, and now getting pottery orders, there are few corners of Cornwall I do not know. Unfortunately journeys on business do involve a time-table of some sort! On one trip I remember sitting above Boscastle harbour munching some sandwiches and wishing I could just stay there for a few days in the quiet and sunshine. Still, as I say, these trips have increased my ground-work knowledge of Cornwall, and I shouldn't do badly on a Cornish quiz programme, I fancy. But after all these travels, and though I immensely enjoyed coming romantically down into some tiny village like Portloe, or into Fowey or Looe, or driving along the wild north cliffs past New quay - still I should without hesitation plump for West Penwith as the most beautiful and exciting part of Cornwall.

In the meantime, while the St Hilary Pottery was bringing in some money it was patently not enough to keep two partners, and in due course Bill decided to leave and open a pottery shop with Biddy, over at Mousehole, where they are working to this day. Jess then settled down to a pattern she has followed ever since, of making pottery on a part-time basis, with concentrated periods during the season and long breaks in the winter.

One result of the unforeseen development of what had been begun as a hobby into an active little business was that we were confronted with the problem of what to do about the younger children. During the spring after starting the pottery Jess had almost literally waddled off the wheel to give birth to our sixth and last child, Dilys Genevieve. By now Stephen had joined Martin, Gill, and Jane in daily attendance at the village school, but now that she would be working on her own, it was impossible for Jess to cope with Demelza and Genevieve at the same time.

So began the saga of our helps. Someone told us that the best place to advertise was in the *Lady*, and that if we were prepared to take someone with a small child of her own, we should have no difficulties. Well . . . we advertised and someone wrote, and in due course I had a wire to meet her at Penzance station. No doubt the peremptory nature of the wire should have given us some faint warning, some fleeting glimpse of what was to come, but it didn't. Dutifully I put aside my morning's work and drove the six miles into town to meet the train. At the station I scanned the passengers getting off the train and was just concluding that our help had missed the train when I became aware of an elegantly dressed young woman standing by the door of a first-class compartment. In her arms was a small infant, curled up in a beautiful Paisley shawl.

Upon approaching and making inquiry I was given a gracious smile and acknowledgment and directed to the luggage van. There in a row stood a mammoth luxury pram, four suitcases, a trunk and several other articles. While the new help stood by I laboriously carried her possessions out of the station and loaded them into the car. When all were squeezed in Queenie and her baby got delicately into the front seat and were driven to their new home.

While, perspiring somewhat, I unloaded all the luggage and carried it upstairs, the elegant young lady made herself comfortable on our sofa, still nursing her infant.

'Isn't she sweet?' she said.

'Delightful', agreed Jess. 'Er, we have some children, you'll be able to-'

'I wonder if you have some milk; Baby would like some milk.' Jess went in the kitchen and heated up some milk. When she brought it back

Queenie took it with a smile and proceeded to feed her baby. While she was doing this Jess decided she had better get on with making lunch. When this was ready our new resident tucked her baby away in the pram and sat down and ate a hearty meal.

After lunch we sat back expectantly.

Queenie rose and looked around.

'Would you mind if I took baby for a walk? She does like her afternoon parade.'

We looked at one another, and said nothing. Queenie went off for her walk. Jess sat and looked at the dirty plates for a long time, then carried them off to the kitchen.

When baby came back from its walk it was tea time. Jess had made a nice tea, scones and strawberry jam. I think Queenie enjoyed it. Afterwards she put baby to bed, an operation which seemed to take rather a long time; by the time she emerged, Jess had fed our children and put two of them to bed. Gill and Jane who were still up sat and stared at Queenie in awe; but Queenie seemed to take very little notice of them. She announced, instead, her intention of unpacking - and this little job occupied her for the rest of the evening.

Ah well, we thought, it must be strange for her, she needs to get settled in. But the next day was exactly the same; Jess ran around making meals for Queenie and on two occasions I was called in to help her move her huge trunk - If you ask why we didn't speak to Queenie about the realities of her position and purpose, I can only meekly reply that there was 'something about her'. Her pram, her clothes, her accessories, her baby and her self - all belonged to the lap of luxury. Everything she had was obviously of the best, spotlessly clean - by comparison our own clothes and things seemed incredibly shabby. It became increasingly obvious that one just couldn't ask such an aristocratic being to wash dishes or sweep floors!

We stood it for several days, until Jess and I were hardly on speaking terms, and then, miraculously, Queenie herself put us out of our misery. She came to me one morning and explained, quite sweetly, that she was afraid it wouldn't suit her here. The children were rather noisy and kept baby awake, and the air was not to her taste. Later that day I loaded her things up into the car and drove her back to the station. In the evening we felt happy for the first time for nearly a week.

A joke? Not at all. That was merely the first of our little dramas. For our next help we decided it must be someone we interviewed first. In due course we chose an obviously unaristocratic working woman called Kathleen. She too had a small child and no husband, but we agreed that she looked the hard-working type, and accordingly she moved in. And quite hard she did work, too, which we decided almost made up for the rather objectionable ways of her little girl, who spent most of the time hitting one or other of our children, or turning on taps and electric fires.

Still, we decided it was worth it. Alas, after two weeks, there were ponderous footsteps up our drive. Opening the door I found the light blocked by two huge policemen. I looked at them guiltily, thinking of lapsed dog licences, and any other offences for which we might be liable. They certainly looked stern: however they inquired not for one of our family, but for Kathleen. And when I took them to her, I saw her face blanch as they eyed her sternly, and my own heart sank. Here, I knew, was fresh trouble.

It was, too. Kathleen, it seems, was not exactly as I had imagined. She had nimble fingers. She had been to prison twice. And when she left her last employer she had taken with her a collection of blankets, sheets, jewellery, plates, money . . . . The policemen had a complete list. They found them all in Kathleen's room.

We felt sorry for Kathleen, but it was out of our hands. She and her child were whisked off - and we were back where we started.

'Well,' said Jess with a shrug, 'I suppose it's as well it came out now, before anything happened.'

Alas, I discovered, things had happened. Missing were jewellery, underwear, materials - gone into the limbo, with Kathleen. But we were too disheartened to do anything about it.

After this, we laid down a new rule.

'No children. Definitely unmarried, umnotherly types only.'

That was how we came to have Frances. When I come to try to describe Frances, words almost fail me. 'Daughter of Darkness' was someone's phrase, and it about sums her up. She was only 16, but there was something about her that made you aware she was centuries old in cunning and secret experience. Sly, I suppose, was the adjective. She didn't walk, she seemed to sidle. She appeared and disappeared without making a sound. She had a high-pitched giggle that made me jump every time I heard it.

Looking back it seems incredible we ever engaged her, and yet at the time I remember we thought, well she seems reasonably bright, and fond of children, and perhaps a young person could be moulded to our way of life. . .Moulding Frances took years off both our lives, even though she was with us for a mere four months.

It wasn't so much anything she did or didn't do, so much as her ways, her mannerisms. At breakfast in the morning I would be reading my paper, and suddenly behind me would come that weird cackle.

'What is it Frances? What on earth is it?'

Frances would point to some minor headline in the paper.

'See about that fellow cutting his wife's head off with a hatchet? Coo!'

Morbid things fascinated Frances. She had an unerring eye for the headline about the bus crash into a ravine, the mysterious stranger striking again, the wife poisoner, and so on. For a long time we were rather puzzled at Frances's penchant for reading headlines until it emerged that she couldn't read, really, and only understood block letters.

Illiteracy was no real handicap to Frances, however. There was more melodrama and fantasy in her small blonde head than in almost any other head I can think of. If she walked down to the village and back, she was nearly raped three times and definitely assaulted by the poor innocent postman. Men were indeed something of an obsession with her. Baker, grocer, electrician - all who entered Frances's domain in the kitchen were subjected to the curious mixture of leers, winks, and smiles which composed her cinema-obtained technique of flirtation.

Not surprisingly, Frances collected admirers. Gradually it began to dawn on me, in a dim sort of way, that there was a dangerously thin dividing line between her fantasies about what happened on her outings - and hard facts. Nevertheless, I told myself sternly, *that* was none of my business.

Then one day, for no accountable reason, Frances fixed her lascivious eye upon me. One day she knocked on the study door, entered, posed dramatically - and her skirt fell down! She took to leaning heavily upon my shoulder when serving a meal and sometimes, furtively, under the table I would feel a leg pressing suggestively against my own.

Even so, so anxious were we not to add to our chain of misfortunes about helps, we might have carried on with Frances - had we not made the unexpected discovery that when we went out for an evening, leaving our children safely in her care, as we imagined, Frances was catching the next bus into town after us, to meet one of her numerous lovers.

This had to be the end, and the daughter of darkness had to go. For a time we tried to manage without anyone, and then, regretfully, we advertised again. This time there arrived into our midst - Florrie.

Like Frances, Florrie was a country girl. But Florrie wasn't 16 and was no daughter of darkness. She was 30 and plump in the really grand tradition, sixteen stone at least and like all plump people, jolly and cheerful. We watched affectionately as she settled comfortably into her new life. The children adored her, and she adored them. True, she was slow, very slow, about the house, but she did the work and she was honest and well-meaning and cheerful. Good old Florrie!

Alas, fate was never on our side. Down the other end of our lane lived an elderly widower called Ben. Whiskery, rednosed, comfort-loving, we did not hold a high opinion of his qualities. No matter - he cast a covetous eye on Florrie; it was too much. Florrie had never been wooed - but secretly it was her longing to be married, like all her friends. This, for his own reasons of wanting to be well fed and looked after, Ben was willing to offer. Soon the inevitable happened. Florrie gave notice, and we were guests at her wedding in the little Methodist chapel.

Just when we were in despair, my old friend the *New Statesman* unwittingly came to our rescue. I saw there one day the constant advertisement which offers foreign girls *au pair,* and we wrote off. By reply we received a fascinating collection of details, rather like stud pedigrees, together with photographs of several French and Italian beauties.

At that time Anthony Richards, who with Len was a constant visitor to us at the Old Vicarage, was very much a lone wolf, and we used to show him the photographs of the girls and say teasingly, 'Never mind, we're going to find you a lovely French girl.' Anthony would grunt rather morosely, being in a state of cynicism about women, but he approved as we did of the details and photographs of one, Christianne Cherrain, and after exchanging letters, we decided to ask her to come over.

From the moment I met her off the train at Penzance, I knew that Christianne was just right for us. For one thing she was dark and pretty and vivacious, and both Jess and I (and indeed our children) love to have attractive people around us. Then she was so sweet natured and had such a sense of humour - while she even spoke good English - oh, yes, she was going to be all right.

Somehow Christianne fitted exactly into the happy-go-lucky atmosphere of the Old Vicarage. Indeed - alas, from the point of view of her rather stern father, who had expressly asked her to find a post in Cornwall so as to be far away from the sinful temptations of London, the wicked city! - she fell with the greatest of ease into the vagaries of bohemian life. As the daughter of a somewhat prim and fussy Frenchman and a much more ribald half-Egyptian mother (the two parents had long since been separated), Christianne was probably bound to have a streak of abandon in her vivacious person. All the same, when we suddenly received news that her father was arriving to pay a visit, I don't think we could possibly have imagined a more compromising or displeasing first impression. We had driven specially to Penzance station to meet Monsieur Cherrain, only to find that there had been a mix-up and he had arrived an hour before and caught a taxi out to the Old Vicarage. There, he walked into the kitchen to find his meek little daughter Christianne, her hair untied and flowing wildly down to her waist, sitting in a rather provocative position on the edge of the kitchen table - posing for a portrait by Donald! It took us several days of excessive cordiality to thaw M. Cherrain out of his displeasure; but I must say by the time his visit was over we were all great friends. This achievement was not without some cost, both financial and psychological, for it was his custom to drink two bottles of wine a day, and desperately we kept pace. But on the last evening we all sat round a roaring fire and were rather touched when Monsieur Cherrain suddenly sang a little song, and explained that that was the customary procedure in France when you wished to express how much you have enjoyed a stay.

In deference to her father, Christianne had resumed pinning up her hair so that she looked quite prim and decorous. As soon as he had gone we determined to persuade her to un-pin it, for somehow when she let her hair down her character flowed and glowed and she became much more natural. But for a time she was adamant. No, she would not let her hair down. Furthermore, she was going to do as her father said and spend every evening studying German.

This was rather depressing. Even the children became down-hearted. How could we cheer up Christianne We decided the best thing would be to have a party, to invite lots of cheerful people, and let her abandon her worries in the whirl, of the dance.

If I remember right this was the occasion when, after someone had discovered we had quite a sizable old wine cellar through a hidden doorway, Len and Anthony decorated the walls with white-wash over which they drew skeletons, and we lit lots of candles and turned the cellar into a sort of bar. All seemed to be going well, when we noticed, no Christianne. Alarmed, I searched the house, and found her all alone in the sitting-room by a fire.

'Come and have a drink, Christianne.'

'No - I have finished with drinking.'

'Oh, come now - well, let me introduce you to some friends.'

'No - I have finished with people. My father was right, I must study hard.'

'Well.'

I was at something of a loss, but fortunately circumstances came to my aid. Dennis Pattison, who then worked on the telephone exchange at Porthleven, had offered to bring one or two Wrens from the big naval station at Culdrose. Naturally we had applauded this move. But somehow, in the passing of messages, the meaning had become blurred and finally there arrived a party of naval officers and Wrens all looking most decorous and fully convinced that they had been invited to a Vicarage tea party!

Fortunately it did not take very long to explode this myth, whereupon the officers of both sexes entered into the spirit of the party with great gusto - and, incidentally, very soon swept Christianne out of her doldrums .... The next morning, and thereafter, Christianne's lovely dark hair was down and flowing wild.

However, it was not Donald, nor a Culdrose lieutenant who finally awoke Christianne's youthful heart - it was, in fact, none other than our old friend Anthony, the very one for whom, we had joked, we were ordering a lovely French girl. These things do happen, of course, but it was amusing to watch the process. Anthony, of course, fell very heavily, but Christianne was a little nervous at first of becoming involved with a strange Englishman, and there ensued a series of alarms and disputes.

One night Len and Anthony and Jess and I sat round the fire, while Christianne sat grimly up in her room swotting German.

'Go on, Anthony,' urged Len, 'Show who's the master, eh? Up you go!'

Anthony looked at us uneasily, squared his shoulders, and went off. For a time all seemed well, then we heard voices raised in anger and a door slam, and down came Anthony to sulk. Then, wickedly, Len would urge him on again, and back he would trail, to the wooing of his dark lady.

It was amusing, but also rather sweet, and Jess and I were glad for both their sakes to see them obviously developing a very real relationship. We had in recent years seen so many cases of unhappy marriages and twisted relationships, that it was a delight to see two happy lovers.

This was a time of fresh money worries, lately caused by the *Cornish Review* which had finally expired in a blaze of debts. We were not unused to visits from the court bailiff, for in our time we had been summonsed for over-due H.P. payments and the like. But when one day there was an authoritative knock at the front door and outside stood a grim looking man who announced himself as a sheriff, we did rather wilt in our shoes. We learned that with a debt of £20 or over anyone can, if they feel particularly spiteful, take out a High Court Writ, in which case this was delivered by a sheriff, not a mere bailiff. The characteristics of dealing with a sheriff are that he arrives in a car, not on a bicycle like the bailiff; that his costs are about three times as high, so that our bill of £22 became something like £40; and that whereas ordinary judgment summonses give you time to pay, a High Court Writ leaves you twenty-four hours. Since the bill was what we considered a ridiculously high one, we were not in any hurry to pay. But . . . under a High Court edict there is no alternative: if payment is not received in twenty-four hours bills of sale are posted on your property and your goods sold. Somehow we managed to rake together the money and pay off the bill.

Altogether it was a very upsetting time, for we were also confronted with emotional problems of our own. Len and Jess and I had developed a close friendship which though in many ways very beautiful pointed to obvious difficulties ahead. I think we all felt some sort of action would be better than inaction. Jess had often said she wished we could live in London to be closer to civilized things like theatres and concerts. Now I began to wonder if perhaps this might be a sensible solution all round. Perhaps too, I could take a job in publishing which would vastly increase our income and enable us to get straight.

One night I stood in the garden at St Hilary, listening to the wind rustling in the avenue of trees, and watching the sparkling lights of Newlyn and Penzance on the horizon. It was all so peaceful: life in Cornwall was so rewarding, at least so far as I was concerned. But perhaps I had been less than fair to Jess, and she needed a period of more civilized life, in the big city. And perhaps too (no doubt a warning intuitional voice was saying) it might be as well just now if we did make a move far away from Cornwall? Perhaps indeed.

Whatever the motive or reasons might really have been, Jess and I decided it was time we moved from the Old Vicarage. It was not altogether as crazy a move as it might seem. Much as we loved the place, it was cumbersome and awkward, and had never been our idea of an ultimate home, though we had been very happy there. So if we were going to make a move, there was no reason why we shouldn't now rather than later.

All the same, along with the undercurrent of excitement, there was a very real sadness in the air as finally, having heard of a lovely country house to be rented for a week in Kent, we decided to look for a buyer for the Old Vicarage. As it happened we never needed to look far. Word gets round mysteriously in these matters. One evening there came a knock at the door; it was a call from a local builder, the same person who had bid against us at the auction five years previously. He had heard that we might be moving, etc...Within a month the deal had been fixed up.

I shall never forget the last few days at the Old Vicarage. Over everything hung this sense of impending grief and sadness. Time and again we would look at each other and shake our heads in bewilderment. Why on earth were we uprooting ourselves like this? Was it really worth it? Were we really doing the right thing? It was to take many years before we could really answer that question, I suppose. But right then, those last bitter January days, we could not know.

Two days before our departure we held a farewell party. We wanted it to be a good party, a happy party, but inevitably it was not. There was too much sadness, too much conflict, and drinking only made it worse, so that we ended morose and unhappy . . . . The next morning, with cold blooded efficiency the furniture men came and stripped the house. That night, our last night, we all slept in a row on blankets by a fire in the sitting-room. Somehow it seemed quite appropriate that when we awoke the next morning the whole of the outside world of St Hilary was covered in a thick blanket of snow. Snow is almost unheard of in Cornwall, but for this, our farewell day, the snow had come. Cold and sad, we heaved our remaining luggage on top of the old taxi, and took a last look-round. Len and Anthony, faithful to the end, stood in the doorway, ready to lock up when we had gone. I started the taxi engine and executed a slithery run round the drive, then headed for the gate. Our last sight was of Len and Anthony standing in that dear, familiar old doorway. They were both crying.

Chapter Nine

JOURNEY INTO THE INTERIOR

Once upon a time there was an old London taxi-cab containing three grown-ups, five school-children, one six-months' old baby, a cat, eight suitcases, three mattresses, and a variety of old shapes such as tennis rackets, fishing rods, and dolls prams. At 9 a.m. one January morning, in the face of one of the worst snow blizzards of the twentieth century, this old taxi set off on the 360-mile journey from one end of England to the other. At 1 a.m. the next morning it was still chugging along.

I suppose we had thought vaguely about the nature of our momentous journey from St Hilary in West Cornwall to Ashford in East Kent - equivalent to the entire length of the coast of Southern England. But probably the sort of things we had imagined were the pleasures of passing from the heather strewn moors of Cornwall to the rich red farmland of Devon, the lush winding hills of Dorset on to the vast plains of Wiltshire, the forest-thick woodlands of the New Forest opening out on to the sweep of Sussex Downs. What a rich and varied journey it would be.

How different it all was! From beginning to end the landscape was one immense area of snow - and from the moment we started we were far too concerned about whether we should complete our journey at all to bother much about the views. Naturally this tension, coupled with the intense cold in the front of the cab, didn't make for placidity. It wasn't long before Jess and I were arguing about whether the car radiator should be refilled with water. We both knew the radiator leaked badly, but I had fixed my mind on not stopping the car until we reached our middle of the morning point the 'Jamaica Inn' on top of Bodmin Moor. So I did my best to keep going, but by the time the front of the cab was steaming like an express railway engine I had to admit the need for urgent attention.

'There's a garage', said Jess pointing.

I braked and pulled in. Unfortunately I had quite forgotten about the huge load of mattresses and cases piled high on top of the taxi; and the garage had a rather low roof. One moment we were gliding into the garage - the next there was a violent jerk, an awful crunching noise, and screams from the back. As we sat, petrified, Martin poked his head round the window and said (in that smug, maddening way with which young children impart bad news): 'There -you've broken the roof!'

We had, too, a great rip through the leather. What was more, we had slightly damaged the garage roof as well, which didn't please the proprietor at all, so that we felt bound to pay him a little compensation. By the time we set off again, we were somewhat chastened, and we avoided each other's glance for the rest of the way to the 'Jamaica Inn'.

The battle was yet to come. In Devonshire, where the snow had stopped, there had been time for road surfaces to freeze. I began to feel nervous, remembering all those newspaper stories I had read about people stranded in snow-storms and blizzards. At last we came to one dreadful long, winding hill, somewhere near Honiton - lined all the way up with immovable cars, their owners standing about helplessly. Was this to be our end I watched mesmerized as the car in front of us suddenly began to slide from side to side, like a most ungainly ballet dancer . . . until at last one slide carried it into the ditch. Now our wheels began slithering, first to one side, then to the other. I held my breath and gripped the wheel. Slowly, like a squat snail, we crept forward.

Somehow - due probably to the extra weight of the cab - we managed it, we got to the top of that hill. After that we had many similar experiences, though never quite so bad. At last we stopped at a roadside café for lunch. We were all of us, children as well, so emotionally exhausted that we could hardly eat anything. Even the cat refused a bowl of milk. Only Genevieve, unperturbed, drank her bottle. By now, we felt as if we had already crossed England twice over. In fact, we hadn't even got halfway! Meantime the unlucky children, crammed in the back - not to mention poor Christianne with Demelza on one knee and rocking Genevieve's cot, with the other - were getting restive. At periodic intervals the strident voice of Stephen was raised, complainingly: 'When are we going to see the new house?'

We pressed on grimly, through snow and sleet. Yet when dusk fell at about six o'clock, we had only reached Shaftesbury, in Dorset, our half-way stage. One hundred and eighty miles still stretched before us! On we went with our nightmare journey. Through Salisbury and Stockbridge, on to Basingstoke, turning off there for Guildford and Reigate. Often Jess had to nudge me to save me from falling asleep at the wheel. I thought the journey would *never* end - but there at last the signposts began to record the magic word, ASHFORD, and we told ourselves the end was near.

That's what we *thought!* Soon after midnight we drove through the market town of Ashford. Our destination was only three miles on. We took the Folkestone road out of the town. Half a mile on -and then, BANG! An awful lurch and we stopped. I hardly dared look at Jess. I knew it was a puncture. Stiffly I hauled myself out of the driver's seat, groped for the jack, and went round to the rear tyre that had burst. After a few moments I came back.

'Sorry, there's so much weight in the back, I simply can't get the jack under. I'm afraid they'll all have to get out.'

Getting 'them' out, after midnight on a strange cold road in Kent, was not a happy operation. But we managed it somehow, and the children stood around looking like wraiths while I managed to jack up the cab and change the wheel. Then we more or less shovelled them back in a heap and set off on our last two and a half miles.

It may sound too bad to be true but we travelled only another half mile and then BANG ! - lurch - a second puncture. The spare wheel had proved unequal to its tremendous burden. There we were, at nearly one o'clock in the morning of a very frosty night, with six children, in a car that now had only three usable tyres.

Jess looked at me despairingly.

'Perhaps we could find a taxi? We could sort of transfer.'

Sheer horror settled over me even at the mere contemplation of such an operation at that hour. I shrugged.

'Ah, well, if we go very slowly.

And that's how we accomplished those last two miles, at the cost of a ruined tyre.

After that - well, somehow, we weren't altogether surprised to find that the furniture van had never arrived, and we were due for another night on our mattresses. I found some coal and we built up yet another roaring fire. It was, I suppose, well after two o'clock in the morning. We had been on the road more than sixteen hours. No wonder my hands were still trembling from constant vibration! Wearily we sank on to the mattresses and huddled together, ready to sink into blissful sleep.

When we woke up the next morning it was a little like a scene from fairyland. Looking out of the window we saw the whole countryside covered in a thick blanket of white, so that all the neat little fields were covered by one vast sea of snow, and the only breaks in the pattern were leafless branches of trees sticking up forlornly, here and there the thick squat clump of a house. The river which wound along and past an old water mill across the field from our house was a single snaking sheet of glistening ice.

It was in fact several days before we could really take our bearings at Bell House, as our new home was called. It was a beautiful old place, one of those Elizabethan-type houses, which are found a good deal in Kent, with great black beams showing through on the outside walls. Inside there were beams everywhere, too, and the sitting-room was completely panelled in light wood, with a big open fire-place lined in red brick. Our bedroom, in particular, was a lovely room, and adjoining it was a dressing room about eighteen feet long, but only perhaps six feet wide, which made me an excellent snug study.

It was more the sort of house one sees illustrated in *Homes and Gardens* and *Ideal Home* rather than a family home, but two aspects helped to save it from the children's point of view. First, at the top of the house, running the entire floor length, was an enormous attic, with light from five separate dormer windows, which made a kind of dormitory where all the children slept and did just what they liked . . . so there was at least one place where they could escape from ageing parents. Second, the house had about three acres of interesting grounds - a huge front lawn, various subsidiary patches, a grown-over tennis court, a large orchard - and only a minute or two away, the River Stour, with all the fun that offered. In no time at all Martin and Stephen had become keen anglers, and were usually to be found down by the banks of a river which fortunately was not too deep.

Everything about Bell House, Mersham, was solid and gracious, and it stood on the edge of a picturesque patch of countryside, leading to Hythe and Folkestone in one direction, and towards the Ronmey Marshes and Rye and Winchelsea in the other. But having said this, I have said everything creditable that I possibly can about our stay in Kent. If Jess and I had sat down and pored over a map seeking to pick a more opposite place to Cornwall we could not have been more successful than the Ashford area. From a world of rugged and majestic beauty, of lingering mystery, we had passed into the shallow pretty-prettiness of the 'garden of England', without a vestige of any sort of mystery. From the bizarre and eccentric country life of Cornwall, with its pleasing lack of class, we had descended into the very hell of conventionality and snobbishness, a world where the nobility abound and everyone is made to realize the fact. No 'dear golden days' here by any means - who on earth should we share them with! In the pubs everyone looked either suburban and respectable, or aristocratic and snobbish. A man without a tie was an exception, a woman in jeans a rarity - goodness knows what kind of sniggers and leers would have greeted our friends Sven Berlin and Juanita or anyone else who dressed how they wanted, with colour and verve. Why, even the sea - in Cornwall a cascade of green and blue colours - was in Kent reduced to an anonymous, uninteresting dull grey. We walked along the front at Folkestone and Hythe, and even the sands were lost in grey shingle. We went to what we were assured were the 'golden' sands of Greatstones and New Romney and though indeed there were sands, they were lined with mile after mile of the most offensive hotch porch of garish chalets, bungalows and 'houses' I have ever seen. Even a ride with all the children on the famous Ronmey Marsh and Dymchurch Railway - and that *was* fun - was marred by the constant vista of this bungaloid world. Nevertheless my few pleasant memories of Kent are of outings such as a trip on the railway, an afternoon at Dover wandering around the harbour, and one-day visits to Ramsgate, Deal, Whitstable, and Canterbury where there was sufficient momentary interest to pass a single day. Canterbury, indeed, seemed a pleasant town with its definite undercurrent of the past. Alas, we weren't living at Canterbury, but near Ashford - surely one of the most uncolourful towns in England.

No doubt this tirade of hate for Kent is most unreasonable and I am sure that tucked away down its highways and by-ways there are lots of interesting people whom eventually we might have got to know. My point is to make the comparison between Cornwall and Kent. If we had not lived first in Cornwall then perhaps life in Kent might have seemed more reasonable. After all, with its simple extremes between suburbia and 'county', workers and shareholders, it is but typical of the general life in Britain. Cornwall, too, has its quota of these classes but they are neither dominant nor even typical. As our friend Gore Allen once said, Cornish society has achieved a broad equality against that background; in West

Cornwall at least, the easy bohemian life of the artist had been able to flower freely, as it has been able to perhaps nowhere else in Britain, save London.

These differences, which subtly imposed on us all kinds of unwelcome inhibitions, were even symbolized by the two totally different landscapes (not to mention the climates! Kent must undoubtedly be one of the coldest counties in Britain). Perhaps I can best illustrate them by recalling a time, after we had been at Mersham some three months, when Len and Anthony and Donald Swan drove up to pay us a visit. We were all the same people, but in such surroundings much of our old gaiety was strangely subdued; over everything we did there was the dampening mood of Kent. They were only too glad to escape and head back for sunny Cornwall, taking with them an extra passenger in the form of Christiannie, unable to bear the separation from Anthony any longer. We were glad for her sake to see them rejoined, but the departure left us if anything feeling more isolated and depressed than ever.

Indeed Jess and I entered a period of solitariness such as we had possibly not known before. It was not altogether wasted. In Cornwall we had enjoyed going out to meet friends, we had taken a full part in social life. Now there was no one we wanted to see, nothing we wanted to do outside - so we spent the long evenings peacefully at the Bell House, sometimes taking long early evening walks along the river, but mostly sitting at home reading innumerable books and listening to the wireless. At the time it often seemed strange to us that we should sink into this inertia, but looking back now it seems almost as if perhaps we were weighed down by an impending sense of a tragic and personal disaster. What we were living under, had we but known it, was the shadow of May the Eighth.

Every year previously it had been our custom to make a big day of Helston Flora Day, and so this year when Len wrote saying 'How about coming down for Flora Day?' we decided to go. We had by now managed to get a temporary help in and so it was possible to drive down for a long weekend. The Furry Dance took place on the Saturday, so we drove down the day before, having arranged to meet our friends at the 'Sloop', St Ives. I should explain that after that momentous journey up we felt the old taxi had earned honourable retirement and she now stood parked in the garden at Bell House, while we sported the one and only new car we had ever owned, bought out of the proceeds of selling the Old Vicarage - a blue and cream Bedford Dormobile. In this the journey down was a much smoother one, of course, and soon after dusk we drove round the brightly lit harbour of St Ives, delighted to be sniffing Cornish sea air again.

We hadn't long to wait before the arrival of Len and Anthony and Christianne, and two friends of theirs, Betty Francis and Mike Avery. It was pleasant to be all together again, and we exploded into a froth of reminiscent conversation. Len told some amusing anecdotes about Anthony and Christianne's venture into married life. He also told a rather strange story of how every morning he was woken up by a sea-gull rapping on his window-pane with its beak. He had tried every means of frightening it away, but always it came about the same time - tap- tap - tap - tap. I remember being struck by the way Len told this story: although he pretended a little to tell it with a dash of humour, I could sense that somewhere he was disturbed. Indeed he looked rather tired and disconsolate altogether. During the course of the evening Anthony confided in me that they had been rather worried by Len lately, that he had been drinking a lot, and driving very recklessly. We knew that our departure from Cornwall had upset Len a lot in more ways than one, but he was the sort of man who usually went on, who would look forward to new experiences rather than back. Yet there was about him a curious air of defeat and desolation, which is unbearable now to remember.

We finished our evening drinking, and then strolled to our respective cars. It was a new experience for us to have a new car of course, and we rather proudly showed it off. Standing nearby, Len's ricketty old van indeed looked a wreck. Perhaps the comparison riled him for after we had all decided to drive over to Penzance he quickly got into his van and zoomed off. For most of the ten-mile journey we followed behind, but since we could do about twice the speed of a prewar van we finally zoomed past and drove on to the point we had agreed to meet outside Penzance station. After a few minutes Anthony and Christianne drove up and we eyed one another puzzledly, for we knew they had been behind us and Len.

Some instinct worked on us all. We jumped into the Bedford and tore back the two miles towards Long Rock. Just as we came round the railway bend there our worst forebodings were realized. It was like coming upon a film set: dozens of cars were at a standstill, their headlights spotlighting the scene. In the bright fierce light we saw a terrible tangle of cars, wreckage strewn about. In the middle of the road several people were trying to lift the chassis of one car off a badly injured man, whom we realized was Mike Avery, who had travelled with Len... And on the grass verge, head nestling on a woman's lap, unconscious, was Len.

A few minutes later we followed the ambulance back to the West Cornwall Hospital. We were there until two or three in the morning, by which time we had learned that though he had broken an arm and received other injuries, Mike Avery was all right - but that Len's injuries were much more serious. The doctors feared a broken spine.

We went to Betty's house for a few hours rest, and were back at the hospital early in the morning. By now they had sent for a brain specialist. It was all like something out of a novel or a film, a kind of nightmare; only it was happening to Len and to us... At half past twelve we went off and had a cup of tea. Half an hour later we came back. A nurse met us in the corridor and avoided our eyes. Behind her we saw the sister who had been so kind to us the previous evening. She hurried forward, as if somehow wanting to envelop us with her kindly concern. 'Your friend... I'm terribly sorry... He's gone.'

We didn't know what to do. We sat in the Dormobile without speaking. After a while I turned the car round and drove out to Porthleven. We felt we wanted only to be with people who had known and loved Len. Dennis Pattison and his wife Joan had heard about the accident but didn't know Len was dead. When they saw our faces they knew. For the

rest of that afternoon we sat and talked, subdued, unbelieving. After a while I went for a walk along the pebbled sands of Porthleven. I couldn't help remembering the last time we had been there; we had gone bathing, Len the gayest of us all. I stared at the waves sweeping relentlessly over the pebbles. It all seemed so useless, so futile, so unnecessary.

Later that evening we drove back towards Penzance. There was a full moon hanging low over the hilltops. A strangely ominous moon, tinged with blood red. As if by the same instinct, Jess and I felt we couldn't stay any longer. We said goodbye to Anthony and Christianne and the others, and we turned the car and I drove and drove and drove . . . not stopping until we had somehow escaped from that accursed blood-red moon, until we were lost somewhere in the quiet folds of Devon, when we curled up in the back of the Dormobile and tried to sleep. To this day, whenever I see one of those huge and ominous orange moons I am taken back to that terrible day when for so many of us a kind of light went out of our lives.

If we had been depressed in Kent before we were quite desolate now. It was in a way my fault that we were at Ashford at all. Our idea had been to live on the outskirts of London, so that we could attend theatres and concerts and other symbols of the civilized life. By comparison to St Hilary, nearly three hundred miles away, Ashford had seemed very close to London - in fact when we came to live there, we realized it was still fifty-five miles away, a journey which, including a drive through the suburbs of London, takes about two hours. So every time we spent a day in London, we had to start quite early, and if we went to a theatre, there was a tiring two-hour drive back late at night. For this same reason our friends in London were seldom able to come and visit us.

It was not good enough; but then our whole life at Mersham was not good enough. Most of my actions in life are prompted by instinct. So now, instinctively, I sought a way out. We began making trips to London not merely for pleasure, but in order to make the round of the estate agents. By a stroke of luck, we came upon a most bizarre house on the River Thames at Richmond, an old and crumbling place with about twenty-two rooms. The house looked about ready to collapse, and for that reason the lease was going very cheaply at £500. We could hardly believe our luck. There was even a garden leading down to the river. The owner was an eccentric old lady, and she showed us round the house rather guardedly - each time came a confession that there was a lodger in this or that room, a very nice man, perhaps he could stay on. We didn't mind, there were plenty of rooms, we would want to let some anyway.

Suddenly seeing escape in our grasp we took decisive steps. We sold our new Dormobile at a loss of £100, put together all our savings, were ready to pay the whole lease and then, alas, the blow fell. Somehow among all the complicated negotiations between lawyers and estate agents and clients, the deal had been delayed. Someone else wanted the house and somehow, by what means I never knew, although we had paid a deposit, the other person managed to gain the contract.

Now we became quite neurotic. Kent was laying a touch of death on us, we felt. Every time I went to London I had to pass the county crematorium: I began to feel I would never escape its waiting portals. Nor was this foreboding unfounded. Jess was very run down. Now she found she was expecting a baby. It was too great a shock, and she became quite ill. The prospect of having another baby seemed impossible. Fortunately the doctor, too, saw that she was not fit, and after lengthy interviews with a gynaecologist and psychiatrist it was decided that she should be sterilized.

In the meantime we had continued going up to London by train and trudging round the estate agents. Shortly before Jess was to go into hospital for her operation at last we found a possibility in Drayton Gardens, South Kensington. A house not unlike Morrab Place, Penzance, with a garden at the rear. It was very central, and though the lease of thirteen years would cost £1,500, after that the outgoings were very low, about £6 a week, and we could easily let a couple of rooms to cover this.

There began a scramble to raise the required money. We still had most of the Dormobile money, now we scraped every source - an advance on a book, a loan through an Ashford solicitor, another loan from my mother. At the very end, we found we were still needing a sum of about £100, and faced with losing the house otherwise for the one and only time in my life I went to a money-lending firm. In fact they proved quite business-like and straightforward, and it took quite a long time to comprehend that their rate of interest was thirty-three and one-third per cent, per year!

Still, their welcome cheque just balanced the scales, and one February morning the old taxi - which we had resurrected and was chugging along merrily - was once more called into major action. Jess was meantime in hospital recuperating from her operation, but by hook or crook I was determined to extract myself and the six children from this Kentish desolation. And so I did - pressing just a little harder on the accelerator as I drove past the Kent crematorium!

If we wanted to live right in London we were certainly very much so at Drayton Gardens. Suddenly from a world of open fields and trees and distant vistas we were surrounded by houses, double decker buses, taxis, bustling crowds, zebra crossings, and endless streams of traffic. About the time we moved someone decided that Drayton Gardens would make a good alternative route for long distance lorries wishing to cross London from one side to another. Day and night there was never a dull moment, and the entanglements between eight-wheeler lorries going in different directions, as they endeavoured to scrape by the long lines of residents' cars, had to be seen to be believed. The children were delighted. As at Penzance, we had given them rooms at the top of the house, and they used to lean precariously out of their windows watching the ceaseless flow of traffic.

Our end of Drayton Gardens consisted of two slightly dilapidated rows of Georgian fronted houses all owned by some property trust and continually being let out and resold and relet on fairly short leases. It was an interesting road. One end ran into Old Brompton Road and the gentility of South Kensington - but the other end, by the Forum Cinema, came into Fulham Road, and a very different, much seedier world. It was also the beginning of the Chelsea area, beatniks and smart pubs, poets and painters and debutantes. Buses ran at either end for the West End, and South Kensington Tube Station was just down the road. In ten minutes or so we could be in the West End visiting the cinemas or theatres or Soho restaurants and bars; while nearer at hand we had all the culture we could wish for - Victoria and Albert Museum, the Natural History Museum, and the Science Museum.

Cornwall seemed a long way away. Sometimes I would lean out of one of the top windows watching the sun sinking in the western sky, thinking wistfully of the view from Sennen Cove, or the cliffs at Portquin. Our 'country' life now consisted of a trip to Richmond Park, and pleasant as that was it was not quite the real thing. I thought about the big trees swaying in the wind at St Hilary, that old tower standing up on the sky-line - what was happening there now, I wondered? I imagined the boats lined up in Newlyn Harbour, the hum of voices in the 'Ship' at Mouse hole - the wild seas at Land's End, the lonely moors at Zennor - how could I imagine I could escape from all that!

Leaving Cornwall for me was curiously like trying to leave a lover - absence, far from making things easier, merely deepened a sense of loss and sometimes even despair. Jess has often declared that from the moment I left Cornwall I was, like a true Scorpio, working to get back there, and no doubt there is something in that. However, it was certainly not a conscious plan or I should never have so resolutely signed my name to a thirteen-year London house lease.

We certainly settled down to a London life. Martin had by now passed his 11-plus and became a pupil at the Sloane Grammar School, whose headmaster Guy Boas was a famous authority on Shakespearean plays - for Martin, alas, a greater attraction was Stamford Bridge across the way, and Chelsea's blue shirts. Gill was attending an enormous new comprehensive school at Fulham. Jane, Stephen, and Demelza had struck lucky - the L.C.C. school which they joined was on the point of being demolished and all the pupils were transferred to the ultra modern new L.C.C. show school in Old Crompton Road. Artists and architects might argue about its aesthetic qualities, but it was certainly the last word in luxury with bright new equipment, sensible functional desks, everything that could possibly be needed for children. Whenever I read about the latest billion pound government programme on new rockets and warheads, coupled with some further reduction in educational building development, I think of that new school, and the comparison with so many primitive, miserable, shocking buildings which children are forced to use, and I don't know whether to weep or explode with anger. If we really cared about our children the parents of Britain would rise up and demand an end to the futile arms race and the use of the money so carelessly squandered to build new schools, new hospitals, and generally to further the health and welfare of our nation. And, while on the subject of children, if anyone were to raise the hoary old stories about East is East and West is West and never the twain shall meet, or talk about the irrevocable difference between black skins and white, I should like to have taken them along with me each morning as I took our youngest child, Genevieve, to the big L.C.C. nursery at Cheyne Walk, overlooking the River Thames. Here, as one entered the 3-year-olds' section, a little piccaninny girl would be playing chase-me with a couple of cockney children - over there two delightful Malayan 'yellow' skins would be romping with some 'white' skins - in another corner a Chinese child, a Mexican and two Scottish children were engrossed in some other game. Truly it is the children who should inherit the earth: they alone show wisdom.

We were glad, for our own sakes as well as hers, that Genevieve was also at school all day, for it meant at long last that Jess and I were free to get on with our own work. In all our travels Jess had stuck to her electric kiln and wheel: now we set up a basement room as a pottery studio. We still sent supplies to a number of shops in Cornwall and now I found one or two local shops in Chelsea and Kensington that gave us fresh orders. For myself I had made a small but cosy office on the ground floor, with a window looking out on the long narrow garden, dominated by an old swing. Here I found I could work just as effectively as in Cornwall. Not only did I not need a view for writing, I can even get along without privacy. I can write in a room with children coming to and fro, with music blaring and other distractions: indeed I have produced some of my best work writing both in such conditions and against a time limit (and more than once while ill). There is nothing particularly creditable about this. I was brought up as a reporter on a busy evening newspaper, working in a room shared with twelve other reporters all hammering away on their typewriters at the same time conducting flippant conversations out of the sides of their mouths and occasionally barking into phones that never stopped ringing.

For some time past I had taken to writing articles about pottery making for the do-it-yourself kind of magazine. It seemed to Jess and me that although there were quite a number of books about the art and craft of pottery they were all a little too technical and theoretical for an absolute beginner who wished to equip himself or herself for making pottery at home. Above all there was literally no book at all which combined between its pages not only instructional advice but practical information on how to go about starting a home pottery, and, especially, where to obtain the necessary materials. We decided to write the sort of book which we hoped would fulfil this need, and in due course it was published. It was called *The Pottery Book*, and in it we dealt with the art and craft of pottery, outlined training schemes that are available, gave the names of equipment makers and pottery societies and pottery books, supplied detailed practical advice on equipping a spare room as a pottery and explained how to start a small pottery. Profusely illustrated with photographs, including an excellent sequence of the act of throwing a pot, the book went very well, and even now has a steady sale. It brought us many letters especially from housewives who felt their lives to be rather empty and wished to take up some creative pastime. Some time later Jess appeared on the B.B.C. Television programme 'Mainly for Women', demonstrating the art of throwing and describing how to start a home pottery - and once again we were very interested in the number of letters received. Undoubtedly all over the country there is a hunger in people to be using their talents creatively. There are some pundits in the pottery world who frown on such temerity and sneer at amateur potters; but surely this holier than thou attitude is in itself a damning self-indictment. There is room in the world for the amateur as well as the professional. As I have said earlier in this book, I always prefer the professional exponents. But that neither gives me the right, nor would I wish, to censor the creative urgings of a single human being. The more people seek, however crudely, to fashion a pot or paint a picture, the fewer people, in the end, will wish to use their hands to manufacture bullets or engage in other purely destructive work.

One of the pleasures of being back in London was that I was able to resume many of my old contacts in the writing world. By a coincidence the headquarters of the Society of Authors was in our own road, Drayton Gardens, while the P.E.N. Club centre was not far away at Glebe House, Chelsea, the lovely old Queen Anne house left to the Society by the novelist Henrietta Leslie. At Glebe there is a beautiful reception room with a grape vine growing out of the middle of the floor, and here regular social gatherings are held, usually with a talk or debate, followed by a glass of sherry and a general discussion. Now we resumed the habit of attending these, if only for the friendly get-together afterwards. As it happened we had returned at a very appropriate time. Each year the International P.E.N. holds a great world-wide congress in a different world capital: this year it was London's turn. A whole week had been set aside for a packed programme of event, and Jess and I decided to treat ourselves to a holiday.

It was a curiously stimulating experience. From the moment we arrived at the Tate Gallery for the glittering opening reception, when some two thousand authors and their wives and friends gathered together in spacious rooms hung with famous paintings, a note of gracious enjoyment was struck. The next seven days we wined and dined as never before. Luncheon at the Guildhall, cocktails at the Royal Festival Hall, sherry at the Mansion House, not to mention innumerable private gatherings. One of the most pleasant of these was a cocktail party given by Cecil Woodham-Smith, a dignified white-haired old lady well known for her penetrating biography *Florence Nightingale*. This was held at a stately home somewhere off Sloane Square, and the door was opened to us by a butler-steward extraordinary who spent a great deal of time plying us all with bottle after bottle of champagne. I can remember comparing notes on our Welsh ancestry with Dilys Powell, and an interesting conversation with Alec Waugh, but the rest is a beautiful haze, broken only by the contrast of finally getting home to find waiting us a pile of bills and a summons!

In fact the pointed contrast between our private poverty and this public luxury seemed emphasized during that week. Once again we were very hard up and I had been reduced to selling books and gramophone records. There were also, of course, the pawnshops of Kings Road, into which my evening dress was due to go the moment the Congress was over...Sometimes during that week we hardly had enough money to get ourselves to and from the various Congress events, yet this very craziness of the situation seemed to impart an extra gaiety to our enjoyment. Many of the authors attending were, of course, very wealthy indeed, and we used to notice their expensive suits and luxurious cars with a certain awe: yet I am sure no one enjoyed themselves any more than we did.

In this we were encouraged by encountering an old friend, Dannie Abse, who like ourselves was in his thirties and therefore young by comparison to most of the delegates. With Dannie we shared quite a light-hearted approach to the congress, observing delightedly some of the inevitable feuding and jockeying for influential positions that went on. Like Jess Dannie comes from Cardiff, where his brother Leo is now an M.P., so we formed a strong Welsh contingent. As far as possible we attended the same receptions, so that if things became too dull we were always able to have each other's company. Throughout the week working debates were held at a Regents Park College. I remember many fascinating talks on the writer's craft by L. P. Hartley, Rosamond Lehmann, Cecil Roberts, John Lehmann, Cecil Day Lewis, and many overseas visitors. The international element was of course, the *raison d'etre* of the Congress, and we made many welcome contacts with writers of other countries, finding - as painters, musicians, and other artists find in their spheres - that true internationalism always exists in a shared art or craft. This atmosphere of international friendship reached a triumphant conclusion at the final banquet held at the Savoy Hotel. I should imagine almost every English author of any note was present there that night to hear speeches by J. B. Priestley, Angus Wilson, the late Charles Morgan, and Andre Chamson. Altogether it was a grand occasion which we were glad not to have missed.

The next morning - back to realities. I was still writing regular items for the B.B.C. and a number of magazines; now, with access to good libraries, I began writing a number of historical articles for the London *Evening News,* as well as some talks for the B.B.C. overseas service. But always the free-lance writer is dogged by this cursed uncertainty and irregularity about payment. Often our daily bacon was literally saved by delivering a small pottery order to a shop in Chelsea, or failing that by collecting rent from two small rooms we let out. Once again, living in a large house, we were driven to think about letting further rooms. Now we decided to let off the basement rooms as a self-contained flat - and so embarked on a series of somewhat amusing additions to the household. These ranged from a lugubrious Hungarian refugee who slept all day and played his guitar to his friends all through the night, to a most odd Australian writer who continually button-holed me for my opinion of Proust or Joyce, who paid the children as much as 15s to clean his room out, and who finally departed in a frantic rush to catch the boat train to France as if pursued by fifty devils. At last we let the flat off to Guido Morris and his wife Jane, whom we had known in Cornwall, and with Jane and several small children around as well as our own, the family house settled into even more of a family atmosphere.

Somewhere about this time we resumed contact with Norman Levine, and his wife Margaret, who had been married originally from the Old Vicarage at St Hilary Church. Like me. Norman was finding a writer's life a hard and upsetting one, especially with a growing family to support. We used to discuss ways and means of improving our lot. One day we hit on the idea of bringing out a publication which would consist of nothing but book reviews. At that time papers were not very generous in the space they gave to reviewing books, and we figured that there might be a demand for a magazine which did. We also reckoned that the magazine should finance itself - indeed we should be able to distribute it free - because we should be able to capitalize by selling off review copies of books sent to us. This of course is a perfectly normal procedure, though the public may not know much about it. There exists a number of firms in London which do nothing but buy review copies from reviewers, for later sale to libraries. Prices vary, but it should be possible to obtain 50 per cent of the published price. Thus we reckoned for every £1 book we would raise 10s and in this way we hoped that we would be able to bring out a useful magazine which would pay for itself and leave us perhaps £10 a week each. Alas, it never quite worked out like that. We duly wrote off letters to some three hundred publishers explaining our plans, and soon the books began to come in. But not fast enough. There were neither as many as we had hoped for, nor was the range of publishers as embracing as was really necessary. Hopefully Norman and I went ahead writing our reviews. I think we had about fifty books each, and wrote individual reviews of them all, many of them requiring much effort and work. But the supply of books only dribbled in, spasmodically, and finally we were drawn to the conclusion that though we had hit on a good idea, we lacked the resources really to put it over. To honour our promise we brought out a single issue of *Review,* as we called our paper, and distributed it as planned. But in that very first issue we had to announce that it was also the last!

It was all, at least, experience. One of the interesting sidelights was the revelation of the traffic in selling review copies. At one shop which bought review copies, regularly every Friday a taxi would draw up and out would step the literary editor of a national newspaper - to begin unloading over a hundred books, on which he might collect £50 or so. We heard of many similar cases. As I say it is all quite legal, and I am all for writers capitalizing as much as they can; but it often seems that publishers must waste an awful lot of copies of their books. I am sure I could make a better job of the publicity side than giving away about a hundred copies, of which perhaps only twenty will actually be reviewed.

Sometimes in London Jess would put pressure on me to 'take a job'. Authors who have worked on their own for twenty years are more or less incapacitated for gainful employment under someone else, but now and then I would make an heroic effort - usually in some subterranean way managing neatly to deflect the eventual offer so that I didn't take or didn't get offered the job. I always remember one occasion when, reflecting that even Sydney Graham spent a year in such a job, I applied for a well-paid position with a firm of advertising agents. Their offices were in Red Lion Square, and as I approached I remember my footsteps automatically slowed up - indeed I walked up and down several times before finally entering. The director I saw was most charming, but he must have summed me up in an instant. 'Now look here, old fellow, just tell me frankly - do you really want to spend the rest of your life writing advertisements,' How could I possibly answer, 'Yes'

Mind you, I am probably more adaptable, at least to editorial work, than most authors. I have done a great deal of editing of one kind and another, from writing the material to seeing it through the printers, and there is probably a job in this line which would suit me and which I could do well. But in general even this work can be done on a freelance basis. The longer we were in London, and the more it became evident that I was earning money in much the same way as I did in Cornwall - i.e. through the post - the more I, at least, began to wonder why on earth we were not living away from all the smoke and smog and bustle and hustle. So, although on the surface life went on fairly normally, and Jess and I pursued a pleasant enough social life, somewhere the old Scorpio was indeed at work, moving inch by inch westwards.

At first I persuaded myself that this restlessness was of a general rather than a specific kind, and indeed for a period I think we quite genuinely believed we had found a possible alternative to the old call back to Cornwall. This was what might be called our 'boat' period. I have always been fascinated by the idea of having a boat of my own, and of embarking on a voyage all round the world. After all, this is quite a practical proposition for a writer. Unfortunately I am a very unpractical person, and in my heart feared that I should be most incompetent in charge of such a voyage. At the same time, just as at the age of 40 I first learned to swim, so I kept telling myself that there was no reason why I shouldn't learn how to handle a boat. And indeed, with Jess's active encouragement, I enrolled us both in L.C.C. navigation classes and for the whole of one winter we drove out once a week to Greenwich, there to learn the intricacies of fixing a course. Accompanied by a mixed bag of clerks and office workers we sat and dreamed of world cruises while, with what in real life would be the most fatal mistakes, we plotted our way from Dover to Calais and Southampton to Le Havre.

Meantime, impatient for some more dynamic action, we hit on the idea that perhaps we might actually buy a large boat and live aboard. Once the idea was implanted in my romantic soul it took deep root. Soon our home became littered with boating magazines. I wasn't interested so much in the articles, as in the pages of advertisements at the back about sloops and yawls and cruisers and motor yachts. Because the sort of boat we wanted would have to be pretty roomy to accommodate a family of eight, so too the prices were alarming - nothing much under £1,000, and many running up to £3,000. We would be met at a harbour by a natty little gentleman in a peaked cap and ferried out to some gleaming white yacht, and duly shown over its luxurious quarters, while all the time our bank balance stood at about £2.10s. Yet this was not exactly false pretences - throughout our life I have found that when we definitely want something then somehow we spin into action and produce results. I knew that if we were to find just the right proposition, we would be prepared to sell our lease and raise money in every way possible.

Once or twice, too, it seemed that we had literally found our dreamboat. Once was up near Brightlingsea, where we went to view a 75-foot converted Thames barge belonging to a director of the big electrical firm, G.E.C. Perhaps because of this fact that boat was equipped to the teeth electrically - there was an electrical laundry, sliding doors that revealed wireless sets and radiogram, not to mention superb rangefinding equipment. But what impressed us was the roominess. There were five or six separate cabins, as big as normal rooms, as well as a wonderful huge lounge with its own fire-place. Down below was like being in a luxury mansion - yet on deck there was the sea air, and a couple of 200 h.p. engines to start purposeful movement. The price, alas, was £3,500, and we couldn't have raised this, though hopefully we made a much smaller offer.

On another occasion we spent a week-end with Sven and Juanita, now living in the New Forest, so that we could view two possibilities - one a luxury yacht at Lymington that had just returned from a Mediterranean voyage, the other a converted Dutch barge at Hamble. The latter, with its gypsy look, appealed to us most, and we hesitated a long time about this one, especially as the price was more reasonable at £1,500. I think we might even have taken the vital step if I had not received an urgent and anxious ten-page letter from our friend Donald Swan, who had worked in the Navy and in cargo ships, and who was, rightly no doubt, absolutely horrified at the idea of my being 'let loose' on the sea in sole charge of seven other lives. His advice was an angry No, No, NO! Morally he was right, perhaps, but I have often wondered since if perhaps we should have (not literally!) taken the plunge. Ah well, there is still time. At least we are now nearer to the sea than ever before.

As some compensation, perhaps, we enjoyed two very pleasant holidays on the River Thames. On one occasion we rented a bungalow on an island at Henley, with the use of two boats and a punt. However this only, so to speak, whetted our appetite, and on our next holiday we forsook the land altogether, renting a 35-foot motor cabin cruiser for an epic journey from Thames Ditton up to Goring, on the River Thames. This experience might have been less un-nerving were it not for the presence of

Genevieve, still a very small child. The other children were self-propelling and could look after themselves, but each time we approached a lock my attention would be diverted by a wild scream from Jess:

'Genevieve - she's going overboard!'

The first time this happened I whirled round, let go the gear and just in time grabbed Genevieve by her knees as she was about to topple over.

The boat, with a reverberating crash, hit the lock door and bounced back. Within a few seconds the water seeping out of the lock had swung our boat round so that she lay exactly across the entrance, causing what I suppose on the roads would be called a hold-up.

At this stage I became aware of a benevolent, brown-faced weather-beaten man in a blue uniform bending over the edge of the lock. As I cowered in fear before the expected wrath, he spoke gently, as to a child, and gave me a few simple instructions about how to use a boat-hook to push the boat round, and then how to tie her up to wait until the lock opened, and so on, ad *infinitum*. Like all the lockkeepers - twenty-three I think there were in all - we encountered during our journey, this one was almost excessively tolerant of behaviour which must have seemed to him bordering on lunacy. As we progressed, and I rammed lock after lock, or at the least got our bow stuck between the white posts that were all that stopped us being swept over a weir, I found that it was never the patient lock-keepers, but rather sniggering groups of children and holiday makers who rubbed salt into the wounds of our hurt pride.

'The fleet's in port!', they would chortle. Or, 'Three cheers for the Admiral!'

And when, as sometimes happened, we ran aground through going too close to the bank, they lined up in rows to watch sardonically while Jess and I and the older children heaved and pushed and rocked the boat in our efforts to get free.

Somehow repetition of these experiences bred in us a sort of hardening, so that we even ceased to feel humiliation. But nothing overcame my allergy to locks. From the moment we sighted one to the moment of nosing our way out, probably knocking some innocent waiting boat into the bank en route, my knees were jelly, my heart in my mouth. I could never overcome my lost feeling without a brake to apply. As we glided into the lock my one thought was somehow to lasso one of the bollards (mooring posts to you) with one of the innumerable ropes lying around our decks. As I also had to stay at the wheel, this entailed my shouting wild, peremptory instructions to Martin, already jumpy because he has inherited my expect-the-worst nature, and to Gill - less jumpy, but easily wounded by imputations of inefficiency.

'Throw the ropes! Quick! Jump - jump ashore. Oh you fatheads ...!'

So the stream of invective flowed from the petty tyrant that these terrible locks had made me. After three locks Gill would no longer speak to me. After I had replaced her with her mother, one more lock sufficed for a quick marital exchange of views which resulted in Martin and I having to manage the locks for the remainder of the trip.

So we meandered up the river, through lock after lock. No sooner were we free of the tentacles of one than something in the very air warned me of the impending horror of another. Penton Hook, Bell Weir, Old Windsor, Romney, Temple, Hambledon, Boulter's, Sonning, Mapledurham - they often had delightful names, matching their pretty gardens and romantic surroundings. For Jess and the other children, reclining lazily on the cabin roofs, they represented part of a pageant of quiet English beauty . . . but for Martin and me they represented minor nightmares, filled with bollards and warps, ropes and fend-offs, sudden alarming ascents or descents which invariably found the boat floating out into the middle, necessitating one or other of us making a wild, quite dangerous leap from the shore on to the boat.

And then there was always Genevieve. By some demonic instinct, she indulged in the full flower of wickedness at locktimes. If she was in the cabin, her blonde head would be thrust out of a port-hole, thus to be in immediate danger of being crushed against the lock walls. If put in the cockpit, within seconds (yes, I timed her) she would have climbed over the side to get into the water. And if taken on the cabin roof...

The wonder of it is that I survived at all. What's more, though but dimly, I seem to recollect moments of pleasure between locks, of course. The green beauty of meadows at Cookham, the rich old world charm of Marlow Church, the faint thrill of coming up the Henley Regatta course after passing the incredibly still and lovely Medenham Abbey...yes and a night moored by Hambledon Lock, and taking the children for that strange single-file walk over the bridge that crosses the wild, frothing weir.

Yes there was a lot to be said for boats, and I wondered why we had never explored their possibilities when living in Cornwall. Well, at least, perhaps we could find our way back there again! That spring I managed to engineer a fortnight's family holiday at St Ives, where we rented a house overlooking the harbour, and wallowed in all the old familiarity of early sunshine and lovely blue seas and seeing lots of old friends. When it came to driving back to London I think I wasn't the only one who felt regretful. Encouraged by this resumption of old links, I rented a cottage near Ludgvan for the whole of August, and we spent that month back in familiar haunts.

But we weren't back in Cornwall yet. There was a long, hard winter in London, with ice and snow and fog and smog, when for days we hardly went out of the house. Christmastime itself is always lively in London, with all the decorations and bright lights, and the children enjoyed that. But Christmas Day and Boxing Day we spent fairly quietly, and we couldn't help remembering those great gatherings at the old Vicarage. It was at times like these that Jess also felt most drawn to those past days. I think it must have been at such a time that finally we made our great decision - we would aim at a return to Cornwall. My reasons were simple and uncomplicated: I just desperately wanted to get back into an atmosphere where I felt much more at home, where I genuinely felt that children would be happier and healthier. But I knew that Jess would like some better justification, so I pointed out that if we could sell the lease of the house in Drayton Gardens that would give us a nice lump sum in hand to put down on a house in Cornwall as well as get straight with our financial affairs.

Unfortunately, things did not work out quite so simply. We advertised our house without expecting much difficulty in selling it, and indeed we had a stream of prospective purchasers, but somehow, one by one, they fell out. My memory of this period is a little dimmed because after helping to nurse Jess through an illness I suddenly went down with virus pneumonia for the first, though alas not last time in my life. Virus pneumonia has a rather shattering effect: one is simply laid low and cannot get up or get about or do anything except lie weakly in bed. Worse still, the convalescent period lasts weeks and weeks and weeks. So now Jess, herself hardly recovered, had to run the house and look after an invalid, and at the same time show round prospective house purchasers. On top of all this, my sudden incapacity to work at all meant our income abruptly came to an end. This is one of those crises that free-lance workers inevitably have to face. So bad were things, indeed, that for the second time in my life I had to apply for assistance from that very good friend to authors in distress, the Royal Literary Fund. I know very little about the constitution of this body but I am personally acquainted with quite a number of young writers with families who have literally been saved from absolute destitution by a timely grant of financial aid from the R.L.F. Its work is carried on fairly discreetly, but in my opinion, and on practical experience, it does a really helpful job.

Thanks to the Royal Literary Fund, and then my gradual recovery, we survived this difficult period, but we were still faced with the problem of selling our London house. It seemed for the moment that we just could not sell it, and so we fell back on the alternative idea - to let it out in rooms and thus once again achieve our dream of having a regular income. It seemed a practical enough arrangement, and so on the strength of it we advertised in the St Ives paper to try to rent a cottage there, the idea being to get back down and take our time about finding a new home. I accumulated a list of five possible houses, and travelled down overnight to spend a day visiting them all - returning to London tired but triumphant to tell Jess and the family that I had rented a place for us and that we were due to move down in the following October. Suddenly everything was a tremendous rush. We advertised rooms, converted the top into a flat, interviewed prospective tenants, drew up agreements - at last as September drew to a close we began to gather together our things. For once I did not mind the autumn nights drawing in. Never mind - soon we should be back in a part of the world where autumn meant sunshine and clear skies and blue seas, not smog and diesel fumes.

In the last week of September we had a round of saying goodbye to our friends - all of whom, I noticed, significantly, seemed to envy us very much for our move -and completed arrangements for letting off 21, Drayton Gardens. At last came the time to load up the Bedford Van which we were now running. Finally, nearly three long years after our unhappy departure, we were once more bound westward - the prodigals returning at long last to their favourite land.

Chapter Ten

THE SEA'S IN THE KITCHEN

From the moment we drove down the long slope into St Ives and saw again that wonderful vista, the tiny dolls' houses clustering around the harbour with the green hump of the island behind and beyond the blue sweep of the sea, I think we felt very conscious that we had come to our journey's end. In all our journeyings about Cornwall it was always to St Ives that we had come back repeatedly, as if for sustenance. Now there was an enormous relief to be back, to be able to give way at long last to a sense of really belonging somewhere.

But of course two adults and six children can't just walk into a permanent home like that - least of all in St Ives, where property is scarcer and prices higher than almost anywhere else in Cornwall. To give us a base to work from I had taken a furnished cottage with the somewhat romantic address, Virgin Street, and though the winter rent was cheap enough the conditions were appallingly cramped for a large family: the entire area of the cottage would not have taken more than half our drawing room at St Hilary. As it was we were all sharing bedrooms, and eating and sitting in one small living-room, so that the winter was something of a strain. To add to this, in the middle of one night I awoke to hear Demelza screaming and after shouting to her several times to go to sleep I got out of bed to find the house full of smoke - thick, billowing, choking smoke. When I opened the door to try to go downstairs I had to shut it again to keep out a blast of hot air and flames. The house was on fire! - and it had no rear windows or entrances at all. I called the children down into the front bedroom, and then clambered out of the window and managed to drop down to the street outside, at the same time yelling out 'Fire Fire!' Soon the people around us were astir, and while with another man I opened the front door and went in and threw buckets of water on the flames in the living-room (clothes drying over a fire had dropped down and caught alight) Jess handed the children out of the window one by one, to be rushed off and wrapped up and given cups of tea by kindly neighbours. In the end the fire-brigade came, and we extinguished the flames: but had it not been for little Demelza's worried cry in the night . . . who knows?

As a place to work in Jess and I had managed to rent a condemned cottage in Back Road West. It consisted simply of one room down and one room up. We converted the bottom room into a pottery work shop and showroom, and the top into an office for myself. It was a quaint corner cottage, approached by a flight of stone steps, and when we hung a wrought iron sign outside, made by our friend Jack Richards, the whole effect was rather striking - at least I suppose so, for during that summer we had hundreds of holiday-makers coming up to take a look round. This was our first experience of direct contact with customers and we viewed it with mixed feelings. On the one hand, especially early in the summer, there were many most interesting callers, intelligent and cultured people, who appreciated the art and craft of pottery, many of them from abroad. On the other hand, especially in August, there were floods of people who not only had no feeling for pottery but seemed incapable of knowing the difference between a hand-made article and a manufactured one (and in pottery there is quite a difference). The only time when the two kinds of visitors might be said to have a common meeting point was when Jess sat throwing at her electric wheel. Then everyone just stood and watched, with open-mouthed astonishment, this living revelation of a craft that is nearly as old as mankind itself. It is at moments like this that I become more and more convinced that it is the artist and craftsman, rather than the politician, who may lead the world to its salvation. Art knows no barriers, whether national or racial - artists are unified by their common simple purpose, a search for truth, for revelation. They are, or will be, the true priests of our new world - unless, of course they are obliterated by the cock-a-hoop scientists.

After a tedious winter spent in Virgin Street we moved to a small cottage near the Wharf, and still we had not been able to find a permanent home. It was not for want of trying. By now I was haunting the estate agents, and we were continually inspecting potential houses. In such a mood we were nibbling at every conceivable bait. Converted landing craft at Lelant, old cottages out in the wilds of Trencrom, ex-Army huts on the Lizard - anything, anything in the world other than small rented cottages. Fortunately, none of these scatter-brained ideas came to anything.

And then we took our walk along Porthmeor Beach. St Ives has several beaches, but of them all Porthmeor is the wildest and most beautiful, the least spoiled - oh, without doubt the most romantic. It is also one of the few beaches (I imagine anywhere) where the houses are literally on the beach, so that the sea comes surging right up to their back walls. It was along the soft sands of this beach, one spring afternoon, that Jess and I took a walk - if not weighed down with cares, at least feeling pretty worried. Should we buy somewhere out in the wilds. Should we commit ourselves to the adequate but somehow unattractive house in the back roads! We must do something, we couldn't go on living in other people's dolls' houses at huge holiday rents. Our capital was draining, we would have to borrow heavily anyway to buy anywhere. What should we do?

'Ah,' said Jess dreamily. 'I know where I'd *like* to live where I've always wanted to live. There!'

We were at that moment just passing the glass doorway of the only house with a door which actually opened directly on to Porthmeor Beach. In days gone by the sands had risen up and completely covered that door, but at last the council had put bulldozers at work and cleared away some of the mounds. Now you could walk off the sands straight through those glass doorways. At least you could have done if the doors had not been firmly bolted and shuttered, almost forbiddingly so.

We climbed on the single step which separated sand from door and peered in between the rows of shutters. Everything inside looked long and empty and unused; here and there a chair or table standing with a strangely unwanted, forlorn look. But it had not always been so.

'Do you remember!' said Jess softly. 'What would it be, ten years ago?'

At least that. We had been in St Ives then on our own, enjoying a break from tiny demanding children (though not so many of them then). Many things about St Ives had been different then, and one of them had been that these glass doors stood wide open and you were invited inside to enjoy Cornish Cream Teas. Inside the impression was of an endless shadowy cavern, for the room extended indefinitely on and on (its actual measurement was, and is, some 65 feet). About halfway down the room was an enormous oak side table that literally groaned under the weight of good things - plates of homemade scones, fruit cakes, short-cake biscuits, bowls of fresh fruit, jars of blackberry jam, slabs of cheese, pickles, onions, a hunk of ham, and a large shallow bowl of Cornish cream. All this, and heaven too, was offered *ad* lib - you were invited to help yourself to a second helping - for a mere 2s. 6d. a head. Little wonder that the restaurant was usually crowded: but there was more to it than that.

The proprietors were an elderly couple with kind hearts, and much too easy-going a disposition, who were intuitively sympathetic to the artists of St Ives. One of their failings - or triumphs depending how you look upon things - was a tendency to give some of the poorer artists regular free meals. In theory this should have been covered by the revenue from normal holiday-makers, but somehow, owing to the proprietors' unfortunate habit of buying cream and other luxuries at retail prices from cash-conscious Cornish farmers, this revenue was never as expected. Life there was always gay and amusing, with intellectual arguments in the kitchen until three in the morning, and people went off to the four corners of the earth vowing they would recommend all their friends to come and stay - yet somehow, things never went right financially. In the end, long after we had returned to London, we heard that the business had packed up, and the house was for sale. At the time we had exchanged knowing, perhaps wistful glances, but there was then nothing we could have done and eventually, we heard, the house was auctioned off. But often since, in our secret hearts, I think, when we thought about St Ives, we really thought of the St Ives which that house represented, doors opening on to a sandy beach. Atlantic waves on your doorstep, a world of sunshine and sand and waves, and of artists at work, of a curious escape perhaps from reality - perhaps to reality.

Now we stood peering in at a lot of ghostly memories.

'It doesn't seem occupied', said Jess.

I stepped back and looked upwards, spying curtains.

'Oh, I think it is you know.'

We stepped back and looked about us, a little sadly. We knew that the house extended back a long way, and that the front entrance was in a road leading round to the sea. Of course it must be occupied, and no doubt was busily functioning as a guest house or something.

I looked at jess, and then shrugged.

'Come on, let's be on our way.'

We tramped along the sands, and then walked up the slope that turned into Porthmeor Road. It was not really on our route to go along Porthmeor Road, but suddenly Jess spoke.

'There's no harm in just knocking at the door. You could ask.'

'Ask what?'

'Ask if the house is for sale, of course.'

As in the best story books, miraculously, it was. It would be tedious, and perhaps unwise, to go into the full ramifications of how we raised the money to buy St Christophers, a process involving mothers, banks, solicitors, building societies and, in the end, even friends and acquaintances. The general reaction was disbelief, suspicion, scepticism. Building societies all clung stubbornly to a conviction that anyone buying a house with eight bedrooms must be going into the guesthouse trade: in vain we pointed out that we had six children and would be glad of the rooms. Banks on the other hand were impressed by the house, but less by our income and earning possibilities. Mothers and friends, bless them, shared a little more of our own woolly and unfounded optimism. Solicitors threw a cold light of reality upon the whole confusion of proceedings - sometimes too much, so that the whole deal seemed off. But in the end, though we could never feel really quite sure who owned the house, indubitably we were in possession.

The first day, like Army commanders planning a campaign, we allocated the troops. Martin and Gill, as the two elder children, were given the two largest bedrooms; Stephen and Jane received the two medium sized rooms, and Demelza and Genevieve were, rather forcibly, ushered into one medium room.

'But the others have got rooms of their own!'

'I want a room of my own I'm not going to sleep with Melza!'

'I don't want to sleep with Genny!'

There is a simple answer to this sort of fruitless argument. A bunk bed. The bunk bed we obtained was ex-Army type, probably rather uncomfortable, but it completely took Demelza's and Genny's minds off their bone of contention. For the next hour or two they climbed and jumped happily about their bunk bed, while we continued our dispositions.

Here perhaps a word or two about the layout of St Christophers. It is an unusual sort of house, not attractive so much in itself or its shape, but for its position. Its front stands innocuously enough on a corner of

Porthmeor Road, an ordinary gable type of front such as many suburban houses have. From that end the onlooker might simply see a house with two front rooms on either side of the glass front door, and three bedrooms above. But once entered, the house begins its surprises. The entrance room has a door at the far end which, when opened, reveals a vista of unending corridor, flanked with doors of innumerable rooms and meeting at the end with a door which, when opened, fills with light - for here is our own sitting-room looking right out upon the beach. Then again, turning right on entering, there is a short flight of stairs leading downstairs - and once again the long endless stretch leading to the light and the sea. On this floor, too, only turning away from the sea, is a very large kitchen, so large that to this day it has defeated all efforts to make shape and sense of its odd proportions. It is indeed a kitchen with something of a history, as I shall now relate.

We were asleep when Martin called. It was, after all, about six o'clock in the morning. What he was doing up at that time I can't imagine: in the ensuing circumstances of the time it didn't seem to matter very much. Martin has a straightforward approach to disaster. Whereas Stephen, with a macabre twist of mind, likes to dwell on all kinds of hypothetical and horrible happenings: 'Fancy, if Demelza was run over by a steam-roller, who would bring me my breakfast?'- Martin simply gets his pleasure out of announcing hard, stark, fearful facts.

'Dad,' called out Martin's clear, crystal-clear, voice, suitably inflected with foreboding. 'You'd better come. The sea's in the kitchen.'

'Mmmmmn? ' I said.

Beside me, Jess stirred angrily.

'For goodness sake tell him to shut up.'

'Yes', I said. 'Do be quiet, that's a good boy. I can't think - '

'DAD!' shouted Martin through the keyhole, like a foghorn. 'Come quickly - it's everywhere!'

It was, too. In the kitchen, in the sitting-room, in the café one long endless sea of it, about six inches deep and for all we knew gathering depth every moment. Carpets were covered, books were awash, furniture was tilting, debris was accumulating everywhere. I stood half way down the stairs, still half asleep, staring upon this sudden transformation of a scene which I had left the previous evening all spick and span and tidy. I could hardly believe my eyes: when I saw Martin and Stephen in Wellington boots, carrying buckets and heading for the sea door, I had to.

'Jess!' I called weakly, unable to shoulder the burden alone. 'You'll have to come - *the sea is in the kitchen.'*

It took us two or three hours to deal with the crisis. Fortunately the tide, in the meantime, took a turn, as one might say, for the better. With the receding of pressure we were able to begin sweeping unwanted water, in long organized waves across kitchen, sitting-room, and café floor and out of the door on to the wet sands outside. The children all enjoyed it, joining in with the sort of will one would have welcomed on other less

exciting occasions, such as washing up after dinner for eight. Martin took charge, uttering the orders, 'One, two, three - push! One, two three - push!' - upon which Stephen, Gill, Jane, Demelza, and little Genevieve, armed with a variety of instruments from brushes to dust-bin lids, bent down and literally pushed the water on its way. There were deviations, of course, Stephen persuaded Demelza that there were strange fishes to be seen swimming around the fire-place, and when she bent down to see for herself, gave her a gentle but decisive push in. When he tried to do the same to Genevieve, Gill leaned across and clouted him. Thus was the jungle law preserved.

But in general the children were far too interested in this unusual and rather bizarre situation. So were Jess and I, though in a less happy-go-lucky way. We were worried less about the sea, as what would be left when the sea had departed. We had reason to be: the carpets were heavy and sodden with sea water . . . we were to waste several days trying to dry them off before outside advice, and the evidence of our noses, told us that this was not the right way to go about things.

'What you want to do', said old Mr Ward, the carpenter from up the road, 'is to wash them down in fresh water - takes away the salt, you see.'

So then we had to get bucket loads of fresh water and carry them from the kitchen to the yard where we had hung up the now dry carpets and make them wet all over again - but really, that is another story.

We weren't insured, of course: we'd only been in the house a few days and hadn't got around to it. Still, it was some comfort later to find out that no insurance company would cover us against sea damage.

'I mean to say, would you?' said the insurance agent, leaning out of the back door and watching the Atlantic waves pounding up the beach. 'Would you, now?'

'Hey, come in', I said hastily. 'Let's bolt the doors quickly. We don't want the sea in again. I've just washed those damn carpets.'

It was impossible not to know that St Christophers had been a guest-house, even though our purposes were more private. Every room was painted in the standardized and horrible chocolate brown and cream so beloved of conservative boarding-house keepers. Every room had its standard little wash basin, its standard little built-in cupboard, its standard little lamp sockets. No doubt before the furnishings had gone, each had its standard little bed and its standard neat carpet. There even lingered about the rooms a curious aroma of past lettings, a sense of anonymous humanity, so that it was easy to close one's eyes and visualize the scenes.

But we were lucky. This was our home at last. We could make of it what we wished. And one of the first things we could do was to wash away the sad taint of these past days, to strip down the walls, to give a new coat of paint - to bring colour and life to a somewhat dowdy interior. We began work on the day we first moved in and with the aid of several good friends, achieved something of a transformation within a week. We stripped off wallpapers, painted walls white to give more light, did the woodwork in blackboard paint, hung up a few paintings we possessed - in the children's rooms some of their own efforts - and generally gave the place a new brightness.

Next we tried to sort out the living arrangements. Sharing small cottages with six children had merely enhanced our conviction that they needed a sitting room - and so did we and never the twain shall meet, or so we hoped. We had our room, a small but lovely sitting-room looking over the sea but what about the children? For how long could they be left below, running up and down the 65-foot-long rooms, or worse, riding bicycles over the lovely wood floor? At one time indeed there seemed a danger of their taking over the whole of the lower floor. But we had to think of our own plans. Yet the children must have a general playroom. In the end we compromised, calling upon old Mr Ward, who with mystifying skill took a few sheets of hardboard and built a folding partition across the middle of the long room - one half making a room for the children - the other, seaward half; remaining intriguingly empty, to await our further plans.

In their room the children had an old-fashioned suite which we picked up in a sale for £2, a green cord carpet which would have seemed enormous anywhere else, but was rather lost in a room which still measured over thirty feet long, and a very long kitchen table with a renovated plywood top. Not a lot to go on, perhaps . . . but . . . enough. On the second day, we found the covers off the couch and pinned on by tin tacks around the edges of the table.

'Big Chief Running Water's Tent', said Demelza. Demelza is the Wild Western of our family. Where other children catch fish or go swimming or ride bikes, she becomes a Red Indian chasing or chased by cowboys. Sometimes she is also a cowboy, or maybe a Red Indian cowboy; but at all events she wears a holster, sometimes a feathered cap, and twiddles toy guns around her hands. As a pacifist and a supporter of nuclear disarmament I disapprove of all this, but so far have been unable to explain things satisfactorily to Demelza. There are many good reasons, one would imagine, why a girl of 9 should not rush around brandishing a tomahawk and yelling out bloodcurdling threats - more reasons, for instance than even against a boy doing such things. But Demelza will remain unaffected by all arguments. Temporarily bereft of her hatchet or Colt, she will adopt another favourite role, old time boxer, raising her bony little hands and banding them furiously. 'Come on now, do you want to box? Shall I box you?' Since the inevitable follow on to this is a flurry of windmill-like blows, all delivered with ferocity and force, I invariably take the coward's way of retreat: comforting myself with memories of Demelza crying out harrowingly at night because of some suspected shadowy movement, and clinging to me with her tiny trembling body.

To break up the monotony of thirty feet of walls on either side of the children's rooms, Donald Swan kindly presented an enormous canvas, after the style of an old master, depicting the patron St Christopher standing naked in the water bearing a baby to safety on his shoulder. For

some reason this painting with its faintly religious aspect had a curiously depressing effect on the company. Then one day Gill got to work with some crayons, and though the result was scandalous and even a little salacious, it introduced a welcome touch of good humour: after that we grew quite fond of the picture and it hung in a position of honour. The fact that Stephen and friends sometimes used it for darts practice was, I strove to believe, in a way another mark of respect.

The piano came a little later. I was at a furniture sale in Penzance and could not help noticing the pianos - there were in all six of them. Five did not even fetch a bid. The sixth and last one I could not resist, and it became mine for 5s.; it was of course one of the old upright ones, but in quite reasonable condition. I went round to the nearest furniture remover and inquired the cost of transporting it nearly ten miles to St Ives. 'Three pounds', he said. As there was no alternative, we arranged the deal. A day or two later we had to remove a large window pane and do some work with a hacksaw in order to get the piano into the children's room. Naturally, as is the way with these things, it was many months before we put back the window pane, and for some time the room was icy cold, until Martin thought of filling the space with an old suitcase. In the meantime the piano was installed, and a succession of small children, including most of our neighbours', took turns at trailing up and down with one, or maybe two fingers. We thought this was the most horrible sound we had heard, until later on Gill, who has a faintly musical ear, picked out a complete tune, *Who's Sorry Now*, and played it over and over and over again. Fortunately after a period as part of a Red Indian ambush place, the piano suddenly went out of favour - only recovering its interest when Jane and some friends turned it into a shop counter, collecting all manner of objects which were stored inside the piano's innards.

A television set and an old gramophone completed the furnishing of the children's room, and no doubt provided them with much amusement. But nothing could compare with their favourite game - which was to slip into the farther end of what had once been the long room, open two glass doorways on to the beach, and then take high speed running long jumps out on to the sand. This was a game which attracted quite an enormous amount of both enthusiasm and followers. The latter, children of neighbours from all directions, accumulated into such numbers that often teams would be formed, and whole afternoons devoted to the famous St Christopher Long jump. One of the great attractions, of course, was the element of the unknown: you could never be sure what unexpected hazard lay waiting outside. It might be a large Alsatian dog, a deckchair, an old lady with a parasol, several small children - or even, via Martin's sense of humour, a large hole dug in the sand and covered lightly with cardboard and sand. I was too old a hand to get caught by this one, but Jess one day practically disappeared down such a hole, and for some time afterwards could be seen grimly chasing Martin up and down the beach.

This particular beach game became much more popular, and twice as dangerous and exciting, later in the year when, following complaints by residents of the rising sand, the local council employed a bulldozer to clear away huge mounds. As a result our door was no longer level with the sand but some five or six feet *above* sand level. This would have necessitated urgent structural work had it not been that, much to our surprise, we discovered that there already existed a set of wooden steps. Evidently at some previous time the sands had been low, and these wooden steps which had been put in place had stayed there ever since. Now, having been buried in damp sand for some years, they were in a state of general rottenness, but they served for the moment, and we were able to concentrate on the new version of our game - jumping and clearing the steps. This was really quite simple: the new excitement was that now, in addition to its being a long jump, it was also like the coming-down part of a high jump. You took off and soared through the air, and then down and down *and* down. I don't know how long the game might have gone on had it not been for the unfortunate day when three of the children chose to jump at the same time and landed in the middle of a serene picnic party of old ladies in wide-brimmed straw hats. None of them were seriously injured, but their subsequent legal claims convinced me that it was time to put an end to this particular fun and games, and I began applying restrictive practices, like fines.

What really finished things, however, was the disappearance of our steps. I have already indicated that our house stands on the very edge of the sea, and sometimes even succumbs to its entry. Many other times, however, the sea is frustrated, and its huge waves pound in angry impotence against the stony foundations, splashing spray all over the glass doors, and even the windows above. It is on occasions like this that the sea, like any other bully who is thwarted, attempts to take it out of something else - in this instance, the weak link, our old wooden steps.

First the sea cunningly washed away huge mounds of sand, so that suddenly one day, descending the steps, I was aghast to find them ending with space between the bottom spar and the sand. This meant that they were simply hanging on by their top attachment to the floor of the house. The next tide soon put an end to that. We watched out of the top window, unable to do anything, as one huge wave after another crashed against the steps, tugging them this way and that. Even so we did not really believe nature would win the battle. Later, we went to bed, though perhaps we slept uneasily. In the morning, a local fisherman called round. 'Them your steps on the rocks?' Them were, alas, smashed to smithereens.

The effect of this, as I was saying, was to put a stop to the jumping game - not because any of the intrepid children were afraid to jump into space, but because they were all too lazy to make the long walk back to the front door, since with no steps it was impossible to come in the back way. In due course our old friend Arthur Slater, one of the Lamorna woodchoppers, made us another pair of steps - but by then, fortunately, the children had other interests.

Besides, we too had our plans. Already we were like some double-edged industrial automaton, myself tapping away daily at the typewriter, Jess in the next room grimly throwing pots - slaves to the eternal quest for money and more money with which to feed and clothe and keep our growing children. Sometimes it is quite frightening to pause, and then to realize that we dare not pause, that everything about our large family life is geared up to a level where for us there is no prospect but work, work, and more work. It is bad enough for me at the typewriter, continually having to concoct new ideas for articles and books over and above those that I genuinely want to write (I don't want to imply that writers do not sometimes benefit from the crack-of-the-whip of a commission - but sometimes they like to pause a while). But it is worse for Jess, whose work is so essentially physical. However, now we had plans for adding a third string to our output - we would continue the beach café at St Christophers, serving ice creams and tea trays, and soft drinks, that sort of thing.

During the winter we cleared out the long room, and with the help of Mr Ward, our old carpenter friend, installed a smart modern snack bar, with urns and cookers and ice cream machines neatly laid out behind. We draped lengths of old fishing nets up and down the walls and over the ceiling and installed subdued lighting. A few visits to sales soon procured dozens of tables and chairs, and we spent long hours painting these all a simple bright red. Next came the ordering of cutlery and china plates, though Jess herself would be able to provide her own pottery coffee mugs and jugs.

We had no experience of running even a beach café, but it seemed simple enough, and in the long run so it was. As I was tied up with my own work and keeping an eye on the pottery showroom in the summer, and Jess herself would be fairly busy with pottery, she decided to take in a partner on the working side of the café. I am all against partnerships myself, from bitter experience, but at least Julian brought a lot of gaiety and amusement into our lives, along with a certain chaos. He was a flamboyant good-looking young man who would walk around St Ives in the evenings wearing a bright red cloak and a carnation in his lapel, usually with his curly fair hair tinted a light blue or green. In a town formidable for its level of gossiping Julian was more than capable of holding his own - indeed he had a talent for embroidering and embellishing which personally I found rather amusing. This is such a dull and dreary world of ours that we should welcome and applaud those who have courage enough to stand out and carve a niche of their own, however bizarre.

Julian was staying at Trewyn, a large and gracious old manor house in the centre of St Ives, belonging to another friend of ours, John Milne, a sculptor. Most of our friends in St Ives tend to be artists of one kind and another. This might seem natural enough, since I am a writer and Jess is a potter. But in St Ives the situation is somewhat complicated. Every summer art students from London flock down, taking part-time jobs as waiters in cafés and thronging into the 'Sloop' and the 'Castle' at every opportunity. The result, at least in the summer, is a surfeit of painters so that the general public, not surprisingly, develops a certain antagonism to the rows of beatniks lining the harbour walls in the afternoon sunshine. It is perhaps indeed a pity that so many beatniks and art students and would-be artists crowd into one small town, but do not think we should be too hasty in dismissing them. In this day and age of mass production and conveyor belts, atomic arms race and metropolitan rat races, what is unworthy about a desire to flee from it all to a place like St Ives, where there is not only the beautiful scenery and brilliant lights, but also the atmosphere well known to be sympathetic to the artist Which person is going to contribute most to the human good - the non-thinking semi-automaton of a man or woman who daily knocks rivets into a warship or equips a bomber aircraft or, dutifully wearing his radiation-proof mask, works on some terrible nuclear weapon - or a young, still idealistic (unwashed if you like) beatnik who merely wants to sing a song or write a poem or paint a picture? I know whose side I am on, and the more I learn of the criminal actions and values of our so-called statesmen the less surprised am I to meet yet another pathetic escaper to the comparative peace of Cornwall. Of course it is no escape really: the bell tolls for us all and we cannot help hearing its mournful, warning peals. But at least if we attempt in our lives to be creative rather than negative, we are surely one step nearer salvation.

Living now in close contact with the artists of St Ives I returned to a task which I had begun during my *Cornish Review* days, namely the writing of a short history of the art movement in Cornwall. I do not mean an art criticism, for I am not a painter and have no wish to enter the already overcrowded field of art reviewing, with all its petty feuds. What has always fascinated me has been the physical effect of Cornwall upon artists, and this has seemed to manifest itself most clearly in the case of painters and sculptors. There is also the subsidiary interest of the development of such a continental thing as an art colony, here in Britain. Accordingly I now began collecting material for a book which was eventually published, lavishly illustrated with photographs and reproductions, under the title of *Britain's Art Colony by the Sea*. In the book I tried to portray the gradual growth of the art colonies of West Cornwall over about seventy or eighty years, and at the same time to describe the different schools of painting culminating in the one now on the ascendant, the modernist abstract movement as represented by Barbara Hepworth, Ben Nicholson, Peter Lanyon, Bryan Wynter, Johnny Wells and others. No such record existed previously and I think that the book must provide a very useful introduction to any newcomer to the area. Some day, though, I should like to forget about art colonies and simply analyse the mysterious relationship between the artist at work in Cornwall, and the land and sea around him, covering not only painters, but poets and novelists, musicians and craftsmen, and so on.

Writing my book brought me closer into contact again with many old friends among the artists as well as new ones and imperceptibly we ourselves merged into the social life of the St Ives art colony. I have touched on this earlier in this book, but I would repeat that although it can be beset by personal feuds and head-hunting ceremonies, there can be a unity and familiarity which can be very sustaining and stimulating. There are many lively discussions in pubs, numerous gay parties in studios or out at remote cottages, frequent amusing gatherings such as the annual fancy dress arts balls. Morally I do not think the life of St Ives is any better or worse than in other parts of the county: wives occasionally leave husbands or vice versa, someone has an affair, someone runs off - but this happens all over the country. And as I have repeatedly said, in what I consider the important sense of the word 'moral', St Ives is a more moral centre than many other places. Most members of what are called the art colony have thought enough about life to take a stand, to try to follow a conscious way of life, that of the artist. This means, in most cases (not all, I agree) that there is a basic feeling for human values. It is, I think, no accident that artists are at the forefront of such movements as the Campaign for Nuclear Disarmament, the Abolition of Hanging, and various international friendship schemes. In many ways the artist is often the world's conscience, if only because he cannot help himself, and this must have its effect in personal relationships, which, though they may seem to outside eyes eccentric, are usually guided by honesty and integrity.

As that year drew near its close Jess and Julian fell out over a variety of café organizational problems, and since then we have found it simpler to run the café on our own. But before the inevitable crisis there was a summer -indeed that summer, 1959 - that was gay and almost idyllic. With the café steps leading right on to Porthmeor Beach, which is easily the nicest and least spoiled of St Ives beaches, the café soon became a centre for all our friends, apart from the hundreds of holidaymakers. As one sunny afternoon followed another, so the queues formed for ice creams and beach trays, and often we were forced to call extra helps. Sometimes

Gill and Jane performed very efficiently behind the ice cream counter, but the trouble with children and a café is that supplies mysteriously diminish. We have long ago come to the conclusion that with six children in the same house as unlocked supplies of sweets and ice creams and other delectables, a certain percentage must be allocated for 'Losses'.

What was pleasant about the café was that, owing to its unusual situation, it was impossible to pretend all was work and no play. There were always slack periods, or times when a friend would take over, and then Julian and Jess and the children and I would slip on our bathing costumes and run down to the waiting waves. 'Waiting' is hardly the adjective to describe the average Porthmeor sea. Our beach faces north, and consequently takes the full force of various north or northeast winds, while there are several fast and powerful currents. As a result at almost any time of the day or night there are long powerful waves surging over the vast flat sands.

And this brings me, quite naturally, to surfing. In our household surfing has become what perhaps watching football matches or following the dogs or collecting stamps is to another. That wonderful golden summer, we all became surf-happy. As it happened part of the café trade was hiring out surf-boards, so we could usually find a board (for Stephen we even had a smaller board made). Thus armed we would stride out into the frothing seas - to embark on one of the world's most delightful and exhilarating pastimes. I find it difficult to describe the art of surfing in words. It is, I sometimes think, almost a mystical experience - indeed more than once, on an early summer evening at Porthmeor with the tide coming in in vast long rollers, I have found myself with several other surfers, strangers perhaps, and caught us glancing at each other with a kind of wonder in our eyes as we picked ourselves up after soaring in like birds in flight. Perhaps flight in the form of gliding, or maybe skiing - perhaps these are the nearest analogies. It is impossible really to teach surfing, it is just a question of practice, practice, practice. At first you may flounder and splash and even temporarily be bowled over, but don't despair. Always try to catch a wave just before it breaks so that you are swept in triumphantly on the crest of its journey. To do this judge approximately at what point the wave is likely to break, position yourself there, holding the slim surf-board in front of you with the bottom end tucked into the pit of your stomach and your hands at full stretch, gripping the top ends of the curve. Wait until the wave is almost on you and about to break - then fling yourself forward.

It is, I suppose, a little like loving - or indeed living. And if I had to search for ten years for a more fitting image to symbolize the theme of this book I do not think there can be a better or more appropriate one with which to describe our family existence. Our life has been rather like an eternal surfing - an endless launching ourselves into the unknown in the hope that we will be carried onwards towards the shore. Experience may have taught us that perhaps that shore may never quite be reached, but it has at the same time made us more proficient in the craft itself. We have learned the value of several sources of revenue, however fluctuating:

when the writing fails, there is perhaps the pottery, when the pottery is out of demand, there is suddenly the summer beach café, and so on. It all makes life a complicated and chaotic affair. If you can perhaps imagine the following things all happening at once under one (admittedly long) roof: a pottery furnace glowing, wheel spinning, typewriter tapping, café heater booming and clanking, four radios blaring, dogs barking, cats miaowing, old cats spluttering, hamsters gone broody, unexpected visitors, phone ringing, and children, children, everywhere (some not even our own) - then you have some idea of the daily situation here at St Christophers. It is a situation that must often seem to outsiders complete chaos and almost unbearable, and of course often it is. It seems an eternity since I sat in my little room in a self-contained solitary castle at Portquin, peacefully brooding . . . . But then there is, as always in life, the reverse side to the coin; when Jess and I look out of a window and see our sun-tanned children running happily into the sea, or watch their bright-eyed faces sitting around one of the eight birthday teas of the year, or perhaps turn and survey them, in bewildered amazement, all squashed into the back of a very old car. . . That sort of thing, I suppose, can almost compensate for the traumatic moment with which I may as well end this memory of a restless decade:

'Dad, you'd better come! The sea's in the kitchen!'

Bonus Material

Steve Newman on Denys Val Baker

from an article first published in 'The Boards'

"When our family settled in St Christopher's, a long rambling house overlooking the Atlantic rollers at Porthmeor beach, St Ives, I was under no delusions about the difficulties ahead. The trouble with a freelance writer's life is that it's rather like being on a perpetual roundabout: one moment a story has been sold or a book taken by a publisher and there's money in the bank, the next moment there are bills everywhere and no money and a bank manager breathing down your neck. My output as a writer could be reasonably prolific, but it was doubtful if even a story a day would keep all the potential debtors away... No, there was only one thing for it: as had proved to be the case in our previous homes in Cornwall, Kent, and London, we should have to develop a second and perhaps third string to our bow - and pretty quickly too..."

The above is the opening of Denys Val Baker's, *The Door is Always Open*, first published in 1963, which is a sequel to his first piece of family autobiography, *The Sea's in the Kitchen*. Both volumes were best sellers and were followed by a further twenty-four titles that not only followed the growth, and the often hilarious antics, of the Val Baker family as they grew up in one Cornish dwelling or another, but also followed them on idyllic, and often scary and downright dangerous, adventures in their sixty foot ex-Admiralty Motor Fishing Vessel, *Sanu*. There didn't seem to be too many dull moments in the Val Baker households, whether on land, crossing the Bay of Biscay, or heading up the Seine to Paris.

Denys may have described himself modestly as being 'reasonably prolific' when in fact he was hugely prolific with, apart from the aforementioned twenty-six volumes of autobiography, fourteen novels, twenty-three collections of short stories, eighteen non-fiction titles. He also edited forty-one literary collections that included stories by Fay Weldon, Hammond Innes, Alan Sillitoe, and Edna O'Brien, plus numerous anthologies of ghost stories and stories of the supernatural. He has written hundreds of newspaper and magazine articles; and if that wasn't enough founded, edited, and published, the prestigious literary and arts magazine, *The Cornish Review*, that often featured the work of such eminent Cornish writers as D.M.Thomas, Jack Clemo, Charles Causley, and W.S.Graham, amongst many others.

And in such books as *A View From Land's End* and *Britain's Art Colony by the Sea,* Denys Val Baker also chronicled the lives and works of many Cornish writers and artists whose reputations and work may, at best, have fallen into neglect, or at worst, disappeared altogether. It is impossible today to write about the Cornish literary and artistic landscape, and its huge legacy, without referring to Val Baker's work. It is also obvious, even to the casual reader, that Denys Val Baker was, and still is, a literary giant.

As Martin points out in his introduction, both of Denys' parents were Welsh, from the North Wales seaside town of Llanfairfechan. Denys Baker was born on the 24th of October 1917 in Yorkshire. His father, Captain Valentine Henry Baker, M.C, D.F.C, was stationed at RAF Cramlington, close to the town of Poppleton, just a few miles from York, where his wife, Dilys Eames (the daughter of a prominent Llanfairfechan family), was living and where Denys was born.

Captain Baker, known as 'Bake', had been invalided out of the army after being wounded at Gallipoli in March 1915, and as Tim Scott writes in his biography, *The Cornish World of Denys Val Baker,* Valentine Baker:

...volunteered for military service again, and in the Spring of 1916 was posted to the school of Aero Flying at Reading for a training course. A few months later he graduated and joined the famous 41 Squadron of the Royal Flying Corps.

Bake's impressive reputation as a flyer, not unnaturally, led the authorities to decide that he would make an ideal instructor for training new pilots. From the summer of 1917 to the end of the war, Bake turned out many good flyers. During this period he was promoted to Flight Commander and later, Captain.

What Tim Scott doesn't mention (although 'impressive reputation' hints at it) is that Baker, before becoming an instructor, also saw a longish period of active service with the RFC in France and is reputed to have shot down between fifteen and twenty enemy aircraft. He earned his Military Cross for low level strafing attacks on German troops and artillery positions, an extremely dangerous occupation for the relatively slow aircraft of the time. So dangerous in fact that all of Baker's comrades in 41 Squadron were either killed or badly wounded. Baker's last year with the RAF (1920-21) was spent in the Secret Codes Department at the Air Ministry.

Back in civvy street Bake earned his living as a flying instructor, teaching such illustrious pupils as the Duke of Windsor, the Duke of Kent, and Amy Johnson. For a time he worked for Vickers-Armstrong before becoming the chief pilot for Airwork Ltd at Heston.

In 1934 he founded, with his friend James Martin, and third partner, Francis Francis, the Martin Baker Aircraft Co Ltd which immediately began to develop what became the prototype for the MB3 fighter, a versatile and elegant aircraft that could easily have seen service had Valentine Baker not been tragically killed during a test flight of the aircraft in September 1942. Whether as a direct result of Baker's death or not the company went on to develop and manufacture the life saving ejector seat.

During the late 1920s, as his father was teaching royalty to fly, Denys was firmly ensconced in a boarding school in Sussex. But when let out for the summer headed back to North Wales to spend family holidays in Llanfairfechan. And it was during one holiday that he had an encounter with an elderly spinster, a Miss Jenkins, as Tim Scott describes, who...

...lived alone in a huge granite house. Regarded as rather odd and consequently left alone, Denys befriended her when one day he helped her home after the old motorcycle she rode had broken down, and was invited to call for tea. He found, although she lived a private life, Miss Jenkins was not 'odd' as the locals made out and he visited her on several occasions.

He later wrote; 'I suppose Miss Jenkins' loneliness must have touched a chord deep in me, without my knowing...' Denys was fascinated by the rambling old house, and one day remarked to her that he would like to live in a big house on his own. To his surprise Miss Jenkins' face went almost dark with anger, she stamped her foot several times, and her black eyes glowered.

"Child," she said, " You must never, never talk like that again. Because when you grow up," and her voice softened suddenly, " When you grow up, my dear, I want you to fall in love, to marry, to know what it is to have a real home, children of your own, a whole fulfilled life..."

Which is of course precisely what he set out to do on a personal level, but at the same time always remembering the deep melancholy that seems to have surrounded Miss Jenkins (who comes across as a latter day version of Miss Havisham, albeit with rather more anger and spirit) that is repeated often, at varying levels, in Denys' fiction, almost like the background wash an artist might add to a canvas.

After leaving school Denys knew he wanted to be a writer, any sort of writer, and with the help of his father, who fortunately knew the executive head of Northcliffe Newspapers (then as now one of the biggest publishers of regional newspapers) he managed to get a job as a junior reporter with the *Derby Evening Telegraph,* where he worked for two years before moving to London to join the *Advertiser's Weekly* which, because of its less demanding regime than the *Telegraph,* gave him more time to write freelance articles for a variety of journals and magazines and develop his fiction writing skills. During this time he also set up Methodical Publications Ltd which, before going bust, published three self-help titles on how to make money.

Although enduring almost daily bombing raids the London publishing industry of the early 1940s was undeterred, inventive, and varied, and Denys soon moved from the *Advertisr's Weekly* to become the managing editor of *Shelf Appeal,* a much respected but short lived literary weekly. When that publication folded a few months after Denys took over (probably due to paper and cash shortages and not any lack of ability on Denys' part) he also received a welcome letter, and an even more welcome cheque for five guineas, telling him his short story, 'Wedding Anniversary', had been accepted by the long established *Weldon's Ladies Journal* (the first British magazine to be published exclusively for women in the 19th century), which gave away free dress-making patterns with every copy and was, undoubtedly, a hugely influential publication for the aspiring writer of 'romantic' fiction in those war torn days.

During the late 1930s Denys had become increasingly distant from his father and, perhaps in part because of his father's experiences in the First World War, and his cutting edge involvement in the creation of fighter aircraft, coupled with Denys' own deeply held pacifist beliefs, he took the very brave step of registering as a Conscientious Objector as soon as war was declared in 1939.

After the publication of that short story Denys also decided he was going to try and make it as a freelance writer and editor, and as some kind of homage,Denys, after his father's death, started using the name Denys Val Baker; although recent research has discovered that Denys' middle name was indeed Valentine.

Denys made his first trip to Cornwall in 1941 after reading an advertisement in the *New Statesman* about a self help community that had been set up in Tintagel. And being the incurable romantic he was Denys travelled down to Cornwall only to find himself "…cooped up in a tiny cottage with a half mad professor of music and an extremely eccentric wife, both of them in their seventies…the whole set-up was like something out of a novel." And although he hurried back to London to get out of the clutches of the mad professor and his wife Cornwall had cast its spell.

And it was at this time, and probably as a result of Denys' pacifism, and the eccentric people with whom his son was consorting, that Valentine Baker stopped communicating with Denys entirely and cut him out of his will. But, as Tim Scott recalls, "…Denys always believed a reconciliation was possible, [although] this was sadly not to be, for in September 1942 news came that his father had been killed." Although Denys and his father may have become estranged it has to be said that Denys was Always rather proud of Valentine's racy lifestyle.

Denys worked with various pacifist groups in London helping victims of the blitz, and it was during this time and while he was living in a vegetarian-based community Youth House in Camden that he met and fell in love with Patricia Johnson, a young woman who shared his socialist and pacifist principles. They married in May 1942 and spent their honeymoon in Cornwall - not far from Bude on the rugged north coast of Cornwall - in a cottage belonging to the theatre producer and writer, Ronald Duncan, now perhaps best remembered as the librettist for the

1948 Broadway production of *The Rape of Lucretia,* and his production of *Don Juan* at the Royal Court in the mid 1950s.

It was around this time that Denys also started his own literary magazine, *Opus,* which had a statement of intent that reads more like that of a political party than a literary magazine (but then why shouldn't it?):

The policy of Opus *is to emphasis the importance of the individual, to fight for freedom of thought and expression, to propagate the philosophies of brotherhood and universal understanding - and to provide a platform for the encouragement of those ideals.*

Which is not a bad set of ideals. *Opus* later changed its name to *Voices* and published some of the earliest writings of W.S.Graham, Wolf Mankowitz, and Henry Treece.

After their marriage Pat and Denys moved out of war torn London to the much quieter town of Tring in Hertfordshire.

Apart from running his own magazine Denys also took on the editorship of several other literary publications such as *Writing Today, Modern Short Stories,* and *International Short Stories* that included work by such writers as Dylan Thomas, Elizabeth Taylor, Anais Nin, and Pamela Hansford Johnson. He was also the first editor to publish the work of the American novelist Henry Miller in Britain.

1944 saw the publication of Denys' first collection of short stories, *Selected Stories* (and the birth, in August, of his son Martin), followed in the autumn of 1945 by his first novel, *The White Rock,* which is set in North Wales and uses many of Denys' own childhood experiences. He received an advance of £350 for the book, which wasn't bad for a first novel in 1945.

But that Cornish spell that had been cast over him just a few years earlier was working its magic and in 1945, after reading yet another advertisement in the *New Statesman* (edited in those days by Kingsley Martin) for a furnished house, which, as Denys writes in his 1976 book, *A View from the Valley,* was...

...to let near Land's End and on spec took the house for six months - it turned out to be Carn Voel, the Porthcurno home of Bertrand Russell's second wife Dora, a rather bleak place with long views down to the sea around the Runnelstone and Porthgwarra.

Here for the very first time I got to know all those marvellous walks along the cliffs to Treen and Lamorna, to St Levan and Land's end...

My holiday at Carn Voel undoubtedly gave me an unquenchable thirst for Cornwall. Many times after that, back in London, I would go along to Paddington and spend some time there watching the bustling crowds boarding the trains with the magic name 'The Cornish Riviera'. How I used to envy those travellers. Ah, well, one day...

In the end the beginnings of my permanent Cornish life were due once more to an advertisement which caught my eye in the New Statesman. *It was an appeal to help with starting a repertory theatre in South Cornwall. Just at that time*

[1948] *my first marriage had collapsed and my life was at a standstill, and so this seemed like a sudden direction. I wrote off enthusiastically and got a letter back from Victor Thompson, founder of the Studio Theatre, Camborne, saying that I was welcome to come and join them in their venture. This consisted of a group of young actors and actresses and other enthusiasts who had taken over the lease of a former grocery shop, and were turning it into a modern little theatre. Had I known my Cornwall better I would have sensed at once that Camborne is hardly the most obvious site for a studio then - but then it's all experience!*

Although Denys enjoyed his stay in Camborne he soon set off in his Austin Seven for Cornish pastures new and eventually parked his tiny car in Falmouth where he joined a professional theatre company, The Avon Players, which had the fiacial support of the newly established Arts Council of Britain. Denys was quickly allocated a publicity job that took him all over the district...

...but now everything was on rather a grander scale. Many well known local people had given the theatre their support: Howard Spring, the novelist, was our chairman, for instance, and he and his wife used to entertain the cast to sumptuous tea parties in the lovely grounds of their beautiful home, The White Cottage. One way and another our social life was very pleasant. We soon adopted a little pub nor far from the theatre where many lunchtime sessions were held. At first I found the brittle theatre talk, peppered with 'darlings' a little unnerving, but I found I got used to it all.

By his own account the break up of Val Baker's first marriage had been quite amicable, with their son, Martin, spending holidays with his mother, and term-time with his father. So, as a consequence of this agreement, father and son set off for Cornwall and a rented cottage (found for them by the potter Bernard Leach) on Trencrom Hill, high above St Ives.

But it would be in 1949, after meeting and marrying his second wife, Jess Margaret Bryan (who, by the mid 1950s was an extremely talented and respected potter, and later a psychologist), and returning with her and Martin to that cottage above St Ives that Denys Val Baker began to publish the *Cornish Review* and establish a literary reputation second to none.

Throughout the 1950s Denys wrote a couple of hundred short stories, many of which were broadcast by the BBC (stories that consolidated his position as a master of the craft), several novels, God knows how many magazine and newspaper articles, and at least five non-fiction titles.

And then in 1962 came the first of the autobiographical volumes (now re-published by Humdrumming), the aforementioned *The Sea's in the Kitchen,* followed in 1963, by *The Door is Always Open.* I seriously believe these two volumes changed popular English literature forever, effectively creating a new genre that only H.E.Bates had hinted at in his fictional/semi-autobiographical Uncle Silas and Pop Larkin series. But what Denys Val Baker was able to do that was different was use his keen novelist's eye, his inbuilt sense of humour, and his particular writing skills - skills that came out of the lushness of D.H. Lawrence and the tantalising yet solid structure of Somerset Maugham - to make them utterly unique and now, twenty odd years after the last one, remarkable social documents not only of a large family growing up, but of a nation coming to terms with ever changing political and social values.

Let me leave you with this quote from his 1981 family saga, *A Family at Sea*, that introduces another member of the family, their boat, *Sanu*...

From the moment, with the help of a professional boat deliverer, Geoff Scott, we brought Sanu *safely down from Southampton to her permanent berth at Falmouth our whole way of life changed. (I don't know whether to say radically or alarmingly!) For Jess and myself there was a new kind of overhanging worry, a niggling anxiety. Is she all right? Will the chain hold? Did we shut off the sea cock? What about the Calor gas? Are all the portholes closed?*

Denys Val Baker died in the summer of 1984.

Steve Newman
Senior Editor, Humdrumming

Other Denys Val Baker Titles

NOVELS

The White Rock	Sylvan Press, 1945
The More We Are Together	Sampson Low, 1947
The Widening Mirror	Sampson Low, 1949
A Journey With Love	Bridgehead USA, 1955
The Titles My Own (as David Eames)	Bless, 1955
The Faces Of Love (no 4 revised)	1967.
As The River Flows	Milton House, 1974
Company Of Three	Milton House, 1974
Don't Lose Your Cool Dad	Milton House, 1975
Barbican's End	William Kimber, 1979
Rose	William Kimber, 1980
Karenza	William Kimber, 1980
One Summer at St Merry	William Kimber, 1980
Frances	William Kimber, 1980

SHORT STORY COLLECTIONS

Selected Stories	Staples and Staples, 1944
Worlds Without End	Sylvan Press, 1945
The Return Of Uncle Walter	Sampson Low, 1949
Strange Fulfillment	Pyramid Books USA, 1959
The Flame Swallower	J. L. Lake, 1963
The Strange and the Damned	Pyramid, 1964
Bizarre Loves	Belmont Books USA, 1964
Strange Possession	Pyramid, 1965
Strange Journeys	Pyramid, 1966
The Face in the Mirror	Arkham House USA, 1971.
Woman & the Engine Driver	UnitedWriters, 1972
A Summer to Remember	William Kimber, 1975
Echoes from Cornish Cliffs	Kimber, 1976

The Secret Place	William Kimber, 1977
Passenger to Penzance	William Kimber, 1978
At the Seas Edge	William Kimber, 1979
The House on the Creek	William Kimber, 1981
Thomasinas Island	William Kimber, 1981
The Girl in the Photograph	William Kimber, 1982
Martin's Cottage	William Kimber, 1983
At the Rainbow's End	William Kimber, 1983
A Work of Art	William Kimber, 1984
The Tenant	William Kimber, 1985

EDITED BOOKS

Preludes (Poetry Anthology)	Opus Press, 1942
Little Reviews 1914-43	P.E.N. Books, 1943
Little Reviews Anthologies	Allen & Unwin
(1943, 44, 45, 46, 47/48 and 49)	
International Short Stories:	W.H. Allen, 1944.
Writing Today	Staples & Staples, 1943-46
Modern Short Stories	Staples & Staples, 1943,44
Selected Stories	Staples & Staples, 1944
Voyage	Sylvan Press, 1945
Writers of Today	Sidgewick & Jackson, 1946
Writers of Today	Sidgewick & Jackson, 1948
Modern British Writing	Vanguard (N.Y.), 1947
One and All (Cornish Stories)	Museum Press, 1951
London Aphrodite	Bridgehead USA, 1955
The Moods of Love	New English Library, 1960
The Tastes of Love	New English Library, 1966
The Ways of Love	New English Library, 1969
The Dreams of Love	New English Library, 1969
Haunted Cornwall	William Kimber, 1973
Cornish Short Stories	Penguin, 1973
Cornish Harvest	William Kimber, 1974
Stories of The Sea	William Kimber, 1974
Stories of Country Life	William Kimber, 1975
Stories of the Night	William Kimber, 1976
Stories of the Macabre	William Kimber, 1976
My Favourite Story	William Kimber, 1977
Stories of Horror and Suspense	William Kimber, 1977
Personal Choice	William Kimber, 1977
Stories of The Occult	William Kimber, 1978
TWELVE: Women's Writing	W.H. Allen, 1978
Love is for Lovers (as D. Valentine)	William Kimber, 1978
Women's Writing 2	W.H. Allen, 1979
Stories of the Supernatural	William Kimber, 1979
The Sea Survivors	W.H. Allen, 1979
Stories of Fear	William Kimber, 1980

Women's Writing	Sidgewick & Jackson, 1980
Cornish Ghost Stories	William Kimber, 1980
Ghosts in Country House	William Kimber, 1981
When Churchyards Yawn	William Kimber, 1982
Stories of Haunted Inns	William Kimber, 1982
Ghosts in Country Villages	William Kimber, 1983
Phantom Lovers	William Kimber, 1984
Haunted Travelers	William Kimber, 1985

AUTOBIOGRAPHIES

The Sea's in the Kitchen	Phoenix House, 1962
	Humdrumming, 2006
The Door is Always Open	Phoenix House, 1963
	Humdrumming, 2006
We'll Go Round the World Tomorrow	1965
To Sea with Sanu	John Baker, 1967
Adventures Before Fifty	John Baker, 1969
Life Up The Creek	John Baker, 1971
The Petrified Mariner	William Kimber 1972
An Old Mill by the Stream	William Kimber 1973
Spring at Lands End	William Kimber 1974
Sunset Over the Scillies	William Kimber 1975
A View from the Valley	William Kimber 1976
The Wind Blows from the West	William Kimber 1977
A Long Way to Land's End	William Kimber, 1977
All This and Cornwall Too	William Kimber, 1978
A Family for all Seasons	William Kimber, 1979
As the Stream Flows By	William Kimber, 1980
Upstream at the Mill	William Kimber, 1981
A Family at Sea	William Kimber, 1981
The Waterwheel Turns	William Kimber, 1982
Summer at the Mill	William Kimber, 1982
Family Circles	William Kimber, 1983
Down a Cornish Lane	William Kimber, 1983
The Mill in the Valley	William Kimber, 1984
When Cornish Skies are Smiling	William Kimber, 1984
My Cornish World	William Kimber, 1985
Cornish Prelude	William Kimber, 1985

LITERARY MAGAZINES PUBLISHED

Opus: Quarterly (1-14) in London	around 1940-1943.
Voices: Opus renamed	around 1943-46
Cornish Review: Quarterly	1949-52 & 1966-74.

OTHER TITLES

| Paintings from Cornwall | Cornish Library, 1950 |
| Britain Discovers Herself | Johnson & Co, 1950 |

How to be An Author	Harvill Press, 1952
The Pottery Book	Cassell, 1959
Britain's Art Colony by the Sea	Ronald, 1959
How to be a Parent	T.V. Boardman, 1960
The Minack Theatre	George Ronald, 1960
Pottery for Pleasure & Profit (as D Eames)	1963
Pottery Today	O.U.P., 1961
Pottery (as Henry Trevor)	Constable, 1963.
The Young Potter	Nicholas Kaye, 1963
Cornwall for the Cornish	Porthmeor Press, 1964
Thy Neighbour's Wife	1964
The Timeless Land	Adams and Dart, 1973
Fun With Pottery	Kaye & Ward, 1973
The Spirit of Cornwall	W.H. Allen. 1980
Let's make Pottery	Warne, 1981
A View from Lands End	William Kimber, 1982

The Door Is Always Open
Denys Val Baker

The second installment of Denys Val Baker's
autobiographical series

Available with classic reproduction cover and a new
contemporary design cover
ISBN 1-905532-19-9 - Classic Cover
ISBN 1-905532-25-3 - New Cover

Coming Soon from Humdrumming
www.humdrumming.co.uk

The Cornish Review Anthology 1949-52
Denys Val Baker

A selection of features, stories, reviews, poems and
paintings by many famous and some forgotten names
from the heyday of the arts in Cornwall

ISBN 1-904537-36-7

Softback 176 pages - £9.99

Published by Redcliffe Press Ltd of Bristol

Available June 2006

HEMINGWAY GOES TO WAR
By Charles Whiting

ISBN 1-905532-20-2

Ernest Hemingway was a literary giant of the 20th century and a hard-drinking man of action. As the fighting in the European Theatre of Operations (ETO) reached its climax in those months after D-Day, in 1944, Hemingway spent his time as a war correspondent with the magazine Collier's Weekly, based at the Dorchester Hotel in London, in various locations throughout France (eventually making his 'HQ' at the Ritz Hotel in Paris) and in Luxembourg and Belgium.

Hemingway witnessed first hand the D-Day landings from an LCVP (Landing Craft Vehicle and Personnel), but didn't land himself until July, something which riled him for the rest of his life as his then wife, journalist Martha Gellhorn, managed to land on Omaha Beach in the early hours of the 7th June. By his own account Hemingway saw frontline action at the Battle of the Bulge, and flew on bombing missions with the Royal Air Force.

British military historian and novelist, Charles Whiting - who fought with the British and American armies in 1944 and 1945 - is the first to examine in depth Hemingway's bloody trail through war-torn Europe, chronicling the brave, yet troubled,personal life of that most famous of American novelists, and assessing the impact of World War Two on Hemingway's physical, emotional, and mental condition.

Hemingway Goes To War reads like a thriller and is a must for all Hemingway fans and those fascinated by the latter stages of WWII.

Charles Whiting is a best selling author of over 300 books and lives in York.

DEADBEAT
BY GUY ADAMS

ISBN 1-905532-02-4

"I think you're missing something, what did you notice about the woman in the coffin? ...She was breathing. Not a common habit amongst the dead."

It's the middle of the night and, in a dark suburban churchyard, a group of men are loading a coffin into the back of a transit van.

But why would you be taking a full coffin away from a graveyard and, more importantly, why is the occupant still breathing?

The matter obviously needs thorough investigation by the best, most capable authorities.

Which is a pity as the only two witnesses are a pair of drunken ex-theatricals with reasons of their own to avoid the police.

Tom Harris (nightclub owner) and Max Jackson (habitual barfly) are on the case.

God help us...

"...a world away from the bloated procedurals that have come to dominate the crime field, harking back to a time when fiction could be quirkier and less boundary-conscious. Tell a good tale, be scary, be funny... easy to say it, much harder to pull off. Deadbeat manages all three."
- STEPHEN GALLAGHER
Author of Oktober, The Spirit Box and Valley of Lights

Deadbeat is the first in a series of adventures set in the secret underbelly of contemporary London, a place where the dead walk, magic can be bought on street corners and anything is possible.

Frankly, it's just like every other Pulp Crime/Horror/Zombie/Comedy/Thriller you've ever read.

DEADBEAT : DOGS OF WAUGH
BY GUY ADAMS

ISBN 1-905532-14-8

"High on life..."

There's a new drug running rife amongst the Undead community. Once ingested it simulates all of the symptoms of the living, faster pulse, perspiration, the intoxicating rush of blood through your veins...

Not that Max or Tom would be stupid enough to try it of course, they're far to busy smashing their senses to a pulp working their way though Deadbeat's new cocktail menu.

But when people start vanishing from the Soho streets and some of their customers disrupt big band nights by keeling over dead for the second time they decide it might be worth looking into, if only to stop profits dropping too far.

Which, in a lifetime of bad decisions, may rank as their worst yet.

Deadbeat: Dogs of Waugh *is the second in a series of adventures set in the secret underbelly of contemporary London, a place where the dead walk, magic can be bought on street corners and anything is possible.*

Frankly, it's just like every other Pulp Crime/Horror/Zombie/Comedy/Thriller you've ever read.

THE IMAGINEER
BY GREGORY ASHE

ISBN 1-905532-00-8 - SNOWSCAPE EDITION
ISBN 1-905532-01-6 - FIRE EYE EDITION

"If it were that easy, we'd all be heroes"

This is not it. The world you know - normal, safe, boring - is just a stepping stone to other worlds, other places. Places of magic, monsters and limitless imagination.

Like most eleven year olds, Charlie Whittaker always hoped this was true. Now he knows it is.
Because somebody's kidnapped his Uncle and he's forced to give chase.

Leaving normality far behind...

He will make friends on the way: the enigmatic Lashram, the absurd Squintillion, the noble Algernon. He will see sights that will make the wildest dreams of his life seem bland.

But will he survive long enough to enjoy them? There are horrors out there, ravenous cannibals, lethal assassins and, of course The High Lord Jethryk – a man who wears shadows torn from his victims and could snuff out all life in the universe using no more than his smooth fingertips.   There is, in fact, only one power Jethryk doesn't possess, a power he intends to steal from Charlie's uncle.

By whatever means necessary.

It's all about story you see, and the power of imagination, one false word and creation as we know it will cease to exist...

The Imagineer *is a beautifully illustrated novel that hearkens back to the child in all of us, a modern fairytale that will excite older children and adults alike. There are other worlds to explore: sometimes wonderful, sometimes terrifying, always spectacular.*

All you have to do is believe...

SWANN & PARKER:
THE CRIME OF THE CRIMEA
BY STEVE NEWMAN

ISBN 1-905532-06-7

In 1882, when Henry Donaldson, one of Britain's most acclaimed actors, is murdered on the stage of the Memorial Theatre, Stratford-upon-Avon, during the first performance of The Crime of the Crimea, the rest of the cast, and several members of the public, find themselves under suspicion.

It is another case for the intrepid police duo of Detective Inspector Swann, and Detective Sergeant Parker, of the new Criminal Investigation Department of the County Police Force.

But nothing is at it seems. What secrets are being kept? And what lies told? And who will die next? And is everyone really who they say they are?

Can the old sleuth, and ex-soldier, DI Herbert Swann, and DS John Parker, unravel the dramatic twists and turns of this horrific, hilarious, sexy, and darkly gothic, murderous mystery?

Steve Newman has created in Swann & Parker a 19th century detective double act that will live as long as crime fiction exists.